Fire from the Mountain

Fire from the Mountain

The Making of a Sandinista

BY OMAR CABEZAS

Foreword by Carlos Fuentes

Translated by Kathleen Weaver

CROWN PUBLISHERS, INC.
NEW YORK

Published by Crown Publishers, Inc., One Park Avenue, New York, New York 10016 and simultaneously in Canada by General Publishing Company Limited
Originally published in the Spanish language under the title *La Montaña Es Algo Más Que Und Immensa Estepa Verde* by Editorial Nuevo, Nicaragua.

Manufactured in the United States of America

CROWN is a trademark of Crown Publishers, Inc.

Library of Congress Cataloging in Publication Data
Cabezas, Omar.
    Fire from the mountain.
    Translation of: La montaña es algo más que una inmensa estepa verde.
    1. Cabezas, Omar.   2. Frente Sandinista de Liberación Nacional—Biography.   3. Guerrillas—Nicaragua—Biography.   I. Title.
F1527.C2813   1985   972.85′0830924   85-1305
ISBN 0-517-55800-9
10 9 8 7 6 5 4 3 2 1
First Edition

Acknowledgments

The English translation was prepared with the assistance of Gonzalo Zapata, Casa de Cultura Nicaraguense, San Francisco. Special thanks are also given to Asa Zatz for his help as an editorial consultant.

Foreword

The Spanish language has given few words to the international vocabulary of politics. Our main contributions are *junta, pronunciamiento,* and *guerrilla,* which are violent words. When I was a child, growing up in the United States with a Mexican head and a Spanish tongue, I remember that violence was a negative trait generally attributed to dark-skinned, marginal, "uncivilized" people. This was during the 1930s. The carnage of World War I had been forgotten. Western amnesia is selective. The United States has a genius for blurring the differences between substance and image, and then pawning off history as entertainment. Gangland wars in Chicago were transmuted into cinematic thrills. Who was truer, Cagney or Capone?

The events of World War II, the horror of the Nazi concentration camps, the Gulag, Hiroshima, the French in Algeria, the Dutch in Indonesia, and the Americans in Vietnam have taught us that no one is exempt from the universality of violence in the twentieth century. It is not a privilege of Latin Americans, Asians, or Africans. We participate in universality through violence. Violence has been variously labeled by Marx as the midwife of history; by Shakespeare as a restless passivity that blows our dust about; and by Saint Matthew as a manner of taking the kingdom of heaven.

Omar Cabezas does not give us such a fixed, grandiose, purely passive, or adamantly active conception of violence. Rather, his portrait of a Nicaraguan youth in the Sandinista rebellion against the Somoza dictatorship is inscribed in the other Spanish word, *guerrilla,* invented by the resistance fighters against the Napoleonic invasion of the Peninsula in 1809. It is a word with a strong declination in the Hispanic world. From Bolívar, Morelos, Artigas, and the Carrera brothers in the wars of independence to Zapata in the mountains of Mexico, all fought guerrilla warfare, using armies of the night. But are we only armies against ourselves? Is guerrilla warfare a particular genius of the Hispanic peoples, in their internecine warfare, in compensation for our defeats in war against the foreign powers, from the Armada to the Falklands?

Or is there an alternative truth? The great campaigns of San Martín over the Andes and of Bolívar toward the victory at Boyacá were wars against the regular Spanish army. Benito Juárez and Porfirio Díaz defeated the French through guerrilla warfare. General Pershing could not capture Pancho Villa in Chihuahua because he could not fight the night of the guerrilla. The Marines could not defeat Sandino in Nicaragua because they could not defeat the hills, the insects, the shadows, the loneliness, the trees, or the fires of Nicaragua.

It is to this landscape that Omar Cabezas now takes us. His first weapon is a language as fresh, funny, direct, and irreverent as any produced by Latin American literature in its history. It has been said that *Fire from the Mountain* is a book written in Nicaraguan. Much of its violence, sensuality, humor, and tenderness (Cabezas is wonderful at the Latin American art of the diminutive) is naturally dissipated in translation.

But it is with this language, first of all, that Cabezas offers us a Latin American life that cannot be expressed otherwise. This is the necessity of his book, its deepest reason—the convictions of the guerrilla. His doubts, his courage, his fears, his greatness, and his smallness are all rendered in this book, both as a sequence and as a simultaneous revelation, as a stream and in a flash, in a way that could not have been done without the recourse to language. A liberated language becomes the vehicle for both a personal liberation and a social, historical liberation. As Cabezas points out, the revolution in Nicaragua not only cost a lot of bullets, a lot of fire, and a lot of lives; it also cost a lot of words.

"Bad words," he says. Dirty words. But made dirty by whom? Stigmatized for what reason? Omar Cabezas's liberation of the language of Nicaraguan violence, insult, and despair as he travels his revolutionary odyssey is, strictly, a liberation of humor, a freeing of the humors of the Latin American body and mind as we face our perennial quandary: We must go forward, because the present is unjust and insufferable, but we cannot kill the past in doing so, for the past is part of our identity, and without our identity we are nothing.

What a difficult and beautiful journey Cabezas takes us on as we consider our quandary of celebrating the present instant, while refusing to give up memory and wrestling with its pains and joys. The tension between memory and testimony in Omar Cabezas reminds me of the fountainhead of our literature, Bernal Díaz del Castillo's *True Chronicle of the Conquest of New Spain*. Bernal wrote the epic of the conquest of Mexico fifty years after the event. The immediacy of the account depends, much as it does in Proust, on the presence of the memory. Omar Cabezas also gives great power to his chronicle by constantly reminding us that he is remembering. "Now I am remembering," he may say, or "I cannot remember very well," or "Now I don't remember anything." The intermittence of memory serves the dialectic of conscience well. Cabezas's book is organized around two spaces—spaces of sound, smell, sight and the spaces of the city and the mountain. These are spaces that are powerfully and sensorially present, or absent, in the measure that they are strongly or dimly remembered by Omar Cabezas. He reinforces this notion by writing, "Idea and memory are man's most intimate things, where no one else can dig."

Because he knows this Omar Cabezas can convincingly take us with him on his trip, both physical and political, from the lyricism of the revolution to the humanity of the revolution. For the danger is always there, in this portrait, as in all portraits, of the revolution and of the *guerrillero*—the danger of the lyrical, the danger of the slogan posing as the lyrical, the danger of the lyrical disguising the historicity of the revolution.

Omar Cabezas chooses ideas and memory, images without sacrifice of politics, and convictions without sacrifice of humor. He gives us a full, moving, dialectical portrait of the world of the guerrilla fighter and then makes his natural and powerful point of the continuity of the struggle in which he is engaged. There is a strong sense of cinema in Cabezas's writing. At times I felt I was seeing one of the great Rossellini films in the streets of the open city, *Rome 1944,* with a hand-held pen doing the work of the bumpy, free, gritty, handheld camera of Italian neo-realism. The liberation through language is also a liberation through images.

These images then have a superb capacity to make the elements live in a natural, almost essential way. Bernal Díaz's chronicle was that of the Spanish footsoldier in the conquest of the New World. That soldier knew how to walk, for his epic was but the continuation of the long re-conquest of Spain from the Moors. Cabezas is not trained. He must learn how to walk, painfully, slowly, over mountain terrain, and he must also learn how to talk and how to act physically. The Spanish conqueror of the sixteenth century was in possession of his body and of his language. The Latin American counterconqueror of the twentieth century must learn both. Cabezas gives us the physical and linguistic realism that the conquistador had no need to evoke (or felt inclined, by prevalent taste, to hide). From Bernal to Omar.

Speech and body in Cabezas go out to meet the elements. From the city to the mountain, the passage is from the fugacious, atomized, brilliant dust-and-light images of heat, dogs, sherbets, blaring jukeboxes, billiards, and more heat ("Everything in this town is hot") to the central, unmoving element of fire in the mountain. The pilgrimage toward the element of fire is approached little by little, by learning first how to touch a hot bulb in a hut, next how to light a fire in the mountain, then how to use fire as a symbol of subversion, and finally how to see a whole town as "a permanent bonfire."

As Cabezas enters the mountain, his sight changes. He is blinded at first, so he must see in the shadow. He must first be deaf to learn to hear anew. He must make the mountain move to "our side," understand it, feel it when it cringes and abandons you, use his senses to have the mountain on the side of the guerrilla, not against him. This task is harsh and painful. It is paid for in loneliness, nostalgia, sickness, and that terrible sensation of being nowhere, certainly not in the center of history, not even in the middle of battle, that feeling Stendhal in *The Charterhouse of Parma* and Crane in *The Red Badge of Courage* rendered so well.

Nothing is more difficult than for a hero to tell of his or her own heroism. The wry and cynical arrivistes to social romanticism—Rastignac, Sorel, Becky Sharp—do not pretend to anything more heroical than ambition, quick wit, and an acceptance of egotism. Dostoevsky's nihilistic counterheroes set out to prove that man can be his own worst enemy and that they prefer unhappiness. Kafka and Beckett tell us that now the hero of the bourgeois world is faceless but not dead, and that he deserves compassion and imagination. The revolutionary hero, too often, has simply illustrated the fairy-tale truth of boy-meets-rifle before settling down to the eternal domestic triangle between two Stakhanovites and a tractor.

Cabezas is not Rastignac or Pollyanna. Rather, there is something both Quixote and Crusoe in him, for he imagines a world and also builds it. Throw in a dash of existential anguish, two drops of Augustinian faith and Thomistic teleology, a measure of Marxist analysis tempered by the above, and a full ounce of Latin American, Nicaraguan, Sandinist brio and consciousness, and the result is strikingly humorous and forcefully dramatic—far more convincing than any monolithic presentation of the author's revolutionary faith.

Cabezas is humorous. He steals condoms from village pharmacies; he is manipulated into erection by a nurse who wants to win a bet; he disguises himself as a commercial traveler to escape detection—he who is seen by the girl Mónica as "appearing to be what you are, the face of a guerrillero, poor thing, which seemed made to order." And when town-meets-village, Cabezas can be as funny as Mark Twain.

Cabezas is dramatic. He loses the city. He is no longer a good-looking young man marching through town in a political manifestation, basking in the admiration of the girls. He loses the information and the repression of the city. He loses sugar and *Jesus Christ Superstar* blaring from ice-cream parlors. He loses sex, women, songs, mother, brothers, teachers, workers, and finds a world without the color blue. He finds the mountain, green, dark, demanding to be heard; the fall of a tree, the direction of the wind, demanding to be seen; a new memory of trees, a new understanding of light and shadow, demanding to be smelled; nature plus his boots, plus his hair, plus his spit, plus the humble olive that gives him a stronger pleasure in the smell of the mountain than it ever gave in the taste of the city.

Omar Cabezas brings all these images, sensations, memories, and ideas of the world together with a sense of continuity where his experience and his person enter the experience and the personality of Nicaragua and its people. Do not forget anything I have recalled. Cabezas will give it back to you a thousandfold as you read his memories and his testimony, but he will give it to you with something I cannot possible offer— the movement, the continuity of a human being living *his* history and discovering it is *our* history.

He leaves León, his city. He is a young man. He reaches

the mountain. There are no more than twenty guerrillas there. He feels like going back. He has made the hardest decision of his life. There is no future. But one morning, after the loneliness, the sickness, and the doubt have been drunk to the dregs, men and women, younger than you, appear, willing to live and to die. You are no longer the youngest; you are part of a continuity. And then one day, late in your life, in the mountain, you meet an old man who was young and fought with Sandino and spent God knows how many years hidden away, and now he is back, with you, older than you, and you find your own history, your tradition, your Nicaragua, your forebears

Then you know what this memory, this testimony taught you. You walk into the mountain, and your present becomes your past. That is, it becomes as valuable as your past. As you climb, as you walk, as you carry your pack, as you fight the National Guard, you go forward by giving your past as much value as your present. You are truly *in* history, not mechanically, not through a simple slogan, not a beatific optimism. You can now speak for yourself and others, past and present; you can now speak for Nicaragua when you say that not even death will wipe off your smile; that the smile you once gave to a girl, you can also give to your death.

I hope, when I finish reading this book, that Omar Cabezas and his country, his revolution, and his memory will not have to smile in death, but in life. Such a human, humorous, dramatic, anguished, and liberating account as his deserves life and a smile more than the mechanical optimism of revolutionary lyrics. This is a tender violence, a new and intimate feeling for the life of the revolution, a feat of the Spanish language and the Hispanic imagination.

Carlos Fuentes
Mexico City
February 1985

Fire
from
the
Mountain

Holy Week

During Holy Week my hometown is a ghost town, with medieval trimmings. Holy Week in León is hot, blistering hot: the pavement is hot, the dust is hot, the car seats are hot, the park benches are hot, even the water out of the tap is hot. Everything in that town is hot during Holy Week. The hair on your head is hot, your thoughts are hot—believe me, Holy Week in León is hot! Look, it's so hot there are practically no cars out in the street. In the center of town there aren't even people—they all go to the sea. I'm talking about the middle class, who live where the streets are paved, where the rich people live, in the center of the town.

You know it's hot when you see the dogs trotting along the edge of the sidewalk exactly where the people walk, because that's where there's a little bit of shade, and even the shade is hot. You also see lots of dogs in the streets, panting along, almost running, with glassy eyes and foaming at the mouth; rabid dogs that run in the street, because people chase them off if they come onto the sidewalk. These dogs just run, pointed straight ahead, never turning, not even to look around—because I guess they'd be even hotter if they turned to look around. I wonder where they go when they get to the far side of town, those rabid dogs. So that's how hot it is in León.

Everything was shut. The businesses, even the houses were shut up. The only place open was Prío's on the corner of the square in an old colonial house with a double-leaf corner door that always stood wide open. Sometimes a breeze through the trees in the park would cool the air, and it would be less hot. (I want to convince whoever's reading this that León is hot. I'm not making this up: it really is hot.)

Prío's, as I was saying, was a two-story colonial house with outer balconies looking out over the square. Inside were about ten tables with rickety chairs, and I remember he had an old loudspeaker that still had power to be heard all over the park. Though usually nobody was in the park, except for one or two people from the local parish sitting on a bench under a shade tree. Mostly these people had nothing to do but watch the scattered cars go by; at the first distant rumble of a car, before it even turned the corner, they perked up, looking to see who it would be, and when it came in sight they followed it with their eyes until it turned the corner and disappeared and was only a noise again . . . and they were left waiting for the next car, to see who'd be coming in that. For as long as I can remember this has been a great way to kill time during Holy Week in my hometown.

Prío was famous because he played classical records; he also served mouth-watering fresh-fruit sherbets and first-rate "burro's milk" candies, dark sugarcane candies that are very tiny and melt in your mouth.

At sixty Prío was a powerhouse, a short, light-skinned guy whom they accused of being anticlerical because he blasted the songs from *Jesus Christ Superstar* at the highest volume on his speaker. The film had played at the González theater on the far corner of the park, and the little nuns from the La Asunción school (on the third corner of the square) went to see it and stomped out in the middle, complaining that it was heresy

2

and an insult to the Lord. That's why they were so mad at Prío—because you could hear that music all the way over at their school, where all the girl boarders in León were studying.

Prío was known as "Cap'n" Prío, and he boasted like crazy about how Rubén Darío used to drink beer at his place and how once when he didn't have any money he wrote a poem to pay his bill. Whenever any big shot came in Prío would trot out this poem and shove it under his nose. Prío's in León was more than just a landmark.

The other place you could go during those dismal Holy Weeks in León was to Lezama's pool hall, a half block down from Prío's toward the university—which was totally dead; the only sign of life was on the walls, where the students had painted anti-Somoza slogans—since there was nobody, not a soul left around. And of course Doña Pastora's little bar was shut up tight.

Everybody gathered at Lezama's—people out of the slums, workers, country folk who came in to spend Holy Week with their families in the barrios. Their relatives would put them up so they could take part in the procession of San Benito and the Holy Burial on Good Friday.

Sometimes I think the rich took off for the sea or shut up their houses just to make sure they wouldn't get caught up in that swarming mass of poor people in the processions—decked out in shirts, pants, and skirts of every color you can imagine. The rich, you see, have always set themselves apart.

Sooner or later, to escape the clouds of dust stirred up by the wind in the slums, some of these poor people from the barrios would start trudging toward the center of town, keeping to the shady part of the sidewalk, until they reached the pool hall. By the time you got to Lezama's you were wringing wet, your shoes were coated with dust, and sweaty bits of black dirt would flake off if you rubbed your hands. Though a few looked elsewhere for a bit of fun, inevitably, as if drawn by gravity, everyone ended up at Lezama's.

Lezama's pool hall had about six or seven tables, one of which, the one right by the door, was for games of carambola; that was for the best players. The hall measured about 50 square feet, with one end taken up by the counter. Behind the counter stood Lezama—a fat man whom I never once saw laugh—and two loud-mouthed women who were serving up drinks like robots; there were also two iceboxes bursting with beer and soft drinks, plus an adding machine.

During Holy Week at least 150 people were jam-packed into the hall, and so many bodies just in off the hot street made it very close and stuffy inside. You pushed your way in from the street through a slatted swinging door, just like the ones you see in saloons in cowboy movies. And *bam!* a sweltering blast of heat, even hotter than in the street, hit you right smack in the face. It was like stepping into a steam bath—you felt limp, drowsy, but there was nothing for it, you had no choice: you either stayed where you were in the hot and dusty barrio, contemplating your misery and wallowing in boredom, or you put up with a bit more heat and could play pool, drink ice-cold beer, and best of all, there was not one speck of dust.

The minute you were inside and swallowed up in the stale air you'd start to make out the different tones and variations of the simultaneous *cla pra pra pon pon bom bom* of the pool balls. And sure enough, that *clic* of a scratched shot.

At the first table, like clockwork—Curro. The best player of all. Master of the carambola—banking shots off one, two, three, or four cushions. Concentrated, imperturbable in the racket, with sweat pouring from his arms, his face, and his back, swigging a little beer after every shot, taking on any and all bettors, or swooping down on some unsuspecting pigeon. You better believe we held our breath when Curro solemnly geared up to hit the ball—50 córdobas could be riding on that shot, and in our flat-out broke state, to win or lose 50 or 100 córdobas in one shot was something. Lezama, unsmiling behind the counter, pretended not to be interested, but whenever it was Curro's turn he watched like a hawk out of the corner of his eye.

4

The roar from the other tables was nonstop, and the voices of the players rose up above the racket of dozens of colliding pool balls: "Do you see that, you've got a perfect shot there; that fifteen is a tough nut to crack!" "Stand back, papa, this is a job for grownups!" "Go ahead, just put the ball in with your hand; you'd like that, eh, chief?" "So you think you've got a shoo-in there. Ha!" "You like picking on babies, don't you?" "Easy now, easy." "Did you like that one, sweetheart?" "Shoot pool, shoot pool." And they set up the tables again.

There were four ceiling fans, but you'd never know it except for the noise. Because no matter how fast they whirled, no matter how they creaked and groaned, you couldn't feel even a puff of cool air. That noise was only good to whirl the jumble of separate sounds into one sticky sound that would hit the walls, bounce off the felt, and finally end up by making you feel even hotter.

Lezama's was a Tower of Babel, a circus, a madhouse. It was hot, noisy, and reeking with the stink of piss. You came in looking for some fun, and finally you would leave, you would have to leave. Do you see what I'm saying? In León there was nowhere to go. Even the whorehouses were shut. The whores in León have always been superreligious; they were all pretty much God-fearing women. They didn't fuck on Holy Days, let me tell you. Good luck finding a whore on Good Friday in León! They started fucking again on Holy Saturday. All through Holy Week the whores didn't fuck; the bars didn't open; the Chinese restaurants were shut. And to top it all off, you couldn't even play kickball. Because that would be kicking the Good Lord and offending him and so . . . what could you do? You could go to Lezama's. There was no place else.

I remember it was during Holy Week that I joined the Frente Sandinista, right after I graduated from high school. It was around March or April of 1968, after the massacre of January 1967. I was with some friends, I remember, walking down the street on our way to study. It was dawn, really early in the morning, when suddenly, out of nowhere a couple of sons-of-bitch Guardsmen stopped us in the street and put us up against the wall and the whole bit. That was the day of the massacre of Managua, but we didn't know it was going on, since there was nothing about it on the radio or in the papers.

When I was a little boy, there was a bar in my barrio that belonged to a fat lady who was always beating up on her old man; it was called Dimas's bar. There were always drunken brawls going on in this bar and the Guard would come in and start roughing up the drunks. That was my first impression of the Guard. They would beat up the drunks; they were like savages, bashing them in the face with the butts of their guns. You could see the blood. It left me sick with fear. I was scared of the blood. Blood's horrible when you're little, right? The fact is I was scared shitless of the drunks and the brawls, though I got a kick out of them when the Guard wasn't there, because drunks are hilarious when they're fighting.

I had my first run-in with the Guard when I was a student at the university, but it was not a direct confrontation—I would have died of fright. My dad was bigger than me and I knew the Guard had got the better of him. But that wasn't what made me join the Frente. A lot of things went into it.

First, my dad came from an opposition family; he was an active member of the Conservative Party. I remember one time Agüero came to our barrio and spoke at a meeting from up on top of a table. Agüero was an old, bald-headed guy with a gigantic adam's apple. The next thing I knew my dad was up on the table beside him holding an electric cord with a dangling lightbulb. The light went out and everything got dark. So my dad yelled, "Turn on that light!" and all the neighbors started yelling, "Turn on that light, turn on that light!" I had the feeling I was the son of a very important person, because everybody repeated what he said. And the light came back on.

Next there was my connection with Juan José Quezada. We had known each other since high school, but we weren't really close until we were students together in our first year at the university. Later, we both went on to study law.

6

Juan José, the son of a doctor who never made any money, was one of those rare personalities. He was very tall but not gawky, and lean and wiry like a foreigner, a German type. He was light, with very fine features, a bit like those classical Greek statues. Curly hair. It wasn't blond, but it wasn't black either; he was definitely a good-looking guy. But his way of dressing was old-fashioned. He always had a special fragrance about him that I think was his brilliantine hair cream. (They sold this stuff smeared on little scraps of paper; it came in red or green or blue and the saleslady would scoop it out for you with a wooden stick.)

Also I remember he was the only one in those days who wore trousers with waist pleats, which was already out of style then (though now it's the John Travolta fashion). And he wore sackcloth slacks, with his shirt hanging out; he only tucked it in on special occasions when we insisted, so he would put on his only other pair of slacks, which were black Dacron and of a really good cut. Of course, since he always wore his shirt out and his slacks were so loose-fitting, you had no idea of the muscular strength of his body until you saw him naked or in his swimsuit.

I admired Juan José for a number of reasons. He was an expert in karate and judo, a killer in karate. You better believe I admired his physical strength, his toughness. Before Juan José left to hijack the Lanica jet, he came by my house to say goodbye, but he never told me why he was leaving. He came over to ask if he could borrow my camera, which he took away with him. I was a bit suspicious, or I should say, I knew he was in the Frente and that something was up, because when he left he said to me, "Okay, Skinny, 'Free Homeland or Death.' " That's what he said. I thought he might want the camera—since he was a bit strange, or you might say a bit crazy—I thought he might want it for something out of the ordinary connected with the Frente. That was the last time I ever saw him or the camera. He hung it around his neck to look more like a tourist when he got on the plane. I found this out because Federico told me later, and he was with him on the plane. It was Juan José who recruited me into the Frente.

As a kid at the university I had already started to hear things, to listen. I liked what was going on, and I started taking part in demonstrations and assemblies, but not as a member of any student political group. On the one hand, I was attracted by all this because it was against the dictatorship, against Somoza, against the Guard; on the other hand, it was a question of class. I was very conscious of being from a working-class family, so when they talked at the university about injustice, about poverty, I thought of my own barrio, which was a poor barrio.

There were only about six houses on my block; some were of wood and others were made out of mud and whitewashed, like the house where Doña Lupe lived; she was an old lady so we called her Doña Lupita; she was married to Don Candido. When they whitewashed her house, we kids would slide the palms of our hands over the whitewash, then smear our faces. We made such a racket there screwing around smearing our faces that Doña Lupita would come out and chase us with a bull's-hide whip. But she was old and couldn't catch us.

So she went to complain to my mom, who told us we had no sense or judgment and should go straight home and start sprinkling the yard to keep the dust clouds down. Because our street didn't have asphalt or paving stones, in the summer huge dust clouds blew up. And when you were eating, a fine film of dust settled onto your plate; we covered our plates with our hands, but the dust still got through, and when we ate it would grit in our teeth. My mom used to say: "Eat, hurry and eat, or more cinnamon will rain down on your plate."

Of course, you are marked by your background. And the Student Revolutionary Front (Frente Estudiantil Revolucionaria, FER) followed a class line. That was my kind of ball game. The funny thing is that Juan José came along and recruited me for the Frente, and then Edgard Munguía, later

known as El Gato, recruited me for FER, not knowing that
Juan José had already recruited me into the Frente.

One day Juan José came to me and said: "Skinny, look . . .
uh . . . do you think you might be interested in a greater commitment to the people and to the organization?" Blood of
Christ! I thought, I know this shit, I know where this guy is
coming from. I knew in my gut, sooner or later this had to
happen; I'd heard talk of it I don't know how many times.
Especially from the Social Christians, the professors, the fathers who sat down for a heart-to-heart talk with their daughters and sons who were coming to study in León and live in
big fashionable houses and eat lunch at Mama Concha's. They
would warn their kids to steer clear of politics. Because politics
gets you nowhere but into jail or the cemetery. Because politics is for grownups, not half-baked kids with no job and no
income. Above all they should not get mixed up with the people in FER or the people in CUUN (Consejo Universidadio
de la Universidad Nicaragua, The University of Nicaragua
Student Council), who were sympathizers of Russia and Fidel
Castro. Besides which all communists were atheists. They
should keep totally away from CUUN and from FER, because CUUN and FER were manipulated by the Frente,
which was full of communists and Russians and Cubans whose
sole purpose was to send people into the mountains to be
slaughtered like sheep. Get mixed up with CUUN and you
were sent straight to FER and from FER straight to the
Frente to be packed right off to the mountains. All this raced
through my mind.

I also thought: Juan José is such a good person, how could
he be mixed up in a thing like that? But then, shit! If Juan
José's involved it must mean the people back of him aren't so
bad! But never mind good or bad, I was scared shitless of getting myself killed. I still had a dim hope that what he was saying wasn't really what I thought. So I asked him, "What are
you saying, with CUUN or with FER?" "No," he said, "with
the Frente." Then he added a word that made me even more

9

nervous: "No, hombre, with the Church," which was a code name for the Frente. That was my first major decision. I knew what could happen to me. But since nothing had happened yet . . . You numb yourself, because you don't want to think about that. Because it's better not to. Because if you do think about it your heart pounds, though nobody knows it. And the thought passes, and you're calm again. An inner contradiction is being played out. But as time goes by what you are doing hits you—even, even when you're screwing.

I imagined that if I said yes they would send me to plant bombs. And just a little while ago René Carrión had put a bomb in Pancho Papi's mother's house, and they had murdered him in prison. And then the mountains . . . Remember, the massacre of Pancasán was still very recent. I thought of so many things, and the more my imagination ran wild the more scared I got.

But you'd better believe I was perfectly composed in front of Juan José. I couldn't let him think I was a coward. Still, though I thought of all those things, I also thought of my barrio. Remember, I didn't have any firm political convictions. I wasn't a theoretician, not even a theoretician! Worse, I had serious doubts about whether Marxism was a good thing or a bad thing. Finally, more out of confidence in Juan José than out of any personal conviction, "Sure, hombre," I said, "certainly." It was more or less a question of manhood. What I mean is, I knew what I wanted. I wanted to fight the dictatorship. But I wasn't very sure, and not only that, I had a sort of fear or doubt, or who knows what I felt, about seeing that commitment through to its final consequences.

Political steadfastness came about little by little. Of course, there are compañeros who've had different experiences. But this was my case, this is what happened to me.

Juan José slapped me on the back and grinned. "Good," he said. "Now I'm going to put you in contact with somebody on such and such a day at a certain time. A guy's going to come by the corner opposite the Zaragoza Church, a short guy, about twenty, you may know him, curly hair, short, combed back, goggle-type glasses with a gold bridge. He's going to say, 'Are you Omar Cabezas?' And I want you to answer, 'Yeah, yeah, yeah, the one who went to San Ramón.' "

I went to the spot. And the guy came by and said, "How's it going, Omar?" as if we were old friends. But it was the first time I'd set eyes on him, and I couldn't think of a thing to say. I didn't recognize him because he had changed more than me. He was an old school chum from San Ramón School, from the primary grades. He'd been studying for the priesthood in the seminary in Managua, and later on in Honduras. Then he left the seminary and joined the guerrillas: Leonel Rugama. My first superior in the Frente.

I didn't know for sure it was him until a compañero came by—Manuel Noguera, a friend of mine with a fantastic memory for faces.

He came up, said hello, then turned to Leonel and said, "Hey, what's up, Leonel?" But Leonel had told me his name was Marcial Ocampo. "What do you mean, Leonel?" he shot back. "My name's Marcial." "Now quit shitting me, you're Leonel Rugama. Don't you remember? We were students together at San Ramón!" Holy shit! I thought, It's Leonel Rugama! No doubt about it. I remembered he still owed me 20 pesos for bread. He had been a boarder at San Ramón School, and I lived at home. So he would ask me to buy him 2 pesos of bread from the vendor who came by my house every morning, and he would pay me at the end of the week. It was all done in friendship. Then all of a sudden he was gone from San Ramón, and I never got my 20 pesos.

Leonel always had a single aim, and as he matured this came to be the basic trait of his personality. Leonel would always pose the question of what it meant to be a man—I don't mean in the macho sense, but in the sense of someone who takes on historical responsibility, a commitment to others. Someone who gives everything for the happiness of others. Leonel's guiding star at that time was Comandante Ernesto

11

Che Guevara, who had been killed only a few months earlier. Leonel based almost all of his political education of me at that time on this one thing—on man's responsibility to raise up others out of poverty and exploitation, and to rise to a higher level on the revolutionary scale. Of course, he also talked to me about historical materialism. I knew a little about it already through some pamphlets I'd read at the university.

Also I remember a political debate at the university. I joined one of the discussion circles that had formed, and Leonel was at the center of the debate. Leonel was Marxist-Leninist and anticlerical. I remember what he said to the group of compañeros that had gathered around to talk. He spoke with a frown: "We have to be like Che . . . be like Che . . . be like Che." His gestures, his mannerisms, his whole way of speaking, all that plus the explosive charge he had inside him, hit me right in the center of the brain: "to be like Che . . . to be like Che . . . ." I came away from the university with that phrase running over and over in my mind like a tape recording. I can still see Leonel's gestures, the expression on his face, the determined way he spoke those words. "To be like Che . . . to be like Che." Of course I never imagined the influence it would have on me later, because, in fact, it was only later that I started studying Che. And this touches on something I really want to say, and I'm not in the least ashamed to say it: I know and came to Sandino through Che. Because I think that in Nicaragua in order to be like Che you have to be a Sandinista. There is no other path for the revolution in Nicaragua.

Strength and Numbers

W ell, I started working. And from that day on I haven't stopped. You know how I felt then? It was like being a little boy when they take you to school for the first time; it was as if that very day marked the end of your childhood happiness. Because you have to become responsible. Something like that happens when you join the Frente, but on another level, less to do with happiness. Because if you are serious and if, as Che said, the organization you are joining is a revolutionary organization, and the revolution is a real revolution, then you're in to stay—until victory or death. Once you join, and as your work and responsibilities multiply, it's like entering a whirlwind. Inside a spiral, right? Because isn't a spiral just a series of revolutions in an evolutionary sense? And you're in to the hilt—you're totally screwed!—and glad of it. Finding houses for compañeros in the underground, or for meetings, or storing things, or for mail drops; coming up with cars, car repair shops; getting information about who Somoza's informants were spying on houses of girl friends of the Guard. So I started to work, doing everything they asked me to do and everything I thought needed to be done.

At that time there weren't any elaborate underground organizations, so the work each person did as an individual counted for a tremendous amount in laying the bases for the later advancement of the work. In León the Frente was just Leonel, Juan José, El Gato Munguía, and Camilo. Remember, this was after the defeat of Pancasán. Really, it was a very difficult time. To decide to join the Frente in those days, looking back now with hindsight, was a very extraordinary thing to do, I really believe that.

The decision to join the Frente had a lot to do, I think, with our practice of compartmentalization, which meant that none of the compañeros knew the details of the organization as a whole. All you knew is what you heard, and the Frente made a lot of noise. We had posters plastered all over the streets, on the walls; we robbed banks, which all the radio stations reported while the whole country hung on the *beep-beep beep-beep-beep* of those famous flashes. With news like that going out to the whole country we saw ourselves as much bigger than we really were through the magnifying glass of publicity. That was beautiful stuff.

I went to Mass in the cathedral of León just to hear what people would be saying in the church lobby after the service—the same sort of thing you'd hear in the stadium before a game. Or on the steps of the building of Letters and Sciences at the university, or in car repair shops, or in the barbershop when the barber was talking to the guy in the chair beside you. And deep down inside you said to yourself, "If they only knew I was in the Frente!"

Now here's something interesting: armed actions of any revolutionary vanguard not only strengthens the masses spiritually and politically, I mean, their effect isn't just outside the organization, but within the ranks, too, raising the fighting spirit of the militants. It's an incredibly delicious thing, and you've got to live it to understand it completely. In secret, in total silence, you know who you are: the vanguard.

All this publicity after hitting the masses bounced back to us, and we had ourselves convinced that the Frente was a real

14

power! But something happened to me, I don't know if it's ever happened to other compañeros, but sometimes in a skeptical or critical moment, or out of awareness or tough-minded pragmatism, I knew, rationally, that we were only a few people, a minigroup, as the Guard always called us in those days. And the compartmentalization worked as a sort of escape valve to give free play to our dreams and our desires. You see, the compartmentalization allowed you to hang on to a shred of hope. So the whole adventure, the challenge you were taking on would seem lighter, less dangerous, see? The compartmentalization allowed you to live a waking dream and feel that it wasn't a dream at all.

I would venture to say that the majority of the people shared this feeling, and every day we had more supporters. Somoza, after forty-five years of dictatorship, was also a factor that made people cling to that hope. Do you see what I mean? The people and the Frente were thinking along the same lines. But sometimes you came crashing down, when smack in the middle of your daily work, your political action, it hit you that really you were dreaming, really you were only a minigroup. Then right away another feeling came over you, like a reserve force or a faith or something like that: you had the feeling that behind the compartmentalization there existed a whole sea of things, people, plans, and resources that you didn't even know about. Such states of mind, or whatever they were, were our daily bread in those days. And time passed, and slowly but surely the work took shape. Then halfway or totally into the process of the revolutionary struggle, when you were very strong, it was a great satisfaction, an intimate, personal satisfaction, to be, as Modesto would say, one more machete carrier in the revolution.

I want to make you see how sad it was and how much it hurt when just as you were getting into the organization and the work, you realized, shit! no way was the Frente a great power. The Frente was just a few people and probably didn't exist outside of Managua, León, and Estelí where a few, bold heroic people had taken up the challenge of history and started to work.

As Tomás once said of Carlos Fonseca, we were like ants, like a hammer blow; we were the stubborn ones, the ones born with iron wills. And we carried out robberies and political assassinations that the press reported because they were direct actions against the dictatorship. Acts of an outrageous daring and political heresy in the world of the bourgeois political parties, the Conservative and the Liberal, and also of course the Social Christian and Socialist; the Socialists would label us adventurist and petit bourgeois in assemblies at the university. They would quote paragraphs from that book of Lenin's, *Ultraleftism: An Infantile Disorder of Communism*.

But the point is when the newspapers and radio and television reported the actions of the Frente, we also were impressed by that. Or I was anyway. The compartmentalization and this phenomenon I'm talking about were like the sweetest, most delicious candy. But like most candy, it only lasted a minute. Then the miserable reality hit: you realized there was nobody out there, and you couldn't help but feel a bit afraid when you looked on down the line. I knew this much—many people would have to die for us to advance. How could I not suspect or realize that as long as the struggle wasn't on a mass footing, had not yet become a popular war, those of us living and working would have to share those deaths among ourselves in the near future. Death scared the hell out of us in those days. But no matter how much you risked your life in the legal aboveground work, you risked it one helluva lot more in the underground. I'd say that the less risk we ran of actually getting killed the more we feared death, and vice versa.

You see, you join the Frente because you believe in its political line. In spite of your fear and all the rest you either do it or you don't. But you can't help but be influenced by the fact that you really believe the Frente is capable of overthrowing Somoza, Somoza's National Guard. You really feel that

16

you've joined up to become one more of those people who are going to kick Somoza out.

And this isn't something that happens when you're only just joining the Frente. Even after six years of aboveground work, when I left for the mountain I went with the idea that the mountain was a tremendous power. We had this myth of the compañeros in the mountains, the mysterious, the unknown, where Modesto was, there at the top. And in the city both the people in the underground and those of us working legally always talked about the mountain as a sort of mythical force. It was where our power was, and our arms and our best men; it was our indestructibility, our guarantee of a future, the ballast that would keep us from going under in the dictatorship; it was our determination to fight to the end, the certainty that life must change, that Somoza must not go on polluting every aspect of existence.

The mountain was our refusal to believe that the Guard was invincible. But sure enough, the reality hit. And you were right on the verge of demoralization when you got into the mountains and found nobody there but Modesto with fifteen other men divided into little groups. Fifteen or who the hell knows how many—what I do know is that there couldn't have been more than twenty guerrillas in the mountains at that time. It made you want to turn right around and go back. Mother-fucking son of a bitch! What is this shit? You are right at the point of saying to yourself, Holy Mother of Christ! this is the worst decision I've ever made in my life. You feel you've started out on something that has no future.

As I've said, the Frente in León was Leonel, Juan José, Edgard Munguía, Camilo, and later on me. There was not even one person in the underground. At least there was Julio Buitrago in Managua, whom you may have heard about. Later I found out there were one or two little urban squads in Managua. I only found out they existed when the Guard killed them and broadcast their names and biographies over the radio. The Guard called the revolutionary activities of the

17

compañeros their "criminal records." That was when Julio Buitrago was the head of all the Sandinistas in Nicaragua. They say he was a good man; I never had a chance to meet him, but Leonel adored him.

People became very attached to each other in the Frente in those days. El Gato and I, for example, and Leonel, became very close friends. I remember on weekends all the students who weren't from León went home to visit their families. We never had any money, so we always hitchhiked to the sea, and people would stare at us because we looked so broke. I remember we used to like being picked up by wealthy middle-class girls. Being total smart alecks, when we got into the car and the little rich girl would look back at us in the rearview mirror, we would smile and stick out our tongues; then she would blush and look away and not look back again; but pretty soon she would look, and every time she looked, we were right there looking back at her in the rearview mirror. It was sort of a game of glances. We loved looking at their skin and the way they moved their lips. When they put out their hands to signal we got to see their fingernails. Their hands were so pretty; hands like that made you wish they would caress you. And when the windows were rolled down and the wind blew their hair, it fell right in front of us on the back of the seat. We loved looking at their beautiful hair. I remember once Leonel wrote a poem with something in it about being "rabid for your hair."

We would get out anywhere along the beach. We hardly ever wore our bathing trunks. The three of us pooled our money, about 20 pesos altogether, and shot off to the Hotel Lacayo or to Uncle Salina's to order a Pepsi each and watch the swarms of rich girls coming in. All of them fantastically good-looking. They all wore shorts—white, red, or blue, or jeans cut off up to the crotch. That would kill me. And it would kill me even more when they turned to walk away. They had long hair or short; dark skin or light. They always went around in groups, and you couldn't decide which one to look at, they were all so attractive. Some of them came in with horrible sunburns—red, red, lobster-red. El Gato Munguía would say, "There can't be more than a tiny spot of white left on their bodies." And Leonel would shoot back, "Great, all the easier then to hit the spot!" At the end of the afternoon we went back to León, hitchhiking again, each of us to our own house. And the next day, Monday morning, like clockwork at 8:00 A.M., we were in the offices of CUUN, or in the university cafeteria, or in the offices of the Association of Letters and Science, or of Law. But there we were, at work.

The work was very hard since it was just beginning. Being so few we had to work that much harder. The more you worked the more you developed your powers. You started catching on to a whole lot of things, and discovering a whole lot more. You were pressed to develop your ingenuity, to come up with answers, to prepare yourself better. Under those conditions I grew up in a more or less dizzying way and in a little while I was given very serious responsibilities in the UNAN (Universidad Nacional Autonoma de Nicaragua, National Autonomous University of Nicaragua) student movement.

First I was in a study circle organized by Leonel. After three months I was putting together study circles in the FER for Leonel and El Gato, under instructions to recruit the best students for the Frente. At one point I had seven study circles going at the same time. By night I was totally exhausted, mentally wasted. I remember the text we used was Marta Harnecker's *Elementary Principles of Historical Materialism.* I knew the whole book by heart, I quoted it so much. At night we worked in the University Club making banners or posters or running off study pamphlets until it got light.

Since we were scared to go home so early in the morning, we slept on top of the ping-pong tables or on mats until dawn. And as more and more days dawned, FER continued to grow. It grew and I realize now that we were also growing as persons. FER was just four persons in the beginning. It wasn't an organization. It didn't have any structure. It was a sum total of four or five compañeros that thanks to God and the Virgin had speaking ability and could address assemblies. FER at that time, the Frente at that time, in León, was mainly a political line, a just struggle. And because it was just, it was dangerous. And for that very reason, there were so few of us at the beginning.

Through University Doors

In 1970 I spent six months underground. This was after Comandante Julio Buitrago died in a gun battle, when the Guard discovered his safe house in Managua. Compañeras Doris Tijerino and Gloria Campos were with him. Security discovered his hideout and the Guard set up a whole military operation around the house, on a scale never before seen in Nicaragua. They surrounded the house, the block, and with a third circle cordoned off the entire barrio. Julio fought it out with the National Guard. He died alone, after hours of resistance from inside that house. He was one of the greatest of the greats of the FSLN (Frente Sandinista de Liberación Nacional, Sandinista Front for National Liberation); one of those who forged the great legend of the invincibility of the Frente Sandinista among the Nicaraguan people. Or I should say the people themselves forged that legend around the Frente. It was a legend based on concrete historical events, and the first of these was Julio Buitrago's heroic battle of July 15, 1969.

The Guard, in a total screw-up, broadcast this battle on television. Sitting in front of the screen at the University Club in León, we could see a huge number of Guardsmen staked out in various spots, in twos or threes, standing behind trees or

cars, kneeling behind walls, or lying flat on their bellies, all firing at the house. There was no sound. We couldn't take our
eyes off the screen—the automatic weapons were spitting out
spent cartridges at an incredible speed; we strained to see bits
of concrete, wood, glass, and paint flying off under the impact
of hundreds of bullets hitting the house. We saw the barrel of
Julio's submachine gun at the balcony window, and the smoke
of his gun bursts when he fired back. Then he was at the base-
ment window, or at another window on the first floor, or at
the door of the second floor that opened onto the street. Then
suddenly Julio wasn't anywhere to be seen, and the Guard
wasn't moving, and nobody was firing. The officers of the
Guard were conferring outside. The Guard started advancing
on the house. Then, Julio suddenly appeared, shooting from
one of those places I mentioned, and the Guardsmen turned
tail and shot off running in the other direction. We ate that up
since you could see they were scared shitless of Julio's bullets.
And when Julio hit some Guardsman we cried out, "Damn
them, they've been asking for it!" A small tank rolled up; you
could see how that cheered up the Guard. It stopped right in
front of the house, about 15 yards back. Nobody fired, not
Julio, not the Guard.

I remember it was afternoon, and the Guardsmen were
mopping the sweat from their faces. There was a long silence
. . . then the tank opened fire. Our eyes practically popped out
of our heads when the tank shattered the wall, exploding it to
pieces. "Maybe they haven't hit him," we said, "maybe they
haven't . . ." When the tank stopped firing you could see the
officers screaming for their men to advance on the house.
Nobody answered from inside, and when the Guardsmen got
really close, Julio started shooting. And the Guardsmen
turned tail again, and the tank opened fire again, and it was
the same thing all over. An endless silence followed. A small
plane appeared. Then all hell broke loose—the whole Guard
started shooting, and the tank, and the plane, almost grazing
the roof, and in a matter of seconds the house was a pile of

rubble. Hunks of iron, zinc roofing, bits of wood, shattered parts of the wall—all hurtling through the air with glass showering everywhere. We couldn't imagine how Julio could possibly be alive. But the Guardsmen were ducking; Julio's bullets were zinging past them; they fell down wounded; and then suddenly something happened that moved us very much: we saw Julio come bursting through the front door, running and firing his submachine gun, and seconds later he started to double over; still firing he doubled over a little more, firing and doubling over until he fell to the ground. We felt like crying, but at the same time we felt that we had an indestructible force.

That was how the father of the Frente's urban resistance died in combat.

You can bet that every last person in Nicaragua with a TV set saw it. And people without a set saw it too, because Somoza was stupid enough to keep showing it for several days on television. People went over to their neighbors' to see it. They saw the Guardsmen shaking in their boots; they heard them screaming through megaphones for Julio to surrender. They saw the tanks—I remember now, there were two tanks. One plane and two helicopters. And Julio, all by himself.

After Julio's death, Efraím Sánchez Sancho took over the main responsibility in the organization. This guy was not only morally bankrupt, but also politically dense on top of that. It was his fault I had to go underground for six months. Because of his sloppy security while underground, a lieutenant in Somoza's Office of Security saw him in a car. The lieutenant's wife, who was with him, recognized a woman in Efraím's car as her next-door neighbor. So looking over to see the neighbor, the guy saw Efraím Sánchez Sancho—and that was it. Two compañeros were also with him in the car; a gun battle broke out and the lieutenant was killed. His wife identified the neighbor as Maria Esperanza Valle, "La Tita," a very close friend of mine. The wife was too shaken up to get a good look at the other two compañeros, but she positively identified me—pure fantasy on her part—as one of the guys in the car. So I had to go underground. What this means is you are now operating outside the law, totally hidden from the Guard, from informers, from neutral bystanders, from your friends, and from your family. You go around under cover, you live in safe houses, you carry a weapon, and have responsibilities of a whole other kind.

But it so happened they needed me in the student movement, because of the experience I had acquired in that struggle. Really, I was being wasted in the underground. And those in command decided I should return to legality, to León— back to the university.

I was very young, physically weak, with no military training, with no possibility of getting any, and there I was with responsibility in the underground.

So we came up with a trick to get me back to León: a visit to the director of the Nicaraguan Red Cross, headquartered in Managua, to ask for better treatment for political prisoners. Bayardo Arce, who was already a militant in the Frente, was working then as a congressional reporter for the newspaper *La Prensa*. William Ramírez was also on the scene as director of the radio program "Extra" on Radio Mundial at six in the morning and six at night. Taking advantage then of the ongoing campaign for freedom for political prisoners, we agreed that CUUN would get together a committee to go ask for better treatment for political prisoners. He asked the Monsignor and a couple of big-shot lawyers to participate, and one morning about ten o'clock this committee from CUUN turned up at the Red Cross. I went directly from the safe house to the door of the Red Cross to join up with the committee, taking the lead and marching right into the building. Sheer nerve! It was risky, since I acted as if I'd never been underground. And the journalists? The journalists, acting like they didn't know anything, started snapping pictures *prac, prac, prac, prac,* and interviewing me, asking all sorts of questions about what we were trying to do.

That same afternoon my picture came out on the front page of *La Prensa*, next to the Bishop and the CUUN compañeros, waving my hands in front of the president of the Red Cross. The caption read: "CUUN delegate Omar Cabezas, *bachiller*, asks the Monsignor and the Nicaraguan Red Cross to intercede with General Somoza to obtain better treatment for political prisoners." This was clear proof that I had never been underground, that I wasn't a fugitive, that if I hadn't been seen in León it was because I was in Managua working with CUUN. That's how I managed to return to my hometown, that very night. The next day, at the crack of dawn, I went to the law school to enroll in a class on Roman law. What a life, right?

Almost immediately after this we started to work with El Gato in CUUN. El Gato Munguía was the first FER candidate to be elected president of CUUN because he publicly admitted being a candidate of FER and a supporter of the FSLN. FER was in power in CUUN from 1960 to 1964. But the candidates they ran for president never stated publicly they were in FER, never mind that they were Marxists! From 1963 to 1970 the Social Christians ran the student government. El Gato was the first CUUN president to be elected by going from class to class repeating over and over that he was a communist, a Sandinista, and a member of FER. That was 1970.

El Gato's election, or I should say his campaign for the CUUN presidency, was frenetic. FER had about one hundred members, most of them first-year students. El Gato's opponent was a Social Christian who took himself for some sort of Adonis. But El Gato wasn't bad-looking himself, and we did our best to help him compete even in that category. El Gato also had blue eyes, but it worried me that his mouth was so big. "Gato," I'd say, "do something about that watermelon," and he'd burst out laughing, flashing his two front teeth, which were big and strong. No, now that I think of it, El Gato had green eyes. And the day of the election he wore a green shirt. After seeing so much of him and hearing him talk so often and applauding him at every speech, even I ended up thinking he was more handsome than his opponent.

And we won. I remember that the vote tallying lasted until dawn. We jumped up and down, we screamed, we sobbed, we jeered at the losers and tore down the posters they had plastered all over the university. We carried El Gato on our shoulders. It was a total collective hysteria—hugs, kisses, sighs, open arms. Finally, we were in power in the university for the first time. Long live FER! Long live the FSLN! Long live Carlos Fonseca! Long live Comandante Julio Buitrago! Until we were hoarse from screaming. And exhausted from all those sleepless nights painting banners and posters and making up slogans or drafting replies to all the questions Edgard's opponents might ask him after his speeches. Exhausted but still grilling El Gato on how to stand in the auditorium, how to hold the mike, on what gestures to make when they asked him hostile questions. Or when he greeted the women voters. Exhausted from lack of sleep and from dreaming on our feet, morning, noon, and night. Exhausted from making love with our girl friends in the brief moments of relaxation. Almost voiceless from yelling so much. But there, on the brink of dawn, with the wind blowing at 3:00 A.M. on the grounds of the Rubén Darío section of the university, we who had been three or four were now around five hundred; we who had been three or four were now the leaders of hundreds of young people who, like us only a few years earlier, were making their first appearance on the scene of student politics. And also like us, many of them, very many, would continue on until victory or death.

You could say this triumph marked a qualitative leap: the culmination of one whole phase and the start of another. The victory of FER in the CUUN elections gave us fantastic opportunities to develop our political organizing work. Just our being in the CUUN offices meant that, first, we had a place to meet that wasn't one of our houses or a student's rented room. It meant we had typewriters, photocopiers, mimeograph machines—and best of all, money! What I mean is, the rise of FER to the leadership of CUUN allowed us to make use of the legal, public structures of the university to advance the work of the FSLN, of FER, and also the work of CUUN. Up to that point we had financed FER by each of us chipping in a certain amount weekly out of our own pockets. And that was just not enough.

We had to steal from the university, from the different administrative offices. The huge handbags of the compañeras were notorious for all the stuff we could toss into them: staples, reams of paper, poster crayons. We swiped glue, staples; anything we could get our hands on, we stole. Can you imagine our joy when suddenly we had 200 pesos at our disposal to buy ten cans of spray paint to make posters and banners? Or to paint our slogans on the walls of the university and the city? Being in power in CUUN meant money for all of that.

Thefts in the alma mater dropped dramatically when FER won the student elections. Students are bandits, right? And I remember the girls' purses were good for other things, too: we took stuff from supermarkets. And I remember they were good for something else—and this may offend the more puritanical. A group of us had a kind of union of couples, and we were all scared to death our girl friends would get pregnant. But how in hell were we supposed to hold out for the safest moment of the natural cycle? The solution was contraceptives. But contraceptives cost a fortune. We found out that a certain pharmacy—the Balladares Pharmacy, about a half block down from Prío's—kept contraceptives in the far right of the first drawer. The corner recess of the counter had a display of magazines: *Cosmopolitan, Screen, Time, Selections from the Reader's Digest*, and some other literature. Take my word for it, stealing contraceptives was the thing! This was the operation: two or three couples would stroll into the store, never just one; being conspirators, we knew at exactly what time the fewest employees would be there, which was at noon, lunchtime. Only one clerk would be left; she had short hair and always wore white; she looked bored, or worse, she looked

27

bitter. Once inside, one couple would undertake a diversionary action, asking for medicine that we knew was kept way over on the other side of the store, so high up that to get it the woman had to stand on a chair and turn her back to the drawer with the contraceptives. The other couple would be leafing through the magazines pretending to read, and *zoom!* the drawer was open. I remember when it was my turn I opened my hand so wide my fingers tingled and grabbed as big a handful as I could. My girl friend was right behind me, covering me in case anything went wrong and keeping an eye on the woman who was getting the medicine; then dropping the contraceptives into the other compañera's purse—mission accomplished. I remember there were some hauls that were good for a month. Can you imagine what that meant? A month without worries, without anxieties. So out we went, hand in hand, motioning to the other couple, as cheerful as could be. We couldn't even wait to get to the apartment to count how many we had got away with. Laughing and kissing each other on the cheek, right in the street.

I think, as they say, we radiated youth in those days. I don't know why but I feel that the students today aren't like that. Not like before, not like we were; they seem to lack spark, brio, both those things. Or maybe I'm just getting old.

That same year, 1970, FER led CUUN in an effort to recruit more members among the first-year medical students. Only fifty had joined, so we set a goal of one hundred new members. Finally, we managed to mobilize all the students, mainly the first-year groups—in León about 1,500 and about 2,000 in Managua. El Gato Munguía led the students, and behind El Gato there we were, always the same people, agitating, organizing, calling meetings, taking over buildings, exploding noise bombs, setting up loudspeakers, sitting-in in front of the university—with speeches, songs, guitars, poems, and dialogues with the authorities and committees for this and committees for that.

New faces appeared on the scene, new faces with a future and destiny nobody suspected at the time: students who after they became active in the struggle for student rights we were able to educate politically. And new figures emerged, new boys, new girls. New smiles like Roberto Huembes's smile with his perfect set of teeth. In those days he was sort of a hippie, going around in a T-shirt and thongs, with dirty trousers and shaggy hair. Or like Iván Montenegro, who was fat (or a little chubby anyway), reliable but lazy, always wearing a Banlon shirt and picking at his face. So on it went, from struggle to struggle, from demand to demand; we went on winning over the best of the students coming into the university. This gave FER fantastic momentum.

We won the struggle for a hundred new members in Medicine, and more struggles came along. We put forward a program for university reform; we studied the reform of Córdoba and wanted to change our own university. We fought to change the content of the courses; and we were able to transfer large sums of money to the Frente out of the coffers of CUUN.

I remember once when they were trying to kick out two compañeros from the Faculty of Medicine, we took over the Law School, a building in the colonial style and a refuge for the most reactionary and obscurantist of the professors. With a couple of honorable exceptions, these professors taught individualistic courses that were a bastion of defense for Somoza's political constitution and an apology for Somoza's peculiar brand of representative democracy; they did their best above all to instill respect for the Civil Code. Everything was perfectly correct and proper—the professors, the courses, the architecture of the buildings. And as if to cast a note of irony over the whole thing, this motto in Latin was inscribed at the entrance to the Law School: SIC ITUR AD ASTRA, which means, "Through these doors one ascends to the stars."

We had a demonstration once in front of the house of the dean, who was a progressive, but still a symbol of authority. The dean was a professor I liked very much as a person, and he was a very Christian man who was always talking about being filled with an unshakable faith. We were always coming up with something novel to motivate the students, to keep up their enthusiasm and morale, in the struggle to win not only our academic goals but the political as well. The point was to come up with an original approach that would lead to further action. We were very inventive in those days. I was president of the Law Students' Association, the famous AED of León. It was then that I decided that our demonstration should move over to the dean's house. Each student had a lighted candle, and when we marched through the street, shouting and singing, all the people came out of their houses or opened their doors. It was about 10:00 P.M. and people in León turn in at 9:00. Hearing our shouts, the men came to the door in their underwear and slippers; some looked startled, others serious, or worried, or amused.

For the people of León the students were a sort of sideshow, because remember, we also staged comic carnivals, with lots of clowning around. And people were delighted because we made fun of Tacho (our nickname for Somoza) and the government. Sometimes there was even obscene stuff in the carnivals—and León is very moralistic and conservative, but the vulgar jokes of the students delighted the people anyway. I think they felt that we were doing what they didn't dare do. Because their neighbors would talk if they thought you were doing something wrong; then the gossip would start, and the good name of one or another Christian would be shot to hell.

The night of that demonstration the women came out in their slips or nightgowns, or rigged up in the craziest-looking outfits, their hair uncombed and without any makeup on. They peeked out of doors or poked their necks out of windows. Many would recognize a boyfriend, or a son, or even me. You could hear what they were saying in their houses: "Look at that crazy fool, do you see him?" "Good God in heaven!" "Look what they're up to now!" "Now see what he's got himself into!" "That little bastard sure has a nose for trouble!"

Since we were singing, and you could see our candles from

a long way off, they thought at first it was a procession for some virgin or of a saint, until we came by their houses. There was no way they would make out the words to our songs from inside their bedrooms, so they peeked out and what did they see but the incorrigible Skinny Cabezas, who was already notorious in town, at the head of the demonstration, candle in hand, chanting and marching at the head of all the students. Some people were sympathetic. But others saw us as just loafers, as students, as if all we wanted was to get by without studying. Because that was what some of the professors and some of the authorities said. But what we wanted was something else.

Finally we got to the dean's house. It was built in more or less the same style as the Law School, and when I looked at it a whole series of things raced through my mind: the obscurantism of so many of the professors, teaching us to believe in and to respect and to defend with the law the sanctity of private property. I thought of what we wanted, and the facade of the Law Building popped into my mind. I remembered the mottos SIC ITUR AD ASTRA and FREEDOM FOR THE UNIVERSITY. I thought, what garbage! and grabbed a can of spray paint from a compañero and stopping in front of the sidewalk of the house, I yelled out to the students, "Do you think that with the teaching they do in the Law School we're going to get to the stars or to the light?" And they all roared back, *"Noooo!"* With a bold flourish and tremendous conviction, I quickly painted in capital letters on the spotless white of the dean's house: THROUGH THESE DOORS ONE ENTERS THE 15TH CENTURY. Because this dean was and is very religious, and in León on the night of the Saint Day of the Virgin of Mercedes, the great patron saint of León, everybody sets out lighted candles on the sidewalks in front of their houses— on the sidewalk in front of the house of my beloved dean, we left that night at least 500 burning candles.

31

Sandino and the Indians

The main thing was we were achieving our goals in these student struggles. Though we didn't actually get the things we demanded in the way of student rights, what we certainly did was mobilize the students around our political line and around our activists; little by little they were beginning to identify with our activists. And there was also what you might call the phenomenon of students at the base beginning to admire the FER leaders. The harder we worked, the more students came out and were organized into study circles, which were then organized into teams, teams that later became cells of the Frente Sandinista. I can't tell you anything specific—since I didn't have access to much information—about the national structure of the underground at that time. I can't give you the details. But my guess is it was very weak.

What I do know is that order after order came in to find safe houses and cars for the underground. Mainly El Gato Munguía, I, and two or three other compañeros were asked, since we were from León. The other students in FER weren't from León, but came in from other provinces to study; they lived in student rooms and their only friends were other students. Not being natives, they weren't friendly with the townspeople. But we were, which made it a lot easier for us to find somebody who would lend a car or offer his house. You went to your neighbors, to people you knew in León, and they would help you.

Once, I remember it was Holy Week—another Holy Week—we got a directive saying we shouldn't any of us leave town, I mean none of the main FER leaders who were all in the Frente. We shouldn't leave León; we shouldn't go to the beach, but should sit tight awaiting orders in the CUUN offices. Because a very important task was coming up. And sure enough, a directive came with word that a "gondola" was on its way and had already reached the frontier, or was in Chinandega, or who knows where. It was a group of companeros who were coming into the country and urgently needed houses. Our orders were to get houses or else. The order read: "Obtain houses, free homeland or death." Which meant no excuses, we couldn't come back until we had a house. The pressure was on—on us and on the compañeros in the underground. Because the gondola had already arrived—was either in Chinandega or on the Honduran border—we headed off, not knowing where, just walking the streets. Sometimes you rack your brain, going over everybody you know in your mind, and you draw a total blank. So we'd just see if we couldn't catch somebody's eye, maybe run into an old friend and have a chance to hit him up for a house. Son of a bitch, I thought, where can I go, where? "Hombre," I said to El Gato Munguía, "wait, there's a way out of this shit." About six doors down from CUUN to the east was a lawyer from the Independent Liberal party, the PLI, Eduardo Coronado, a guy with a working-class background who had his office in the same house where his brother had his dental clinic. "Eduardo, hombre," I said, "I need you to do me an urgent favor. Look, I need a house, for a compañero in the Frente who is passing through town, right?" (If I told him I needed a safe house he'd never do it. You had to say: for a compañero who's just passing through on his way to Managua, who needs a place to stay for a couple of nights, until they come to pick him up.) But the guy turned me down anyway and sent me to a fellow named Blandino who lived a half-block farther on in a house that was also a funeral parlor. So I put it to him—I knew him. So, "Compa," I said, "uh, I need a favor."

The problem was that these guys were old, and I was just a kid. I'm thirty-four; this was in '70, '71. I would have been twenty, twenty-one. What I'm saying is that for them to get mixed up with a kid like me in this sort of thing—it would be irresponsible for somebody old to go along with what I wanted, right? These were old men who were used to getting involved in conspiracies of the old, conspiracies of Conservatives or Liberals, conspiracies that took place in the aisles of fancy cinemas or in the stately mansions of León. To get mixed up with a kid, a rebellious student, a notorious activist, for an old man like that to agree to put somebody in his house—it was a difficult thing. He told me there was no room. "But compañero," I said, "that doesn't matter. Look, in the daytime we can put him in a casket and put another casket on top, and he can spend the day like that. The compañeros are very disciplined," I told him. "Okay," he said, "but what if somebody wants to buy the casket?" "Just tell him it's sold," I answered. But the old guy wouldn't go along with it. "Look," he said, "I know somebody who will give you a hand. Another member of PLI, a Subtiavan."

So I went to meet Tomás Perez. When I explained what we needed, I could see he wanted to help, but his house wasn't really suitable. I went to see it. "Brother," he said, "I'd do it gladly, but in this house there just isn't room." (I should tell you who was coming in the gondola I'm talking about: Tomás, Modesto, Oscár Turcios, Juan José Quezada, José Dolores Valdivia, René Tejada [whose nickname was Tello]—the very cream, our top people! The whole group that had just been in Cuba, and I think even Vietnam.) So the compañero had to say no, but he told me he knew a guy he was positive could do it; he would guarantee it; we would go

34

find him right away. But the guy wasn't home; he was marching in a funeral procession in Subtiava. We went to the cemetery. "Look," Perez said, "I'm not going to go with you to talk to him, because I'd be compromised. If he says no, he's going to think I'm in the Frente and I'll be screwed. I'll point him out, then you get his attention and take him aside."

We had already started very discreetly to mix in with the crowd of mourners. "That's him," he said and pointed to a particular guy. So I went up and stood beside the guy as he was talking to a group of people. I tapped him on the shoulder and winked, and he saw I wanted to talk to him. I wasn't a friend of his, but he knew me, I was so notorious in León. "Brother," I said, "I want to talk to you about something very sensitive." "Sure," he replied, "gladly." We hung back behind the others. "Brother," I said, "a compa is coming." The important thing then was for him to make up his mind. At that point it didn't matter whether it was for one compañero or two or for one night or three days; the important thing was for him to agree, to make that decision. So I laid it all out and he said, "Gladly, compañero, of course." A Subtiavan by the name of Magno Beruis.

What a relief! I struck out on foot for the University Club and, no shit, it was far—block after block. I came in wringing wet. "Find anything?" I asked the compa. "Zero, brother." "Well, I have! I've got a house." "Is it clean?" "No, brother, it's not, but it's a house." "Where is it?" "In Subtiava." "Fantastic! Let's get going."

That was it. But they didn't come. The people from Chinandega didn't come, and the man was left waiting. When I went by to tell him they weren't coming, he just said, "Fine. You let me know when to expect them so I can be ready." He'd already talked to his wife; her mother and brothers lived right next door, so he had told her that a friend of his was coming from Managua, a guy who'd run off with a young girl and was being hounded by her relatives, who wanted him to get married.

By the time the gondola got in we had another house. I had run into Joaquín—Joaquín Solís Piura, who is Vice Minister of Health today. He just got back from Europe, from Switzerland, where he had done a postgraduate degree. He was CUUN president during the student massacre of July 23 in '58. So I put it to him. He'd never met me but he had checked up on the new leaders, so he knew who I was. Anyway, I ran into him, he came through immediately.

So when the gondola arrived, we had two houses, and from then on the Subtiavan was our collaborator. But the men in the gondola were just passing through on their way to Managua. So I started to do political work with this man.

His shack was on a dusty road in Subtiava, an outlying barrio, a barrio of Indians. The Subtiavan Indians were there even before there was a León, even before the Spanish Conquest. The shack was isolated, about 30 yards away from the next house, which belonged to a guy we recruited later on. The yard was huge, like a big empty lot. I suggested we should study, that he should talk to his brother and get some people together to study—not mentioning the Frente, but saying it was university students, coming into the barrio to do consciousness raising. But the house was tiny and uncomfortable—overrun with kids, and his wife always there cooking, making *vaho* day and night, which she sold on the street. We couldn't study there. So he sprinkled the yard, and right by the door we rigged up a board, which hung from the roof; we attached an extension cord with a lightbulb, about a 50-watt light I guess, and we set out five, six, maybe seven chairs that he had rounded up somehow—he was a natural leader. It was just a preliminary effort, a sort of shot in the dark that would later on bear important fruits, as you will see. So the guy invited five or six people, right? I went there about three times. We started out with the Communist Manifesto, and I became friends with the people who came, all Indians. Some were farmworkers, one a taxi driver, others were quarrymen or connected with fishing, or worked tiny farms in the barrio.

Subtiava is on the outskirts of León, toward Poneloya and the sea.

You could see when I talked that they were taking it all in with their eyes; it was as if their eyes were refracting my words to their brains; who can say what the process was, but the thing is they were listening, listening, listening. The ideas would travel from their brains to their eyes, and by the look in their eyes I knew their world was turning upside down. Their heads were being turned around; every moment they were discovering an incredible number of things. But it was all happening too fast, you could see that in their eyes too. They were filled with enthusiasm and so we recruited more people.

But I was so notorious, we decided I should stay away. First, because it was a safe house that was going to be used again. Second, because sometimes the neighbors came by and looked into the yard and there we were, five or six guys under the lightbulb and me, a notorious student with a pamphlet, all sitting on little chairs or benches or three-legged stools. So FER, or the Frente through FER, appointed somebody else to do the work in that barrio. Iván Montenegro Báez was put in charge, "Fat Man" Montenegro, who by that time was a lot more mature.

Our work in Subtiava took off like wildfire, but very quietly and out of the light. And we started presenting the image of Sandino in Subtiava. The Indians had a leader, a historical figure, who more than any other was representative of their people: Adiac. We presented Sandino as an incarnation of Adiac, then Adiac as an incarnation of Sandino, but Sandino in the light of the Communist Manifesto, see? So from shack to shack, from Indian to Indian, ideas were circulating: Adiac . . . Sandino . . . class struggle . . . vanguard . . . FSLN.

Gradually a whole movement was born in Subtiava. Here I want to make you see how these things were interrelated. We started penetrating other barrios in León, through the relatives of Subtiavans who had moved there when they got married or for whatever reason. We set about recruiting these relatives and this was how we made our initial contacts with the Subtiavans in other barrios. I'm talking about La Providencia, Reparto Vigil. There was a time when FER was going to organize a special branch to deal with the barrios. Now our influence was not just in the high schools; we had grown not just in the university; FER was beginning to have a real presence in the barrios.

Since it was always the Frente behind FER, when the work in the barrios reached a certain level the Frente said, "Fine, now FER can forget it. The underground network of the Frente will take over from here."

And they started transferring cadres from FER to work in the barrios in direct contact with the Frente. They started setting up committees to try to get electricity, or water, or whatever was needed. And sure enough, very slowly the barrios began to develop, and local leaders began to emerge. So eventually there weren't so many students coming in. Only a coordinator. And more and more leaders emerged from the masses and started developing their skills. We put the leaders of the different barrios in contact with each other, and the movement of the barrios was born.

It was a fine thing to see, a very beautiful thing.

Fire in the Barrios

W hen I left for the mountains I knew they could kill me. But there's one thing that impressed me deeply and always filled me with satisfaction. You see, I always repeated a thing I'd been saying since 1974: if the Guard kills me they'll have to spray my face with bullets to get rid of the smile on my dead face. That was my vow. Because it seemed to me by that time I'd already done so much damage to the Guard, so much damage to the enemy, so much damage to imperialism that killing me would be a small thing compared to what I'd already done to them.

When I left for the mountains I knew the Frente was behind me, as Frente, as a front. I wasn't going alone. I knew when I left Subtiava a whole generation of students was behind me, but more important—and here I may be guilty of lack of modesty—a generation of students that in some way bore the seal of my own combat.

This was the student movement that later spread throughout the country. For the students we recruited in León went back to their own provinces and initiated work in the barrios. They were the first contacts of the regional underground of the FSLN.

So as I was saying, I left for the mountains with absolute

confidence. Not that I'd come out alive—but confident of victory. Mainly because I felt that Subtiava was behind me. And when I left for the mountains, *Subtiava*, that was power.

In 1972 or '73 we had our first mass demonstrations. Before that only students demonstrated. Never people from the barrios. I remember once we called a demonstration, I can't remember now what it was for, but it brought together two currents, one from the university, the other from Subtiava. We had the capacity to mobilize masses in Subtiava, but in this march it was mainly people we'd already recruited in the other barrios, the small committees. Like all the mobilizations in Subtiava, this one was impressive. One long street runs from Subtiava to the cathedral. We were all to come together in the park in front of the cathedral, the students marching from the university to the park, the Subtiavans from Subtiava.

We had discovered the Indian origins of the Subtiavans and encouraged these as a strength; we tried to transpose the old ancestral struggles of Adiac, their ancient chief. And to remind them how they'd been dispossessed, humiliated. How both Liberals and Conservatives had bullied them and ripped off their lands. How Sandino had rebelled, just as Adiac had rebelled. And then there was the question of the bourgeois classes having all the power.

Before the Subtiavans started marching, they beat their atabales—you know what an atabal is? It's a drum, a kettledrum. So the local committees went all through the barrios beating their drums: *barangan-bangarán . . . barangan-bangarán.* It's a muted, serious sound; it's not cheerful, but it's not sad either; it's a tense sound: *barangan-bangarán-barangan-bangarán-barangan-bangarán.* They didn't look to the sides but only marched straight ahead, *barangan-bangarán-barangan-bangarán.* And people looked out from the vacant lots, over thorny hedges, or out of their houses. And behind the drums came people chanting, "Seven tonight in the plaza, seven tonight in the plaza." People knew, being Sandinistas, this was a directive. So off they went to the plaza. Then, after a brief rally, they headed down the Calle Real, which is the street that goes all the way to the Central Square, the famous Calle Real. So at the head of the Subtiavans, the drums. First the drums, and behind the drums the leaders, and behind the leaders all the Indians. And the first leader was the man I met at the funeral, Magno Beruis.

So, when you saw the Subtiavans on the march, hearing their drums in the lead—*barangan-bangarán-barangan-bangarán*—you saw the stony face of the Indian, with coarse, straight hair, not smiling much. A serious face, not sad, and not bitter either, but grave, with a repressed rage that was just beginning to surface. And you felt a unity in the beat of the drums, a unity of rhythm and face, or of rhythm and step, or of step, rhythm, and face. I don't know what went into that unity, but you saw the Indians, with their Indian faces, marching and shouting slogans, but not in the rowdy tone of the students, who were screwing around, making up catchy phrases. The Indians' slogans were simpler. An Indian would call out, "Which way do we go?" And they all shouted back, "The way of Sandino!" All serious and looking straight ahead, and with gravity. This instilled respect and began to frighten the bourgeoisie. For this was the Indian awakening. The rebellious Indian going back to Sandino and projecting Sandino forward with greater historical depth, forward into the struggle against an exploitative class society. So when you saw hundreds of Indians on the march, all serious—women, children; old, heavy, stocky, tall; rough, strong men—you imagined it wasn't just a Subtiavan march, but a march of Indians that encompassed all of Latin America: the Bolivian Indian, the Peruvian Indian, the Chilean Indian, the Indians of the copper and tin mines, and of the rubber plantations. I realized at that moment they were marching not only in the Calle Real but over all of Latin America, over the Andes, over history, over the future, with a firm, solid step.

So when I left for the mountains I knew they could kill me. But I also knew that this march of Indians was a march of

Latin American Indians, a march of Indians against colonialism, a march of Indians against imperialism, a march of Indians that could mark the end, or the beginning of the end, of the exploitation of our peoples.

So let them kill me! It wouldn't matter, not one fucking bit! Because I knew that Subtiava was behind me.

Subtiava was a permanent bonfire. Because remember, by this time we had discovered fire. Along the line I mentioned earlier about always coming up with new protests and agitational ideas to keep up morale—let's say we were in the ascendancy; the fire was rising. I don't mean political fire, though that too was rising; I mean fire as an element of nature. We started out having demonstrations with candles. Then we got the idea: for every student a torch of pitch pine. But pitch pine was very hard to get hold of since it only grew in the north of the country. We saw that every time we marched with candles the people were curious. So we held a demonstration, early, with small pitch-pine branches. And people came, because the pine torches caught their attention. Everybody knows those processions of the Middle Ages: a few old hooded monks weaving their way through the dark passageway of a castle? Well, in the barrios, in the dark streets, with a row of houses on one side and a row of houses on the other side, it was like the corridor of a medieval castle. Can you imagine, hundreds and hundreds of points of light, the pitch-pine torches flaming in the streets, and us jumping over puddles, climbing up over gulleys, over the rough cobblestones of the bumpy streets of León?

But we found it was too hard to get pitch pine and decided it would be better to build fires in every barrio. We agreed on bonfires since we'd already seen how fire attracts people, since it lights up your face in the dark. People are fascinated by flames; they stand watching the flames, but they are also listening. They are listening, and their eyes and their minds travel from the fire to the words, from the words to the mouth, from the fire to the speaker's mouth. We discovered that very subtle cycle.

So, great, we said, we'll build bonfires on all the street corners. And we did just that. Besides, it was a helluva lot easier to come up with firewood, old planks from the shacks, or we would buy a little. In the barrios people cook with wood, so there are always a few houses selling wood. Five pesos will get you a couple of sticks about a yard or a half yard long. "Rally with bonfire today," we used to say. Then our activists came, five or ten students from the university at the beginning, in the summer, because in the winter it rained. We hauled along a gallon of kerosene, sprinkled the firewood, and lit roaring fires in the dark barrios. Then we started chanting around the fire: "People, unite, people unite!" Or we shouted slogans for a particular cause like, "Free Chico Ramírez and Efrain Nortalwalton!" The bonfires really started taking off about that time, during the campaign to free Chico Ramírez, who's a guerrilla comandante today, and Efraín Nortalwalton, who was a prof from El Salvador.

We noticed that the minute we lighted fires in those dark barrios people would hop right over the hedges bordering the dirt road; they came out of their yards, or over hilly, wooded pastures; through wooden gates, or over barbed wire that sometimes marked the property line of a little shack. Coming out of doors or on their way down the street; the thing is, people poured out from every nook and cranny of the barrio; cutting between houses or across yards, off streets and street corners, they started gathering on the corner, a safe distance back from our activists.

People were gathering. We called to them to move in closer, and the little kids were the first to come up, the five- or six-year-olds. They were the first to start yelling. And they yelled right along with us. We could hear that our voices were louder, the chorus was bigger. But we knew it was just those kids. Right from the start we underestimated those kids; we didn't think they were important. Though yes, we felt a little bit of company; we weren't so alone, so totally isolated. At least those little kids were with us, were a little company.

Before long some worker would come up, a union man, already halfway into it. The unions were weak, tiny unions of León, little groups of craftsmen. Or maybe a woman with a stall in the open-air market, a very militant sector. Or some student who lived stuck away in the barrio. We started shouting in unison. As a few more, then a few more joined in, the others drew in closer, and more and more people gathered. And always the people stood watching the fire and watching us. We started talking. And when we talked we tried to look people right in the eye, as if to imprint what we were saying right on their brains. But it wasn't just that: since we didn't have any structures to work through to contact the people, to study with them, to convince them, persuade them, to lead them to rebel—in those few minutes, when we had this contact through the element of fire—we had to use every ounce of our persuasive power. And more and more people came, and more people and more. And the wood burned down, and we sent for more wood. And more and more sticks went up in flames. And the people went on listening, listening.

We built those bonfires again and again and again. Before long the local people were helping you sprinkle kerosene and set up little twig houses, little towers out of kindling wood to get the fire to light. And we went on building fires, and more and more people gathered; a whole lot of wood went up in smoke. Pretty soon the people had firewood ready, carting wood from their houses, or if they had old tires they brought those, or wood thrown out in the yard. And when our kerosene ran out, and we couldn't get the fire going because the wood was green, they gave us more kerosene.

Well, bonfires began popping up in all the barrios. And little by little they came to stand for subversion. Fire took on this subversive character because everybody in the opposition, all the anti-Somoza people and all the pro-Sandinistas, clung together around the flames. So the bonfire was a sign of subversion, a symbol of political agitation, of revolutionary ideas brought by the students into the barrios. The bonfires were the enemy of the Guard. The Guard hated the bonfires because they brought people together. Fire incites, integrates, unites; because fire gives you courage; because fire makes you feel more protected, stronger. As if the flames were a kind of company.

Really, the bonfires were growing. They became an open defiance, a public conspiracy. The bonfire became a cry, a political slogan, a slogan that gathered strength as the bonfires multiplied and as the masses closed ranks around our leaders, defined themselves and grew in numbers. And there were ten, fifteen, twenty, thirty, fifty, a hundred bonfires all over the city. But the best thing was that as the organization developed, and the work in the barrios expanded to the point where the Frente said, "Fine, we'll take over from here," the best thing was that by that time the students weren't building the fires anymore; the people were building their own fires. In the daytime they were exploited and at night they rebelled. They worked all day and protested and shouted at night. And the bonfires did not consume those cries; it gave them life.

So, when I left for the mountains, it wasn't just the march of Indians I had behind me, but also a chain of fires, a spreading of fires in all the barrios. An unleashing of conspiracy and of rebellion. A people in flames that later became a people in arms, but which started as a people in flames.

What I'm saying is, I didn't go into the mountains alone; I went with a tremendous sense of being accompanied. At first, sure, we were alone, as I said; we were shouting by ourselves, with only that swarm of kids. At that moment we felt a vast loneliness; our only company was the memory of our dead, which gave us enormous life. It cost us a lot to reach the people.

The problem was, we didn't have any organic ties; we still didn't have any ideological or political ties to the people. Because the message we had for the people carried with it danger, expectation, strangeness, and fear. We had to be very persuasive. I discovered something then—I mean a personal political discovery; I'm not talking about figuring out that

water boils if you heat it—I discovered that language identi-
fies. I discovered for myself how language communicates.

Looking out over the faces of the people, I saw the workers
in their caps. They didn't nod yes and they didn't nod no; fat
women with aprons on who didn't laugh but didn't frown
either; their faces were impenetrable somehow, impersonal.
More than once we had the feeling we weren't getting anywhere, that the people didn't understand, that it didn't matter
to them at all. And dammit you wanted to pick up a stick and
beat what you were saying right into their brains. But you
couldn't.

At the beginning that lack of communication was a block.
And on top of that the Guard might come and start harassing
them, or harassing us, or all of us together. I remember once
when I was talking, a couple of swearwords slipped out; then
ha, ha, ha! people smiled when I swore, and looked at each
other. No doubt about it, they were communicating with each
other; they were chuckling, but chuckling about something
I'd said. I realized I was getting through to them. This is important, because it dawned on me then that a swearword or a
crude word used in the right way can be explosive, very sharp
politically. It's one thing to go into a barrio and start lecturing
about the current historical juncture. It's something else to
start talking about how the rich with their fat investments are
off whoring in Europe, see? Because the people start to identify with that viewpoint. They start to discover their own
identity, because we helped them become conscious of their
situation.

This war, then, cost us not only thousands of bullets, thousands of fires, thousands of dead sons; but millions of swearwords went into it, too. Swearwords that were a blend of rage,
hate, hope, determination. Millions and millions of flesh-and-
blood swearwords: "son of a bitch" had a political meaning,
and so did "mother-fucker."

Because of all this I'll say it again: when I left for the
mountains I knew I wasn't going alone. I went with the feel-

ing that thousands of Subtiavans were with me, and thousands of workers from the barrios of León, and thousands of bonfires. What I mean is, I went with the collective defiance that had spread throughout the masses; I went with millions of swearwords that represented all the hatred and aspirations of the masses. Swearwords that were political, because people said things like: "Where are the poor people heading?" "To power, to power!" "Where are the rich people heading?" "To the shit pile, to the shit pile!" I'm talking about a huge pile of shit that had moved beyond the outlying barrios and was starting to dirty the bourgeoisie.

So I left for the mountains with boundless faith. And it wasn't just the romantic glow of that march I was telling you about, but this: behind that march was a whole political experience, an organizational experience, an experience of struggle, in this case in the streets. The masses were being mobilized.

Leaving for the Mountain

When I left for the mountains my morale was extraordinary. Let's say my batteries were fully charged by everything I've just mentioned. I had an enormous amount of political work behind me, plus the intimate satisfaction of having added my small spark to the great fire that was now glimmering on the horizon of the cities.

That was one of the main things that kept me from thinking of deserting when I first got to the mountains. It's a terrible shock to be plopped suddenly into that environment, especially when you're not prepared for it physically. I'd say we weren't prepared physically or mentally. Even though we'd read *The Diary of Che* and writings on Vietnam and the Chinese Revolution, a whole string of accounts, of works on the guerrilla movements of Latin America and elsewhere, we only had a general idea; we had no sense of the concrete reality. So, when they sent us in, they took us first for a day to a little farm on the outskirts of Matagalpa, a place that belonged to a compañero-collaborator, Argüello Pravio I think it was, who was liberated in the action of December 27. Juan de Dios Muñoz was there to meet us, and he put us in a little shack on the grounds. The car that dropped us off didn't go any far-

48

ther. Cuqui Carrión was the driver; I was startled to see him behind the wheel. Before leaving León they had brought us together in a house in the San Filipe barrio, in some new student apartments. They took us there in the afternoon. At dawn a red jeep, a Toyota or Nissan, came to pick us up. They knocked on the door; we loaded in our bags and climbed in back, Iván Gutiérrez, Aquiles Reyes Luna, Denis Palma, and me; a chilly morning, about 3:00 A.M. It was my first trip in an underground car and I was really curious to see who'd be driving and all that.

We couldn't sleep that night, waiting for three o'clock to roll around. Who could have slept, with that incredible tension? Babbling on and on, we just stared at each other, speculating on how long it would take us to come to power. Four years, five? Then one by one we ran through our analyses of the entire national and international situation, in support of the case for five years, or ten. Then the knock a compañero opened the door, and we put our bags in the jeep. I recognized Pedro Aráuz Palacios (whose nickname was Federico) because he got out of the car, then got back in. But the driver stayed behind the wheel and didn't look around. It was dark, and though I think there was a street light on the corner, the light barely reached us; I couldn't recognize the driver, who was wearing a black or a tan jacket, of either cloth or leather, I'm not sure which. He wore a typical worker's cap, like a miner's, and a sort of little towel wrapped around his neck. I didn't want to look at him—that question of compartmentalization—though I really wished I could since I was leaving for the mountains. But that was our training, because it wouldn't have been correct, even if nobody would ever know the difference. It was an inner discipline, a question of self-control.

Later, with the sun coming up—after we'd stopped in Chinandega to drop off one of the compañeros in the underground who was staying there—Federico started talking to the driver. I remember on the highway we had started singing, to keep up our spirits. Not that they were low, absolutely

49

not! Our morale was fantastic; we knew we were setting out on something that we were sure would triumph. What we didn't know was who among us would live to see that triumph. And as it turned out, some of the people in that car died.

That was the question we were all asking ourselves as we rode along in silence in the jeep, at night, when nobody could see your face, when nobody knew what you were thinking. All those things were a jumble in your mind. You realized this wasn't a movie, like some films when at the end all the actors come on screen in tiny closeups, even the ones who had died. It wouldn't be like that for us; we knew that some of us weren't coming back—and of course we didn't know how long the film was going to last. So we sang. We sang with gusto, but I don't know, it wasn't totally spontaneous. It was as if we were clinging to the words of the song, to the forward thrust of the song, so we wouldn't sink into those ideas.

After a while I noticed that Federico was talking to the driver, then—holy shit!—I recognized him—it was Cuqui Carrión, who's a guerrilla comandante today, and who later took part in the action of December 27. I just about fell over. Because Javier Carrión was a middle-class kid. I knew him because he ran around with Claudia and Guaba, who's the brother of Tito Castillo, the present Minister of Justice. I met them in their apartment in León, where Claudia and I used to go to make love—Cuqui would lend us his apartment. They had a soft, polite way of talking in those days; some of them smoked marijuana. I was getting to know them better; they were starting to get involved in our work. They asked me questions, and instead of studying we spent hours and hours talking. They were middle-class kids with lots of money. Not millionaires maybe, but they had the bucks. Some of them were developing politically. They quit smoking dope just like that and started going to CUUN activities and becoming more serious; but they never lost their cheerfulness, only became more responsible, and studied more, too, which was why I was so surprised. Because, well, I'd been ordered to quit going to their apartment to be with Claudia; I guessed the Frente was using it for meetings, among other things. And in fact they were. But actually Cuqui was already the underground driver for Pedro Aráuz Palacios and couldn't afford to be compromised, so they yanked him out of CUUN activities, too. I thought: Cuqui's dropping out, he's lost interest, he's given up the fight, or who knows what. So when I saw him there, Cuqui so deeply committed, I was very happy.

Well, it got light, and about 5:30 A.M. we pulled into the little farm on the outskirts of Matagalpa. We spent the whole day there; I remember they cooked us a hen. They came for us at night, I think in a jeep. A jeep or a pickup truck, I'm not sure. We didn't know where we were going, just into the mountains. We drove through Matagalpa and continued on until we came to a blacktop road, which may have been the road to Jinotega. Then we left the blacktop and started down a dirt road. This was the most dangerous part of our trip so far; we were entering zones where traditionally there had been guerrilla activity, and though you didn't see much enemy surveillance—because they hadn't spotted many guerrillas—there were informers everywhere and some enemy roadblocks. But the compañeros had already cleared the zone; what that means is they had sent a vehicle on ahead to check for roadblocks; when it came back, our vehicle would start in.

It was a trip of about three hours by jeep, again at night. We hadn't slept; we hadn't slept the day before, and we started out at night. The road was awful; it was mountain-jungle, with ravines, steep inclines and descents, stretches of rough ground with banks of mud and a few shacks where we could glimpse a fire burning in the stove—there was no electricity. Now and then we met a car coming toward us. All this for us meant plunging deeper into a mystery.

Because we didn't know when we would start to march. We didn't ask questions either; we'd been trained not to. We didn't know if we were going straight into the brush or if we were heading for a house, nothing. Not who would be there, if they'd have weapons or be in uniform. Our curiosity was killing us, but you reined it in. By that time we had our weapons, our small arms, out in the open. Then all of a sudden we came to a stop. Compañero Juancito (Juan de Dios Muñoz) let out a shrill whistle and a typical north-country campesino appeared. I was more or less familiar with this type, from vacations with my Uncle Victor when I was a little boy. So I knew that face, that type of campesino, which isn't the same as the campesino of León. There's a difference, I really can't say what it is. A small north-country hat and a lousy set of teeth.

It was almost dark; you could hardly see; our headlights were shut off. A half-moon hung low in the sky, but since it was raining and the rain was falling on our jeep and we were getting wet, we didn't appreciate it very much. They wanted us out of the car. We pulled back off the road and all piled out and trooped into a house. Somebody stirred; kids started bawling. It was about eleven at night. A campesino whispered, "Sleep there," on the ground. There were a couple of boards. We loaded our flashlights. We were making some noise and Juancito said, "Ssshhh, quiet." We were barely making a sound, but still he insisted. For us it wasn't noise, yet it was noise, since there were houses in the area, and the least disturbance in a campesino's house at that hour—the sound of a voice that wasn't a campesino voice—could be deadly, because it meant that guerrillas were coming and going, that strange people were arriving in the night. It could mean anything! We didn't realize how the tiniest sound carried, and how dangerous sound could be, any kind of sound, the sound of a blow, a metallic object, a plastic bag, a sack, anything.

Anyway, we switched on our flashlights and looked around for a place to settle down. You had to take the flashlight and shine it up at the ceiling; if you aimed it to the side the light would show through the chinks in the walls of the shack. What's a campesino going to think if he sees the light of four or five flashlights in the neighboring shack when a campesino is lucky if he owns one flashlight? "But compañero, it's just a flashlight." "Turn it off, turn it off," as if he were talking out of his throat. "Don't keep it on like that. Hold it by the other end." And he explained how you hold a flashlight, by the glass; the only light you want is what filters through your fingers.

Well, we were nervous wrecks. Then we heard a noise; there were animals out there—cows. We noticed that Juancito was jumpier than anybody, maybe because he knew who we were—some of the main leaders of the student movement, of FER—and we knew Juancito; and he knew me and the other guy, too, which put some pressure on him. "Go to sleep, we have to start at dawn," was the last thing he said to us that night. The house was right by a road that wound through hills and a valley, with little shacks scattered here and there. We had to start at dawn in order to get through the populated areas, then on into the mountains over local trails and following marks on trees and all that.

Again we couldn't sleep. How could we with that terrible tension, with those weapons we didn't even know how to shoot? I had a huge revolver that rubbed me raw, that son-of-a-bitch gun, and I was superskinny. That damned revolver poked me in all my bones.

About 4:00 A.M. a whisper: "Wake up compañeros, wake up, ssshh!" We opened the thick plastic bags that made so much noise—you have to open them very gently. Five or six plastic bags, *crac, crac*—you could hear it in the road, in the next shack. We lined up everything we had taken out of the bags. Careful with the flashlights, turn the batteries around, because sometimes a flashlight goes on, can light by itself; if you brush against something and catch the switch, the bulb will light. We packed up everything, took our bags, tied rope around them, and started off, about five of us.

And there my Calvary began, the moment I left that house. A new phase began in my physical life, in my beliefs, in the development of my personality, in everything, in maturity, in everything, everything. Because starting at that moment I began to experience a series of feelings like those any human being in those conditions would feel, from the most beautiful to the most miserable feelings.

The first thing the campesino said was, "Not a sound as we go along." I saw him disappear into a jungly, impassable brush. I said to myself, I wonder what he wants in there? It was impassable, but the campesino didn't come back. And there was that jungly, impassable brush. He never said to wait, but I waited, half-expecting he would come back out. The brush was impassable, but the compa didn't return. "And the compa?" "I don't know, he went in there . . . he hasn't come out." It was like a wall, a giant obstacle. I squinted but couldn't see him. "You don't think he went out the other way while you were standing there?" "But I don't see how anybody could get through . . . no shit, take a look." I went in a little and didn't see him. Could it be possible we were supposed to march in this impassable brush? It can't be, I thought. How could we march in that? It was tough going but I pushed on, moving aside the branches along the way he had gone; I noticed a sort of passage, with the brush all beaten down ahead of me. Brush to the side, brush in back of me—I was deep in brush. So that's what this shit is all about. Have I fucked up? I thought by that time I was lost, he was way ahead of me. But he's heading into the mountains, and we're supposed to be going with him . . . son of a bitch! I started marching faster. But I kept falling; I had my bag over my shoulder, but it kept getting caught on those damn branches and falling off behind.

My name in the Frente was Eugenio. "Wait, Eugenio!" We were making a ridiculous racket. We were all nervous because I'd lost sight of our guide, fuck! He'd gone off and left me. I never thought we would go through there. I thought we would go along a little path. I didn't understand what the mountains were. He went straight into the brush, the dense brush, the bastard. I didn't understand this. And it was dark and damp, and I mean freezing. These were northern mountains, with those shitty little trees, young trees the size of a small house. We weren't yet into the mammoth trees but still in the dense brush that had once been mountain jungle, but which had been cleared and now a new brush was springing up. Scraggly trees, but higher than a shack and with every type of vine you could imagine, lianas with tiny leaves or bigger leaves and grasses of all kinds, everything green, right? You had to wade through green, like when you enter the water and go splashing through water; here you dive into green, into vegetation. Or it's like when you walk and go pushing through wind; here you go crashing through green.

Anyway, the campesino went into the brush and pushed on, deeper and deeper in. And we bitched: "That damn son of a bitch." I was all tangled up, my bag was caught, I yanked it, then fell down with it on top of me and got all wet. I picked it up again, slung it over my shoulder, and right away it was cutting into my neck. When one shoulder got tired, I'd shift the bag to the other. I was trying to climb. But how in hell did that damned idiot get up this hill? I said. How can I climb with this bag if my hands aren't free? I didn't know if I should keep hold of the bag or throw it on ahead of me to climb up. But whoosh! I was sliding back, so it was impossible. Then I took it from underneath and tried to hoist myself up with my hand, and down I went—a major battle to go 30 yards with that bag. That bastard. But I couldn't hear him anywhere. And we jabbered on: "Brother, I don't think he's in there." "Eugenio, Eugenio, you don't know where you're going!" "I don't think he's in there anymore." "Eugenio, do you think he's behind us somewhere?" "No, brother, I'm positive I saw him go in there." "But you, what do you know, I suppose you're used to this brush." "Hombre, it's just that I feel . . ." "Just look, look in." "Aha, it looks like he went through there." You could see big tracks.

And in a while the campesino came back out, pissed off, but very respectful to the city man: "Compañeros, I can hear you yelling all the way over there." That was right; I couldn't see him, but he could hear us. He could hear us on ahead; he had experience. He could hear the racket, our screams and squabbling. Because right from the start our good humor went down the drain, our good natures. We hadn't gone 200 yards when we were talking to each other in a tone we had never used before, different even from the critical tone of our study groups in the Frente cell. It was more like when you were little and fighting with your kid brother: "Don't bug me, just get out of my way!" And the campesino was back: "Compañeros, you're making way too much racket. And if you don't speed up, it'll be light and the Guard will see us and slaughter us all." So let's get going! We were running, or I should say we were lost and scrambling to keep up with our guide! We were starting to feel the icy chill of the damp, and we marched for about two hours in real misery.

Our hands were a mess of tiny threads of blood, not bleeding much, but you could see the blood. We had been attacked by a sort of poison ivy. That son-of-a-bitch campesino is immune to pain, I thought. First it got on your hands, then you spread it to your face; you didn't know whether to throw down your pack or put up with the terrible itch; two hours of that, uphill and down, and all of a sudden a big surprise—we ran smack into some creeks, little streams, springs of water. But I didn't see them until *bam!* I was right on top of them. "Look, we can cross over here . . ." A creek about a half-yard wide, but when you waded in it was a deep gully.

You can't see in the mountains. Everything is dark at first, until gradually you start seeing like a cat. You start to differentiate among the dark shapes to make out the lay of the land. But at first it all looked the same. We sloshed through the gulleys, almost knee-deep in water. I didn't know whether to stop and dump the water out of my shoes or what. "Brother, the water . . ." "No, brothers, we've got to hurry or we'll be left behind." But it seemed odd to me not to stop and dump out the water. And I would keep reaching down to my damp sock, and I got all caught up in that, obsessed with that as we

56

went along. Until, finally! we came to a halt. "Is this the camp?" I asked. I hadn't the slightest idea. It seemed as if we had marched for who knows how long; it must have been about three hours nonstop. How far can you march in three hours? I calculated how long it took us to walk from León to Managua on the highway. But that was level and our path was rough, so I figured we had marched about 12 miles.

"Let's stop here; we're going to wait for daybreak." It was already getting light. "Compa, when will we get there?" "Well, at the rate you've been going, if we really speed up, we'll be there in three days." "What?" we said. "Three days to get to the compañeros' first camp?" In fact, it wasn't really a camp but where Silvestre, or Faustino (also known as Valdivia), was. He was there to work in the zone and had a tiny camp where he hid out so he could work in the valley with about three compañeros—he worked with Aurelio Carrasco, and Edwin Cordero was there, and Jorge the baker and two more campesinos. In our group we had Iván Gutiérrez, Aquiles Reyes, and a couple of others. "Son of a bitch, compa," I said to him—you see, I talked to him in the way I knew was best, since I was more educated, to get around him and get information without his realizing. The campesinos are very quick, and on top of that suspicious of city people. I didn't let on, but I wanted to find out when we were going to come out of that hell we were marching through. That poison ivy had just about done me in.

By dawn I was half covered with mud, soaked to the skin, my hands were totally screwed, and we were starved. We had already gone two nights with no sleep and about twenty-four hours with no food; we had no idea, we could never have guessed what was in store for us. Had we known we could have stuffed ourselves with some huge meals before starting out. So we sat down to rest by the bank of a creek about a yard across. "Break out the chow. It's suppertime," the campesino announced. But nobody wanted to eat. Our stomachs were tied in knots. I saw that the campesino had taken out the powdered milk we had brought, the White Lily brand with the green label from the Prolacsa Dairy. He got out a little pail, which was already all dented and banged up, and poured in some sugar, a lot of sugar—when there's sugar they eat things sweet—then he cut a stick, which he used as a stirring spoon, filled the pail to the top with water, and stirred in the milk. Then he drank the whole thing straight down! We just stared, amazed that anybody could drink so much. It was really big, I'm not shitting you, full to the top. And since there was a little milk still in powder form stuck to the bottom, he took his finger, his fingernail, and scraped around the edge and ate that, and was still working to get the last bit out from under his nails with his teeth. Son of a bitch! we said; those poor campesinos don't even drink milk, but he drank it anyway . . . shit!

We started asking questions about the route. "No," he said, "now we're going on a narrow trail, and we'll keep about 20 yards apart. I'll go first." I went right behind him. "Stick close to me," I said; "get too far ahead and I'm lost." So we started marching; we left the brush, passed over a lower ground cover, and came upon another type of brush, different from the first. More a mountain jungle with huge trees, but tangled with all sorts of smaller trees and weeds and grasses and every kind of underbrush you can imagine, so overgrown you couldn't even see the ground. And you couldn't see the sky because the trees were embracing overhead; you couldn't see a thing, only tiny needle holes of blue or white. It started raining before we headed out, and it kept on raining.

I didn't understand why the campesino was so obsessed with our not breaking the brush. "Compa, don't crush the grasses"; "compa, don't snap that branch." At first I thought it was the campesino's love of nature. We, too, theoretically respected nature: we were against all the awful things that had happened in León with the problem of the dust storms, because the whole west had been stripped of trees to grow cotton. But it seemed to me to be overdoing it in the middle of an ocean of vegetation to be saying, "Compa, don't nick the trees with your machete." And when we were ready to march he would line us up, move us apart a little with his machete, then, using both his machete and his hands, start plumping up the grass where we had sat and smashed it down. He also arranged the leaves; he was acting just like El Gato Munguía, who adored plants and had been brought up to take care of them. But these were the things that could betray us.

Anyway, we started marching about 6:00 A.M., in a drizzling rain, exhausted, I can't tell you how tired from marching. My shoulders were shot to hell, my hands raw from the weight of the bag, which was about 25 pounds. We followed a muddy trail that wound deep into the mountains. Horses had left their hoofprints in the mud, and so many mules and horses had traveled that path, all leaving hoofprints, deep holes in the mud, that between the hoofprints was a sort of higher ground, which was where you walked, like on jagged little waves. In winter it was one big stretch of mud, a mudhole, clayish mud. We would slip and *bam!* you were flat on your ass. You picked yourself up but then your bag was all dirty; as you marched along you tried to clean it off, since it was new and covered with mud. But once you had the mud off your bag, where could you wipe your hands? On a branch? You took another step, teetered, put out your hand, and were drenched with mud all over again.

Then it really started raining. We tramped on through the mud; it was impossible to get a good foothold on the ridge between the hoofprints, besides which the rise was muddy, too. But when you marched in the hoofprints you sank in mud up to your knees. And mud poured in at the top of your rubber boots. Wading through mud . . . with your bag all black from being dropped so many times. Finally you said to yourself, "That son-of-a-bitch bag can just stay dirty!" And that's how you learn that nobody in the guerrillas cleans his bag.

I was carrying a shotgun, the one-shell kind that you break open, clack, and put in the shell. My military equipment consisted of that gun and the revolver that was rubbing me raw. I had already switched it to the other side; my skin was so raw that it burned when I sweated, and sometimes it would jab me in the ribs as I walked. I had a big kerchief where I wrapped my shells, since we still didn't have cartridge belts, and I tied it onto the other part of my belt, the opposite side. So I had my shotgun, my revolver, and a handful of shells in the back pocket of my pants; I held the shotgun in one hand, since it didn't have a sling, and the bag in the other; when I got tired I'd switch the bag, which was heaviest, to my other hand. I still hadn't figured out how in hell I was supposed to march— was I supposed to climb by hoisting myself up with my hands? Sometimes I took my shotgun and bag in one hand and tried to climb with the other. But what happened was I'd come crashing down and land on top of the shells and my ass would hurt even more. The longer you marched the more your body hurt, until it got to the point where you couldn't stand it, it hurt too much, you were raw all over. You tromped on, and the farther you went the more tired you got, until a kind of dizziness came over you. Then suddenly a strange thing happened, which happened to a number of us in exactly the same way: we heard a noise that sounded just like a siren: *eeiiiii eeiiiii eeiiiii* . . . an air-raid siren. But there was no siren.

We tromped on, the campesino in the lead, and that constant battle not to be left behind, to keep moving forward, and again and again you fell down in the mud. Then just like that you forgot all about getting rid of the mud, even off your hands. Then to keep my balance I would ram my shotgun up to the hilt in mud and clog the barrel completely. Or when I was slipping, the gun would pop open and the shell would drop out; so I would have to look for it, pawing through the mud with my hands. But when I found it I couldn't clean it, since everything I had was soaked with mud.

I realized that my shells had slipped out of my kerchief— had been dropping out along the way—because a campesino had found some of them. "Go find those bullets, they could give us away," the compañero said. "But they're buried in the mud," I protested. "No, compa, you'd better get going." The last thing I wanted to do was turn around and slog back 50 yards through that fucking mudhole, besides which every inch of my body ached and was raw and sore. We had been better off in the brush where we were before. Can you imagine that nightmare of mud, can you imagine how bad it was if I was longing for the brush? Well, we marched all that day. The bag got heavier and heavier, and we would have to rest, one guy every 500 yards, another every 300, another at 200.

In the distance, a campesino cut across the trail: "Adiós! Adiós!" The campesinos knew we weren't natives, that we came from the city. But they played the fool out of fear, so we wouldn't think they had discovered we came from town.

We noticed that our guide was tromping along very easily there ahead of us. He wasn't covered with mud, except for his boots. He pulled out a spotless kerchief and mopped the sweat from his face, while my kerchief was sopping with mud. I had mud on my hair, on my face, everywhere. Before we were marching through brush, now we were marching through mud. When you tried to get a footing on those jagged waves of ground you lost your balance, your bag swung to one side, and *bang!* it knocked you down, because the bag overwhelmed you. Or you manage not to fall, but the bag pulls you back- ward—*slam!*—or you let go of it and keep from falling but stumble off to the side. One last time I took up my bag and lugged it on. I hoped to God the mud would be level on ahead, but the fact was the trail wound up and down through the mountains, with now and then a deep ravine alongside.

I remember we stopped about four in the afternoon; we were going to sleep, the campesino said. Great, we were stop- ping to eat and then to sleep. We left the trail and went into the brush, about 500 yards in, which is where we would sleep. All this was new to us. "Now pay attention. We're going to enter the brush scattered out, about every ten yards, so keep about ten yards between each man. But before we start in," he said, "we're going to march for a while on the shoulder of the path, out of the mud. Pick up your feet like you're riding a bike and try to put your foot in the same place as the guy ahead of you." We left the path and started marching alongside it over a stubbly vegetation. We picked up our feet the way he said, each of us marching in the footprints of the guy ahead. So, anyone coming down the path would only see one set of footprints. When you're going through deep mud your footprints will eventually disappear. But if you're out of the mud on the vegetation, if you don't want to leave tracks and trample down the whole area, you have to march in the steps of the guy ahead of you, with big strides. So you go a fair stretch like that, 300 to 500 yards, up to over a mile; it was rough and very awkward going because the ground was uneven. The topography was rugged as hell. You couldn't do it; physically and mentally it was impossible to do. It was very hard because it was so awkward. Shit, we said, this son of a bitch is too much. But that was survival in the guerrilla war: not being detected.

One time we marched like that for some 500 or 1,000 yards, sometimes for half a day. It was superawkward; but the moment came when our guide would strike off into the brush, also with giant strides like this, *pam, pam, pam,* into the brush; then the next guy dove in, *pran, pran, pran.* Before long we were back together again in the brush. We didn't want to leave prints either going into or coming out of the brush. So if they were on your trail they couldn't find you. Later the Guard figured out how to follow our tracks. There were campesinos who knew all these tricks, and when campesino-compañeros were arrested, some of them talked. So the Guard learned all these methods. The repression was ferocious; there's no way to describe it. We came up with a thousand ingenious things along this line, but the Guard was always right on top of us.

Fire in the Rain

All day as we went along I kept thinking about the camp; I was spurred on by the thought of the camp, remembering everything they had told me about the mountain. In the city the mountain was a myth, it was a symbol, as I told you before. I wondered what the camps would be like, and what Modesto looked like, how tall would he be, if I had ever met him—all these things. What I mean is the idea of getting to the camp and demystifying, that's the word, demystifying it, once and for all, finally seeing it from the inside, that's what I'd spent almost six years working for day and night, with no Christmas, no Holy Week, no vacations. All because of that mountain. Because of the FSLN, because of that mystery which was growing greater with every passing day. If anything in that hellhole of mud, in that nightmare of mud and raw blisters and exhaustion and discomfort made me happy it was this: finally, on my own two feet, I was approaching it—I was going to see those famous men in person, the guerrillas, people like Che. What would their beards be like, and the battles, and the work with the campesinos? How would they cook? I was going to be in the heart of the Frente Sandinista, in the most hidden, the most virgin part of the Frente, the most secret, the most delicate, the Frente of

Carlos Fonseca and all of that. Carlos: I had never met him, never had a chance to meet him. And all of that propelled me forward.

Maybe it was machismo or wanting to set an example, but I think that more than anything deep down it was a sense of pride, which we all had, that I drew on when I felt tired, or when it seemed I was screwing up the march by being out of shape. Because don't forget where I was coming from— drinking, staying up late, smoking, eating junk, never exercising, then all of a sudden, *bam!* I was right in the middle of something that called for men. Men? Shit! Toughened campesinos! Seeing how useless I felt then on that march after being accustomed to leading student marches on the paved streets of Managua—see what I'm saying, me, the hero of the young girls! Shit! Now I was nothing but a miserable dog. You feel your ideas so deeply, so intimately. Finally, it was not possible that I could fail to come to grips with that environment, but I felt I would never be able to do it. You go through incredibly low moments. You feel absolutely impotent when the first blisters pop out on your feet and your legs are full of sores and raw spots and every step is another spot rubbed raw.

A point comes on the march when it seems that your body and your clothes and everything you are carrying have a single rhythm, one rhythm. As though my heart was beating to the same rhythm as the bullets that were chafing my ass or my legs. Pounding to the same rhythm as the two pocketfuls of bullets. Heart and legs; when you took a step it was as if everything was moving in unison, in unison with your stride, with the bone that was swiveling, with your pistol jabbing you in the crotch. Just think of that jabbing and chafing, how pistol and legs and bullets and blistering shoes and your heart were all pounding, all beating in unison and *bom, bom,* you are marching and your body absorbs all those blows to the skin, and right through your skin, throughout your entire organism as if suddenly a harmony took hold of you, of your whole body, inside and out. And when you put your foot down on the ground, and when you put your foot down once again, it was as if that thud was in rhythm with the hammering of your heart and the rubbing of your pistol and the chafing of the bullets and the blistering of your feet, right down to the flow of your blood and the flick of your eyes when you were looking where to put your foot. Because when you march you feel so shitty, so tired and miserable and tense from trying not to fall, not to slip, that you keep your eyes glued to the ground to see where to put your foot. So, vision and hearing and heartbeat and blistering blows, the thud of your foot, your pistol rubbing and bullets in back and bullets in front—it's all one blow, one movement, one man marching. Then with blow upon blow coming at you through all those smaller blows, of raw blisters and fatigue and the slap of your bag swinging you to one side, and with the next step to the other side, it's all one rhythm with the rubbing and the beat of your heart.

You are thinking, too, as you march, you are thinking back and images arise from the past, and also images of the mystery you are about to unravel. And you feel you'll unravel it all in one blow, with one heartbeat, one bullet, one blistering pain, one gasping breath. Because your breathing is also in step with the other beats. Though on the outside you see only a man marching, actually that man marching is made up of an incredible number of little beats, blistering beats, lung-beats, heartbeats.

I was horrified to think they might be looking at me, so I busted my balls so the stroke would be an elegant stroke, a martial stroke, a guerrilla stroke, a courageous stroke, a noble, masterful stroke. You might say this was machismo or egoism, this business of being an example, of setting an example. And maybe they weren't looking at me at all. I was so curious to see the compañeros face to face, to know, finally—all this gave me strength, so when we stopped to rest in the middle of the march, in that place I mentioned, there were plenty of mysteries; everything was new. I kept a sharp eye on the campesinos, on everything they did and how they did it so I could do it later myself.

"We're going to cook," they announced. And how were we

going to cook, and where? I thought cooking meant setting up camp, setting things up. It was raining, and where were we going to get the stuff to eat; and what were you going to cook in up there, the cooking pots, where were they? And the stove, the oven, and what in hell were we going to cook?

Anyway, when we were marching along we heard a *gurrr, gurrr, gurrr, hoossss.* We thought it must be wildcats or mountain lions, and on the basis of that I made some rapid calculations: *pra, pra,* three tigers, with five shots, one shot per man . . . we'll bring them down with pistols, son of a bitch! And my rifle up to the butt in mud! Okay, with my revolver then, I'll kill it, *bam, bam,* I'll shoot it and kill it. Because campesinos know what to do when five tigers turn up; campesinos know those things, right? So the compañeros must know how to deal with wildcats.

But the campesino told us, no, those weren't wildcats, they were monkeys, Congo monkeys. The Congo monkey is a son of a bitch, ugly, filthy; the meat is tough, brooother! And it stinks. But if you're hungry it's delicious—monkey soup, which is a broth that simmers for four hours. So the campesino gave the orders: "Let's go shoot a little monkey, okay? Give me the .22, come on, Eugenio, you, Eugenio, come on!" he said. Ah, how fantastic to walk without carrying anything, out of the mountain mud, free of weight; I didn't bring my rifle since it still needed to be cleaned; I had taken out the bullets that were chafing me and had them in my hand. My hands and feet were a mess. I didn't want to walk, but what the hell, I wanted to go along to see what it would be like, and to show him I wasn't worn out.

Then I saw the monkeys, a troop of monkeys, droves of monkeys leaping over the branches, incredibly high, in trees 100 yards high, even higher, and monkeys swinging from branch to branch. They were racing over the treetops. Miles of them, hundreds of miles of monkeys in troops.

The monkey is like man. Anyway, the .22 and *bam!* That'll bring that monkey down! A huge monkey, no shit, a good yard or half-yard long, no, about a yard, counting the tail. I could see the monkeys were looking at us just as we were looking at them. I had never tasted monkey or anything like it, but I was never squeamish about food, and besides I came prepared to eat anything. But I wasn't very hungry. We hadn't wanted to eat at all—it hurt us to swallow when we ate—who knows why it hurt to swallow when we started out. What was that? Crack, crack! *Aiiii!* The monkey shrieked when it was hit; we hit it three times, and it finally fell *perrr-bamg*—they come crashing down through the branches. They are very heavy. A monkey can weigh up to 35 pounds; it can even weigh 100 pounds. So the monkey fell. It was the first time I'd ever seen a monkey at close range. There was a monkey near where my grandma lived, a tiny monkey, but it scared me to see it up close, and it was really small. But that was a long time ago. The first time I ever saw a monkey close up, that son-of-a-bitch monkey's face looked like a little old man with a little boy's body, a little old man's face. And we carted it off to our camp.

But what were we going to do with a monkey, where were we going to skin a monkey? How, where, and who was going to skin the monkey, and what seasoning for the monkey? Well, we were all staring, taking it all in. The campesino picked up the monkey, and we carted it off, cutting five pla-tanillo leaves along the way, which are like chagüite leaves; I cut them, *whock whock.* I thought we were going to sleep, to put down our ground covers, but everything was wet, the grass, the jungle. I noticed the campesino was starting to clear a yard or so of brush with his machete: to dig up the dirt, be-cause the dirt on top was very damp, to get down to some drier dirt. "Hey you, go get some stones. In the ravine there are stones." So the boys went to look for stones, and they brought back some that weren't right. "Those stones are no good. Go get some others."

We had finally stopped marching; it was a cheerful mo-ment, our first night as guerrillas. We all felt like guerrillas in that place. We felt like guerrilla men. I had been in that area before with the Boy Scouts, with Juan José Quezada, but that was different. Now the Guard was there. If the Guard came we'd have to fight them. Can you imagine? Not one of us would have come out alive. Except maybe for the campesino, because he could have run, and he had a decent gun.

"Put down the stones," he said. We got a kettle, and he put in the leaves he had set aside; we started skinning the monkey, *ziip, ziip, ziip,* in the rain. The monkey had worms; we got rid of those, and the skinned monkey looked just like a skinned little boy with no head and the tail chopped off; cut off the hands and the monkey is a little boy. We saw that it really looked like a little boy, but we didn't mention it because we didn't want to seem like squeamish women. He took up the pieces of the monkey's hands, the feet, the legs, the tailbone of the little boy—except that it was a monkey—then he tossed the meat into the pot and poured water over it and a handful of salt. Not washing it, just wiping it off a little. The clear water was tinted pink from the drops of blood, because the monkey had not been wiped clean.

Now for the firewood. But how could we build a fire if that damn wood was wet? The campesino went to get some wood; they know all about how to spot dry wood, dry branches that are still growing, that are wet on the outside but dry inside; and the better the wood the less trouble you have, because hard wood is less porous—the water can't penetrate. He returned with the firewood, peeled off the bark, and the wood was dry. But how were you going to get a fire going? Would you start it with a match? Good luck! Who was going to have a match up there? We were watching everything very closely. It was the first time we'd seen this ritual that later on we became true masters of. The ritual of building a fire in the mountains—the real expert was David Blanco. David Blanco was a genius at fire building. That guy could build you a fire anywhere except in water. In the mud, even by a puddle; he would first get rid of the puddle, then build a fire. He's wet, everything around is wet, but he builds you a fire. Fire in the mountain is an art. It's harder to get a fire going than to turn on a woman in the mountains.

The campesino cut little pieces of wood, then cut them in two with his machete, *chop, chop*. Then he took one of the pieces and cut it down still more, then did the same thing with the other sticks, cutting them down into smaller and smaller sticks, until finally there was a pile of sawdust and wood chips, a huge pile of wood chips, then larger chips and larger chips up to little pieces of wood. First he piled the wood chips in the center. He had already rigged up a champa, a plastic sheet, a rain cover overhead, to keep the water from screwing us up. He put the wood chips on the shavings, right on top. Then a bit bigger piece, then a bit bigger, with the biggest ones more to the outside, with the wood chips in the center. Then he took a scrap of boot rubber—boot rubber burns if you set a match to it. So he lit a scrap of worn-out boot rubber that he had in his pack. And very gently, so they wouldn't fall apart, he separated the little sticks and in the center set up a very fragile little structure of chips. The chips have to be touching and very dry; they have to exchange very dry kisses there in a mountain of damp wood. This is the driest thing there is for hundreds of miles around. You drop the burning rubber into the center of the wood chips and they catch fire. As the fire starts burning, flames leap up out of the damp, out of the wet. Fire is born and leaps higher and higher; it travels toward the sticks, starts burning the little sticks, then the bigger sticks and bigger sticks until the fire is roaring. You can hardly believe you are seeing a fire. You dry off, you get warm. It's incredible how in the middle of so much dampness, so much rain, in a dripping jungle, fire can appear.

We put the kettle of icy mountain water on the stones, and before long it was boiling. We switched on the radio and started listening to the news. The sound was barely audible; we had brought along a radio antenna which we hung on a tree to get better reception. So there we were around the fire saying anything that popped into our heads, asking the campesino all sorts of questions. We couldn't stand the suspense any longer: how many men were in there, what were their aliases, what places were we going to go through? About three hours like that, bullshitting and listening to the radio crackling and fading in and out, listening to Radio Corporation when it still "spoke the language of the people."

We listened to the "News at Five." When they realized in the city that we'd all left, it would be an explosion. What leaders would take over? This guy or that guy, did their girl friends know where they had gone? Some of the guys had said they were going to study abroad; others had told their girl friends the truth.

Okay then, the big soup was ready, each of us with his own little pot. We weren't hungry, but how could we not eat when we had gone to so much trouble? Besides, it was hot, and the heat sparked our appetites. We dove in and ate a fantastic meal of monkey. No shit, it was damn good.

Meeting Tello

We left the following day. All traces of the fire and cooking had to be hidden; we dug a hole, threw in the stones, buried the charred bits of wood, ashes, and embers, then threw leaves down and spread them around as if nobody had ever been there. We didn't sleep in our hammocks that night. At dawn we started off through the brush, not through the mud. Another experience, another battle with vines; the bag kept getting caught in the vines. Sometimes you couldn't get through, you had to practically crawl under the brush, dragging your bag—that's tiring.

This time we went another way, which took us to where Evelio (Nelson Suárez) lived, in a place called Las Bayas. I noticed that the campesino stopped about 100 yards back: "Ssshhh," he warned, "nobody make a sound." And he took his machete and rapped it against a tree, *bam, bam, bam*. Then he went off to the little shack about 50 yards away, *bam, bam, bam*—the return signal.

We entered the shack, the kitchen; the kids were in bed; there was a newborn baby. A tiny shack built right out of the brush—of branches and straw with a wood roof. No table, nothing; the bed was built out of the same wood. There was nothing made of artificial materials, not even any home-crafted items, except for a couple of little plastic glasses. That was where we would sleep; they had already finished supper, but they gave us some tortillas.

About 6:00 A.M. we reached our contact point, where Silvestre was. I don't know what I was expecting from this contact, but it really impressed me. I had a talk with Valdivia there. I'll never forget it—when we reached Valdivia in the morning, there were about five compañeros; you see, Valdivia always met the new people and leapfrogged them on to the other compañeros up ahead. On to René Tejada, about two days' march away. I figured when we reached Silvestre we would find a camp, I'm not sure what I was expecting.

In fact, there was a mountain gorge with a gigantic tree fallen across it; it must have just recently fallen, I thought, because its leaves were still green. And under the fallen tree there was a little space between the ground and the trunk. The trunk was massive, with a whole shitload of branches. And the compas were holed up beneath that giant tree, hidden in the huge branches that were so enormous they could hang their hammocks from them. First the signal, three raps. They answered back and faces popped out, but who were they? The usual curiosity.

A skinny guy appeared, and I mean skin and bones, with a face that was elongated, and a beard. A hard face, as if he wasn't very enthusiastic about anything, including us. I was a lot more enthusiastic about getting there and meeting the compañeros and incorporating myself than he was to have us there. It was a dry, serious, even tense business on his part. He was a lean guy, with a big nose, wearing a tan shirt and green pants—not a military green; his clothes were civilian—and he wore a leather belt with a pistol. He was not in uniform, but in something that was between military and civilian dress; guerrilla dress you might call it. I think his rifle was a Garand.

Flavio (Edwin Cordero) was there, too; he's now the representative of the MINIT, the Ministry of the Interior, in the

Fourth Region. We called him the Doctor because he'd been studying medicine. A short, stocky guy. I turned over to him a bunch of letters they had sent from the city.

We set about rigging up some cartridge belts for our bullets, trying to halfway equip ourselves since we were heading deeper in. The camps were deep in the massive trees where theoretically the main body of guerrillas was located. By that time we were hungry, but there was no food, except what our collaborator had brought—three pathetic tortillas and a few beans for the lot of us, a little bite for everybody. The hunger was beginning to get to us.

We chatted a bit with Valdivia, who recognized me—at least I think he did, because he asked about the university, how things were going, the university reform, just small talk. I don't know if he knew my brothers, but it came out in our conversation: "You see, brother, I left to join the guerrillas on a Sunday, and the next Wednesday my brother Chema and I were all set to graduate. Emir was in his fourth year of Economics." I told Silvestre that we were four brothers, and I was sure that the others were going to come up, too. "That's right. If the mother gets at least one of her sons back, that's enough," he said. Son of a bitch, did that hit me like a ton of bricks! If only one comes back, if only one . . . You might say I was seeing from a little closer up the real likelihood of what we were thinking about in the jeep. It was out of the question, it was too much to ask that we'd all come out alive. This was not a film, it was not the movies. And the fact is, I was the only one of us who survived.

Well, they fitted us out up there; they equipped us. We recovered from our blisters, and for the first time in three days I took a shit. "I'm going to go shit," I said. "You know how to do it?" he asked. "How?" "Take a machete, dig a hole, shit in the hole, and when you're finished, cover it with dirt and then with leaves, so there's no trace." This is basic security for the guerrilla. "And how do I wipe myself?" "With leaves, you wipe yourself with leaves. You take a handful of leaves and

73

wipe yourself like that." Fine, that didn't scare me. Off I went with all my sores and blisters—pretty pathetic. I dug a hole, took my shit, then grabbed a couple of leaves. Well, what happened was, I drenched my hand with shit trying to wipe myself; it was impossible. If figured out later that you had to take a huge handful of leaves. I had used just two little leaves and imagined I was going to wipe myself like that! What a mess: my fingernails were full of shit. I dug my nails into the dirt to get rid of it. Then I took more leaves and wiped again. Common sense teaches you, the hard way, that you don't wipe with a few leaves, but with a big handful of leaves.

That night they sent me on to Tello, to René Tejada. We didn't get in that night because of problems on the march. There were two campesinos, veteran marchers. Pedro went in front, with Aurelio Carrasco behind and me in the middle. I carried a pack, right? A pack with huge burlap bags that they put straps on so it could be carried on your back, like the packs in militia practice. Can you imagine, me marching along with Aurelio, with those two expert marchers? I should mention that Pedro, the guy who I told you was in the lead, was one of our top mountain guides. He was our main guide in those days; he had to have been in the mountains longer than anybody; a veteran of Zinica, a son of one of the campesina women of Cuá—there was a song about that. Venancia was his mother.

I felt more comfortable marching. I had my pack and a cartridge belt for the bullets, so that rubbing against my ass was gone. We were off to a good start. I felt sturdier; I had gone through the experience of marching through that hideous brush and mud. I was a little steadier on my feet. The thing is, we had to march at night. We started out with flashlights, always keeping our hand over the glass to block most of the light.

It was my first march alone with those compañeros, those veteran marchers, so I was forced to march better, so as not to be a drag on them. Besides, there was no hope we would stop and rest because one of them was tired. It was just me, and I had to pour it on, give it all I had. I don't know why, but suddenly it seemed that I was sailing along. The campesino in the lead with me right on his tail, I was marching along right behind him. We slogged through banks of mud and I hardly fell down or slipped or anything. Sometimes I saw a campesino fall, but I was hardly falling at all. Finally my legs were adjusting, were toughening up. I had my weaknesses, that's for sure, and lack of experience, but it wasn't like before.

That was the day we got lost. We got lost. We stopped marching at 4:00 A.M., slept, then got up to head into the mountains. But Pedrito got turned around, and we ended up marching again through the brush. I was getting used to shifting my weight from one foot to the other, and by that time I had a rifle sling, so my hand was free—flashlight in one hand and one hand free. I was getting the hang of the topography, figuring out how to get a footing when I was going downhill or climbing up, how to get over a tree trunk, or underneath, without snagging my pack.

It wasn't long before the chafing started in. But this time it wasn't everywhere as before. Basically it hurt around my waist; my belt was rubbing. It hit me right at those two bones at the base of my legs, the pelvic bones. As I marched along my belt would slip down and start pinching me. You're climbing up and it's slipping down and pinching you, and pretty soon these bones are a mess and bother the shit out of you and your pack is getting heavier. And before long your whole body starts to feel like hell, just as bad as before. Raw all over, every step a blow. Your legs get fatigued; the calves of your legs start to ache.

But finally we got to Tello. He was all alone. At first I didn't know who he was; I realized who he had to be when he told me, not what his name was, but how one of his brothers had died. The story of how David Tejada Peralta died is famous—the Guard murdered him, then threw his body into the Santiago volcano. So we met Tello. Tello wasn't like Valdivia, but they had one thing in common—their faces, the expression on their faces. Tello was thin and strong, a thin, strong guy, roughly my height or a bit taller, with short, very curly hair, kinky hair, and with fine features and good teeth. He had tiny little eyes and abrupt gestures—very countrified. He had picked up the campesino way of talking. When he talked to you, even though he was from the city, he sounded just like a campesino.

I'm not sure why, but right from the start Tello began to be close to me, to open up a little. We were with him for about three days; we had to wait for the boys who had stayed behind with Silvestre. I was going up to join Rodrigo (Carlos Agüero) in the main camp about fifteen days' march deeper in. We were all supposed to meet where Tello was, to go join up with the main body of guerrillas. I don't remember if it was on the first or second night when Tello invited me to hang my hammock next to his. As we lay talking in our hammocks I realized that he knew who I was, that my name was Omar Cabezas, that I was a student leader, a guy with some political ability. Sometimes you can't say all you want to say to the campesinos; you have to talk on their level. So when I arrived, Tello opened up to me; now he could talk. He had so many memories and ideas and dreams, all sorts of things, doubts and things he wanted to know about, to ask about, certain things that were going on in the city that he had no information about, and so on.

So he started letting out all he had inside him, something he hadn't done with the campesinos because he thought they probably wouldn't understand. Because urban people are more complex, more abstract, more sophisticated, complicated— their feelings, emotions, ways of interpreting things. And Tello started talking about his family, his belief in the guerrilla war. He was depressed. He was a guy who you could see was hardened by the mountain, the shitty food, the rain. But I also sensed that Tello was deeply lonely. Later he told me he had left behind a woman he had loved very much. It made him very nervous to talk about that. He had rapid-fire gestures; he was very agile, very strong, on the surface a tough, weather-beaten guy. But just scratch that surface and he was capable of crying; you would see how sensitive he really was inside, how tender and human. Tello was a man who was capable of crying out of disappointment. Later René Vivas told me what happened on the march from Tello's camp to Rodrigo's camp. Because of us, Tello cried. Of course he didn't understand that it wasn't possible for us to be any good at that time. But he had wanted us to be much better right from the start. Out of his longing for freedom and for victory, out of his longing to have all that suffering over, or for whatever reason.

As I heard it, he thought he was getting seasoned men, tried and true guerrillas who were used to marching and carrying packs, trained fighters. Then, marching along, one of us burst out, "Okay that's it, we can't go on," and Tello cried, out of disappointment. René Vivas told me that—that he was capable of crying out of disappointment. Tello had an army background, had been a lieutenant in the National Guard and after that had received military training from the Palestinians, who are extremely rigorous. Tello's method of whipping us into shape was brutal. It was a sort of military school along Palestinian lines, extremely tough. His military background was a combination of those two things, which he wanted to pass on to us through a crash course, to us "good-for-nothings" as he called us, fresh from our first year at the University of León, thrust all of a sudden into that unbelievable, unimaginable hell.

Loneliness at the Mountain's Heart

Tello ended up having a big influence on my development. You could say he was one of the guys who influenced me the most in the mountains. Not even
Modesto or Rodrigo had as much influence on me as Tello
and David Blanco.

In a little while more compañeros arrived, the ones who had
stayed behind with Silvestre. And we got together some food,
some cornmeal; we were super-loaded down. We dug up some
weapons that had been buried there to be taken up into the
mountains, and which we could use ourselves. So, laden down
like mules with provisions and two weapons apiece, it was a
helluva lot harder to march. But off we went, about ten or
twelve men, I'm not being exact since I've forgotten the spe-
cifics. We were heading for the center of the mountains, about
a fifteen-day march. It took us about five days, I think, to
reach the camp. You can bet we marched as much in the brush
and jungle as we did on trails. It was our first big march.

First we marched one night, then two nights, then a day.
We started out this time to march for fifteen days, never running into any houses—only an isolated shack here and

there—through an area that if I'm not mistaken was called El Naranjo, beyond Zinica.

You could say that march was our baptism by fire as guerrillas, as veteran marchers. The ones before had been nothing; we barely got our feet wet on those first marches. For the first time on that march feelings of a very different sort began to surface. About two days out you start to feel you can't go on, that your body won't do it, that your lungs won't cooperate. You feel as if your whole body's shaking. Climbing up and down, up and down, with no end in sight. The only noise you hear is the sound of animals in the brush and the sound of trees crashing down, and the falling rain. You don't see colors, and it's always the same compañeros. You get sick and tired of seeing the same compañeros . . . the same footsteps . . . shit! And when it comes time to fight, I said, are we going to have to turn around and go back and find the Guard? Son of a bitch, turn around and go back the way we came! Then haul our asses all the way back up! With any luck, I thought, the Guard will come up to us, and we'll wipe them all out on the spot. Then we won't have to make an extra trip down.

We started to get hungry from marching, marching all day. The third day we ran out of the tortillas and beans we had brought along; by the fourth day we were down to three spoonfuls of cornmeal three times a day. Being that hungry, we shot monkeys, but only at suppertime. Because we couldn't carry them. Though sometimes we did lug monkey meat that weighed down our packs.

To get rid of some weight I wanted to chuck out all sorts of things. But I couldn't chuck the blanket or I'd freeze, and I slept in the hammock—so I threw out books. I wanted to chuck everything: nail clippers, ball-point pen, paper, even things I needed, to make the pack lighter. Because the longer you march the heavier it gets. You put down your foot, and it's as if you're sinking into the ground under the weight of the pack. Or it makes you slip. You think your tail bone is going to crack under the weight of the pack. They weighed about 35 pounds each. When we stopped to rest we plopped down on our asses, *pum*. I remember I plopped down once, and a pain shot through my ass. I let out a screech and jumped up; I'd sat on some poor snake. Luckily it wasn't poisonous, but I didn't know that. And when I felt that seething pain in my ass, *ayiiii, mamita!* I took off like a bat out of hell; I didn't even feel my pack, and the snake took off just as fast! We sat down without looking, just anywhere . . . plop. Right on a slope we would decide we wanted cocoa, and we would sit down. Which made Tello furious: "Bunch of drag-ass loafers, bunch of lazy fuck-ups . . ."

I remember when I went underground Camilo Sesto had a song out that was very popular: "Help me change my thorns for roses . . ." Iván Gutiérrez, who was with us, was in love. One day, he began to sing, and suddenly we heard loud cries echoing in the mountains: "Hellp meee . . . !" That poor guy had sat down and was belting out that song toward the city. To his girl friend, calling her to come and help him, or who knows whom he was singing to; it was as if he was calling out to her. Tello didn't get angry that day; he just laughed.

My feet were one big open sore, and on top of that my socks were wet. The march was a constant struggle. We suddenly realized we craved salt, and we started eating more salt than usual. We were getting dehydrated, and the saga of salt began. We took fistfuls of salt; the monkey meat was salted, and we salted it again and tore into that, or dumped salt on our boiled corn.

We also discovered the true value of fire. You're dead if you can't build a fire in the mountains. Not just the fire to cook with, but the spark, the spark to light the fire. If your matches get wet, what do you do? Everything was in plastic bags inside our packs—matches, your notebook, a photo of your kid—all in plastic bags. You discover how valuable fire really is—for drying you out and to cook with, and even for company, because fire is company, too.

Finally, one day, we got to the camp. The same signal,

three raps. Finally I was going to see and unveil the mystery. We went in, and I remember the first person to greet us was a guy about twenty-eight or twenty-nine years old, a tall, skinny guy with a powerful physique, stronger than Tello or Silvestre. His face was hard but not bitter, with brownish hair, and he had some very nice blue glasses that looked very expensive. But this man's face was different, with his yellow beard, a yellow beard and a pale face. Blue eyes, brownish hair. He wore olive green and carried an R-15 rifle. He greeted us with a smile, the first smile I'd seen since I'd been in the mountains. Do you know what it's like to go twenty days and never have anybody in command, anybody above you, anybody who knows more than you, who's better than you, look at you with anything but a harsh, hard expression—and then this smile? A smile on a hard face, a prophet's smile. His alias was Rodrigo. I found out later he was Carlos Agüero Echeverría. Military head of the guerrilla war, second in command to Modesto in the mountains.

Other compañeros were there, David Blanco, and others whose names I've forgotten. Entering the camp we saw some green plastic rain covers and some rough beds. It was like a camp, about ten plastic rain covers scattered about, big ones, black and green, and some other rough beds built of wood with bags on top. Some of the rain covers had little tables beside them, made of pacaya branches, which look like bamboo since they're green on the outside. And the kitchen area . . . we saw big kettles with cooking pots. This really was a camp. It looked exactly like a camp. Just as I had always imagined. But I didn't see any people. I thought they must be off somewhere, someplace else, but what the—there wasn't anybody else! Just the people there and those of us just arriving. I was coming to grips with this a little bit at a time. I also knew that Víctor Tirado López was with Filemón Rivera on the other side of the Dariense range, about 350 miles from us. My brother Emir was there. We were in the Isabelia range.

When Rodrigo was given his mail, instead of reading it

81

right away he called us together. He wanted to talk to us. I guess he must have felt the same way Tello did, though not exactly, I would say. Because really, his situation was different in the sense that there were eight or ten of them who had been together for months, or years, who knows how long, one year, two, but time enough to have told your comrades the complete story of your life. You talk about your longings, your past, your personal history. You talk about your family, you talk over with your compañeros all the things you think are most important. And everybody knows everything that's ever happened to you, and suddenly there's nothing left to tell. Somebody starts talking and you could carry right on for him.

When somebody new or a new group arrived, it was like hitting the jackpot. What a goldmine of information each new guy was! On top of that they refreshed your memory about things, and you could ask about your neighbors, and your compañeros in the student movement, how their work was going, and how the people underground in the city were doing. It was like an inundation of joy, though six months later the same situation was repeated all over again. It was an influx of new things into camp, new ways of seeing, new opinions, new judgments, day and night, new things, new subjects to talk about, new topics you had never hit upon with the others. Six or seven new compañeros in camp was an inundation. And you saw their faces; you still hadn't sorted them all out. They were new, the names were new; what's so-and-so's name there? It was a flood of information, a flood of company, a breaking up of the accumulated loneliness of the camp. The violent eruption of sociability. The shattering of loneliness. You are scattering the solitude; it breaks up, for a few moments it evaporates. Your presence inundates and irrigates the place with company. It's an extraordinary thing. In fact, I was one of those for whom—I've often said this in the guerrilla war—after months of being in, when you've adapted and been transformed into a guerrilla, the hardest thing isn't the nightmare of the trail, or the horrible things about the mountains;

it's not the torture of lack of food or having the enemy always on your track; it's not going around filthy and stinking, or being constantly wet. It's the loneliness. Nothing is as rough as the loneliness.

That feeling of loneliness is indescribable. And we had plenty of it. The lack of company, the lack of a whole series of things that traditionally the city man is used to having right at hand, to sharing his life with. Loneliness is starting to forget the sounds of cars, the longing at night for electric lights, the longing for colors, because the mountain dresses only in green or dark colors. Nature is green, but what about orange? There's no dark blue, no baby blue, no purple, no lilac and none of those modern colors. Longing for your favorite songs, longing for a woman, longing for sex. Longing to see your family, your mother, your brothers, your compañeros from school. Missing and wanting to see your teachers and the workers and the people in your neighborhood; missing the city buses, the scorching city heat, the dust; not being able to go to the movies. You long for the company of all those things, but you can't have them; it's a loneliness forced on you against your will. You can't leave the guerrilla war. Because you've come to fight, which has been the great decision of your life.

That isolation, that loneliness, is the worst, the hardest thing; it's what hits you the hardest. The loneliness of not being able to kiss anybody, of knowing what it is for a human being not to be able to caress something, the loneliness of never being smiled at, never being touched. Even the animals caress each other: the poisonous snakes caress each other, the wild boars, the little birds; fish in the river caress each other. But we couldn't; we were strictly male, and we couldn't say affectionate things.

So that loneliness—that lack of being petted and fussed over and loved, with nobody to shower you with affection and nobody to shower with affection—that is harder, that stings you more than always being wet and being hungry, than always having to go get firewood, and battling the vines to keep from dropping the firewood and having to pick it up all over again, and wiping your ass with leaves. Nothing was more terrible, for me anyway, than the infinite loneliness of our lives. And the worst of it was, we didn't know how long we would have to go on like that. It led to a kind of forced accommodation. We had to do without the past, without caresses, smiles, colors, the company of a sherbet, of a cigarette, or of sugar, because there was no sugar. A year without tasting sugar; you gradually resign yourself.

On the other hand, you march a short way and fall down; though you're a tried and true marcher you fall about thirty times; nobody ever notices. You cook with hardly any sanitation; you hardly ever wash. Or if you wash it's without soap. Eating is the main thing to look forward to, even though you know it's the same old shit: a handful of ground red corn with salt, a chunk of monkey meat with no seasoning at all, or three spoonfuls of plain cornmeal, or a teaspoon of powdered milk. And as hungry as you are, you have to go do political work with the campesinos. And you go, and get wet, and are shivering with cold and hunger, with no caresses, no laughter, nobody to hug and kiss, and the mud and the darkness of the night, and everybody by 7:00 P.M. lying in their hammocks, each thinking his separate thoughts.

But gradually you are mastering the environment, learning to march. Your legs are getting stronger. You learn how to swing a machete. And as time passes your hair starts to get long. I sprouted a mustache in the mountains. Washing so little roughens your skin. Over long periods of time your cuts and scratches heal and new ones come to take their place, until your hands and your arms are a different color. Callouses form on your hands. And you belch right in front of everybody. You wash out your clothes, you train; and the Guard; and no news from the city; and the repression in the city. It's as if very gradually this mass of men was becoming one more element, a few more creatures of the mountain—intelligent, yes, but like animals, and even worse, like inhibited animals.

This, in a way, was what helped to forge in each of us the steel that was needed to overthrow the dictatorship. Our skin was weathering, the look in our eyes hardening, our eyesight sharpening, our sense of smell keener. Our reflexes—we moved like animals. Our thoughts were hardening, our hearing was more acute, we were starting to take on the same hardness as the jungle, the hardness of animals; we were growing a half-human half-animal hide. We were like men without souls. We were tree trunks, snakes, wild boars, fleet as deer, dangerous as cobras, fierce as mountain lions in heat. And so a spirit was forged that enabled us to endure all the mental and physical hardship. We were developing granite wills in the face of the environment.

To say that the FSLN vanguard was solid was not an idle word. The Frente Sandinista was developing, through action—in city, country, and mountain—a spirit of iron, a spirit of steel, a contingent of men bound with a granite solidity, a nucleus of men that was morally and mentally indestructible, and capable of mobilizing the entire society against the dictatorship. A society in different stages of its development. Because, as the Christians say, we denied our very selves.

Still, and this is another mysterious, contradictory thing, though we were extremely tough and hardened, we were tender, in spite of that hard look in our eyes; if you just grazed the surface of our eyes the pupil would spin, and you would see another kind of expression. That is, we were hard inside and out, but we were also very tender, very gentle; we were very loving, too. We had a sort of gruff affection; it was as if we had stored up all the affection that we couldn't express to each other as we would to a child or a mother or a woman. It was all stored up, accumulated, until we had a well of tenderness, of affection, within us. As if the lack of sugar had created a great inner sweetness, which made it possible for us to be touched to the quick, to make our hearts bleed for the injustices we saw.

We were tough, hardened men, yet Henry Ruiz was capa-

85

ble of giving up his blanket when he came across a shack where he saw a little boy sleeping without covers. He gave it up knowing that it wouldn't solve the problem and that he was our leader and would be left in the mountains with no blanket. We transformed our loneliness into a brotherhood among us; we treated each other gruffly, but actually we loved each other with a deep love, with a great male tenderness. We were a group of men in a single embrace, as brothers, a group of men bound by a permanent kiss. We loved each other with blood, with rage—but it was a brotherly love, a fraternal love. I remember on one march a compañero came across a baby bird in its nest and carried it with him for six days. One of the compañeros farther down the mountain had mentioned that his mother loved little birds, so since he was going to take mail down to the city, he took that opportunity to take the bird with him, to go six days with a tender little bird. Savages like us, battling the vines, fording rivers, marching six miles through rivers, over stones, trying to keep from falling—to save that little bird. Watching out for your pack and thinking how any minute the Guard might come, and death, all of that, with the little bird; battling the environment, sleeping with the little bird. To take it to the compañero so he could give it to his mom. When the compañero received the little bird he just stared; they embraced, and I'm sure he didn't cry. Because he couldn't cry anymore or refused to. It's like that song of Carlos Mejía Godoy's about us always having a clear look in our eyes. There was no selfishness among us.

As if the mountain and the mud, the mud, and also the rain and the loneliness, as if all these things were cleansing us of a bunch of bourgeois defects, a whole series of vices; we learned to be humble, because you alone are not worth shit up there. You learn to be simple; you learn to value principles. You learn to appreciate the strictly human values that of necessity emerge in that environment. And little by little all our faults faded out.

That was why we said that the genesis of the new man was

in the FSLN. The new man began to be born with fungus infections and with his feet oozing worms; the new man began to be born with loneliness and eaten alive by mosquitos; he began to be born stinking. That's the outer part, because inside, by dint of violent shocks day after day, the new man was being born with the freshness of the mountains. A man—it might seem incredible—but an open, unegotistical man, no longer petty—a tender man who sacrifices himself for others, a man who gives everything for others, who suffers when others suffer and who also laughs when others laugh. The new man began to be born and to acquire a whole series of values, discovering these values, and cherishing them and cultivating them in his inner self. You always cultivated that tenderness in the mountains. I took care not to lose my capacity for that beauty. The new man was born in the mountains, as others were born in the underground in the city, as the guerrilla was born in the brush.

The beginning and end of everything is what leaves its mark on the man, what influences him the most. Military training was the start; it was decisive, because there you began to receive a directed knowledge, information systemized so you could assimilate it; that training had a great bearing on our subsequent conduct, development, and way of being.

Students and Teachers

René Tejada (Tello) and David Blanco (Arcadio) gave us our training: Carlos Agüero (Rodrigo) had a hand in it, too. But Tello was in charge. The training couldn't have been more rigorous or severe. Tello wouldn't allow the tiniest mistake; he was always yelling at us; he kept us constantly on the move. Of course, he also had the great virtue of pointing out what we'd done wrong and explaining why we shouldn't make that mistake, all at the top of his lungs. You were crawling along on your belly: "Compañeros, asses down!" he'd shout. "You'll get your ass shot off on a terrain like this, the way you're going over, you can't do it like that." "Put your rain cover up like this, so it won't come undone and you can take it down fast if you have to retreat in a hurry." "Tie these nylon strips to your hammock cord, so when the rain pours down the tree where you've got your hammock it won't get wet—the water will catch and run off to the ground." It was horrible in the mountains when you were sleeping and those downpours came. You got drenched to the skin, your blanket soaked; that was the worst, getting your blanket and hammock soaking wet in the mountains. That meant you had to get up and sleep the rest of the night sitting up.

In the training, Tello taught us one at a time to build a fire, how to cook different kinds of guerrilla meals, how to march, how to put down your feet, all with his typical patience and at the top of his lungs. "Okay, you good-for-nothings, hit the ground," and he would loose a hail of bullets in our direction. He took a gun and started zinging bullets past us, while we dragged ourselves forward on our bellies. He steadied the gun on a little branch, and you had to crawl under his fire. You didn't dare lift your ass or you'd get it shot off. When he lined us up in formation before beginning the daily training he would always connect the military to the political question. He couldn't keep from dreaming a little, whenever he had us lined up. That was when, with his military temperament, his violence, with all his talent as a commander, with all of that, he would talk about the struggle, the *why* of it. Sometimes he would start out shouting and end up as if he was alone, just talking to himself, and saying all those things so as not to lose his sensitivity. Tello was a combination of tenderness and violence.

The training lasted a good month and a half, right in the heart of the mountains. From four in the morning until the light was gone. You know what it's like to be sound asleep and all of a sudden hear that awful call? You end up hating that call. "Up, compañeros"—not "Time to get up, compañeros."

It was always like that with the guerrillas; the officer of the day gave the wake-up call at 3:30 A.M. And we'd been used to sleeping late, because we went to bed late. It was horrible, getting used to hitting the sack at seven—you had no choice—and hauling out at four. We collapsed into bed bone-tired and hungry. You often dreamed you were eating ice cream; you dreamed of banquets. Sometimes your thoughts start to center around food—you think a lot about food at a time like that—and at 4:00 A.M. the wake-up call . . . in the rain. You're all cozy and dry, while those torrents of mountain rain are barreling down, and I mean icy, believe me icy, and you have to get up and take down your rain cover. You take it down for the day, roll up your hammock and go stand in for-

89

mation in the rain with no breakfast or anything. Ten minutes later you're crawling through the mud, after being all dry and sound asleep, with mud all over your body, in your mouth, your ears, your hair, in fifteen minutes. And that Tello shooting at us, making us crawl or march goose step over a rugged, thistly brush. Or slosh through water on our bellies—being shot at in that icy dawn water. You can't see a thing and end up crawling through God knows what.

And physical exercises, they were awful, and even worse when Rodrigo led them. First, running in place, then running for speed, then up-and-down squats, then stationary squats, and exercises for your waist, your legs, your arms, your head. Exhausting exercises, with our packs on. The only thing we took off was our belts, which might cut into us with all that jumping. Finally your legs gave out. Then the order, "Hit the ground . . . hit the ground . . . crawl!" And more shooting at us. But little by little we were shaping up, developing reflexes. The thorns and brambles didn't phase us anymore. Or the mud. We were like animals prowling in our natural habitat, like savages. There we were, practicing ambushes, shooting, daily target practice, military tactics and maneuvers—and always that political orientation. And all the while Tello talking about the new man.

Once after a practice session, when the course was over, we went to look for some corn, about two days' march from camp in an abandoned cornfield. What you ate you really sweated for. We didn't know what it was to deal with getting food every day, cooking it, finding it. We were used to sitting down to hot meals at home, not having to scrounge up food to survive. It was a matter of instinct. Besides, I had never been hungry. What you feel in the city is appetite, as René Vivas said; in the mountains you're hungry. So after the training, first thing, we went for food. By that time we were stronger physically, but Tello was always rough; he always wanted more from us, more and more. It got to the point where we couldn't stand him, it was as if he was a member of the Guard.

We really did like him, but his manner, his personality, infuriated us. I told him that when we talked in confidence—I told you we had become close friends. Even, some compañeros told me when I ran into them about three years later, I'd even picked up some of Tello's mannerisms. It's possible, because you imitate your compañeros. So we set out to march that time, not carrying anything, and full of self-confidence. We were fully trained, with weapons of war—M-1 carbines—and chomping at the bit to take on the enemy; we knew how to hang our hammocks, how to cover our tracks. Tello had explained an incredible lot of things in our training, things we had experienced and learned. So we went for the corn and arrived with no problem, everybody in fantastic shape. But you should have seen us when we dragged back into camp! We found the corn; we already knew how to husk it. We ate roasted corn, boiled corn. In the mountains, when you run out of coffee, you make coffee from corn. You roast the corn until it's burned, then grind it, and that's your coffee. For months, years, we drank corn coffee, with no sugar. It's the bitterest thing in the world, but after a while it starts to taste delicious, and it's even better if you eat it with a roasted banana. A bite of banana all ashy and covered with dirt, and a sip of coffee—it's fantastic. We were hungry there. Once I put away three dozen little bananas, and I was one of the light eaters; there were savages who ate six dozen big bananas. Anyway, the point of this trip I'm talking about was to bring back corn for the whole camp; and also because Rodrigo would be coming back. He had gone out on an assassination mission—to bring to justice some of Somoza's local judges.

We started back carrying about seventy-five to eighty-five pounds apiece, more or less. I remember that when I tried to hoist the pack onto my back I couldn't lift it. I'd been in the mountains for two months. It really must have been heavy if I couldn't lift it by myself, using all my strength. I saw that Tello was really busting his balls to get his pack on; he screwed up his face and in one big lunge, *blunk!* it was on; then he slipped his hands through the straps and adjusted it. When we saw all the weight we were supposed to carry it didn't seem right to us, it seemed like just too much. Sure, we felt stronger, but it wasn't humanly possible. Still, it was no joke, we really had to carry it.

Tello said something then that hurt us all: "Can't you sons of bitches learn to carry the food you stuff in your mouths?" That hurt and offended us; maybe he said it for a purpose, but whatever the reason it was hard to swallow. I remember I said to a compa, "Compa, give me a hand with this shit." So with the compa's help I managed it. Which was how we all got our packs on. The campesinos managed alone, I think; I can't remember for sure, maybe they had help, too. And we started to march.

Really, it was as if you were sinking into the ground; it wasn't muddy, but the ground was squishy with all the water, a clayish soil. When you slip you just about make a pit in the ground. We stopped every 50 or 100 yards. On a little slope of about 200 yards we bogged down at about 150. We just couldn't manage that weight, which kept sliding back; but we busted our balls trying, because by that time we were in a rage. Besides, we felt halfway toughened up by then. But the moment came when we couldn't go on. And we plopped ourselves down.

Tello stomped back, furious. "What do you want, do you want to dump the corn? You better lug that corn or you don't eat," he yelled. "Here if you want to eat you carry the food, you little princesses, crybabies, good-for-nothing little shit-ass students . . ." We had just come from being university leaders—to be talked to like that—but you have to be humble. Besides, we couldn't budge that pack. What he was saying was right, in a way. We felt impotent, good-for-nothing. But we also knew we had advanced at least a little in our development. We had a long way to go, but we didn't know whether Tello kept beating us over the head so we would keep on growing, or if he was just a damn bully who didn't understand.

92

A violent situation developed with Tello, because we stopped dead in our tracks and said no farther. We hadn't had his time in the mountains, which was more than a year. The eight compañeros with the most time in the mountains were Filemón Rivera, Modesto, Víctor Tirado, Valdivia, Tello, René Vivas, Rodrigo, and Manuel. Eight plus Juan José Quezada and Jonathán González, who had died. Eight who had been there a year or a year and a half before we arrived. We were fighting mad. This was no way to teach, no way to form better men. We had already demonstrated a steady improvement. Anyway, it was their fault for sending us in with no warning. But we had demonstrated conviction, political firmness, though physically we weren't worth shit. Later we were expert marchers, pack carriers. But that period of adaptation was hard.

Finally Tello realized we meant business—we were really pissed off, we were armed, and he wasn't dealing with children. It was very tense, since we were raising basic issues, we were questioning him, and he was furious. But we wouldn't put up with that kind of treatment. He strode off for a moment. I think Tello cried then; I can't remember for sure. He went off by himself, and René Vivas went after him. René had been falling down like us under the weight of the corn.

In a little while Tello came back and in a gentle, persuasive tone that he used sometimes when he wanted to, "Compañeros," he said, "you've heard talk of the new man." We just looked at each other. "You know where to find the new man? The new man is in the future, the man we want to create with the new society, when the revolution triumphs." We just stared. "No, brothers," he said, "do you know where he is? He's there on the ridge at the top of the hill we're climbing. He's right there; go get him, grab him, look for him, take hold of him. The new man has gone beyond the normal man. The new man has gone beyond his tired legs. The new man has gone beyond hunger, beyond rain, beyond mosquitos, beyond loneliness. The new man is there, in that supereffort. There where the average man starts to give more than the average

93

man. To give more than the typical man. When he starts to forget he is tired, to forget himself, to put his own self aside—that's where you'll find the new man. So, if you feel tired and exhausted, forget that and climb that hill. And when you get to the top you'll have won a small bit of the new man. We're going to start creating the new man right here; right here the new man is going to be formed. Because the Frente has got to be an organization of new men, men who, after the triumph, can generate a whole society of new men. So, if this isn't just talk, if you really want to be new men, go to it and catch up with him!"

Son of a bitch! We stood staring at each other, staring. Mother-fucking son of a bitch! That's the new man, all right. We agreed with that definition; we all identified with that concept, especially since it had occurred to us that if we wanted to be new men we would have to go through a lot of hardship. In order to kill the old man in ourselves. So the new man could start being born. I kept thinking of Che, of Che's new man, and it hit me then—the enormity of what Che meant when he talked about the new man: the man who gives more to others than the average man is able to give. But at the cost of sacrifices. At the cost of the destruction of his faults, of his vices. We just stared, convinced that Tello was right. That bastard had hit us in our weak spot. Because we all wanted to be like Che, like Julio Buitrago.

So we hoisted on our packs, slipped the straps over our shoulders, looked at each other, and said, we'll get that son-of-a-bitch new man today if it fucking kills us. And we started climbing. By noon the film of the new man was running through my mind—to be like Che, to be like Che—and I swear to you we didn't rest once over a distance where before we would have stopped to rest five times. Which goes to show how sometimes not being clear about things makes you give up at the first sign of tiredness, or back down before the first obstacles. It's not true; a man can always give a little bit more. It's only if a guy keels over or is dead; but while he's still conscious and on his feet and hasn't fallen, he can always give more. And this applies to all activities and all conduct in every sphere of social activity.

We got to the ridge. And Tello saw we had taken up his challenge back there. "We're going to rest, little bits of men," he said. We embraced, and from then on our friendship with Tello was deeper. Because, damn him, he wanted us to get to just that point. First, he wanted us physically to be hard as rocks. Then, on the mental level, the level of will, of consciousness, he wanted to make us indestructible. He even said to us once, "They can kill me now, that son-of-a-bitch Guard." He said it in an almost visionary way. He meant they can kill me now, because there are people here with sufficient steel to maintain and continue this guerrilla war.

And we reached the camp and ate; we felt like seasoned guerrillas. And they greeted us like seasoned guerrillas. And that was a small part of it: we felt that we'd given birth to ourselves, that everything was just beginning. That was the end of the first period of adaptation, the development of that physical indestructibility in the face of the environment, and that moral indestructibility as well.

I remember an anecdote from the disastrous period of that first great shock, that awful time we had, the first of us who joined the guerrillas. Some felt it more than others, of course. Because it wasn't as hard for the workers or the farm laborers. I don't know what the screw-up was, what problem we had created, but once David Blanco said to Rodrigo, "Why the fucking son of a bitch do they send us these shit students, good-for-nothing shit-ass students? Son of a bitch, there are good people there at the university, in the city, and they send us idiots. Why can't they send students like Omar Cabezas, son of a bitch, people who could do something here? But they send us these babbling idiots." "Shut up," Rodrigo answered. "That's Omar Cabezas, that skinny guy over there." I hadn't heard anything. They told me about it later.

We were going through a period of adaptation; after that

we continued our training but with less intensity, more to keep all we had learned fresh in our minds. The veterans had a different relationship with the newcomers then; our status had improved, and we stayed on there in Cerro Gacho, about two days' march from Siuna. Can you imagine, right in the heart of the mountains.

We spent roughly two or three months there, a more or less reasonable amount of time for us to adapt ourselves. We cooked, did sentry duty, all that. Also, little by little, they gave me camp responsibilities; they made me responsible for the political education of the compañeros. I got together some study circles. And sometimes we took turns as officer of the day. They were giving us what you could call military duties, until the compañeros decided it was time to start back to the edge of our zone.

I understood that Modesto and his little squads had to coordinate with some other small squads also operating in Isabelia. Modesto would be coming from the same zone as the other small column headed by Víctor Tirado López; with him were a few campesinos, Filemón Rivera, El Zorro, my brother Emir, and some other compañeros who were in the area. While we were advancing it seemed that Modesto had already sent instructions that somebody should stay behind between Cerro Gacho and Modesto's own position to carry out political work in that zone, to set up a stronger network. A small network existed, but it was very shaky—there were too many stretches, sometimes up to a three-day march, where we didn't have one collaborator among the campesinos. What we had to do was firm up our collaborators where we had them and branch out into new zones that would link up with zones where we had support.

I remember when we passed through Zinica, Tello stayed behind, where he later died; and I stayed in Waslala. It was a new experience for me, since they assigned me to Waslala alone; it was the first show of confidence in me on the part of the compañeros. Waslala was one of the principal zones, the site of the main headquarters of the Guard's counterinsurgency. That was where I was supposed to kick off our political work. There was Lower Waslala, Upper Waslala, and Central Waslala. I think the barracks were in Lower Waslala. I was in Central Waslala. They put me in the house of the only collaborator we had in Central Waslala, the father of Quincho Barrilete, whom Carlos Mejía dedicated that song to. A collaborator who was a local judge, but we had recruited him.

His name was Apolonio Martínez, and he had an extraordinary wife; in fact she was even better than he was. Her name was Martha. A woman with a real desire to improve herself; her mind was very open, very alert and intelligent; a woman with a strong spiritual sense and a strong sense of what it meant to struggle. And a commitment to the emancipation of women. A woman who spoke with affection and tremendous respect for the guerrillas, for the compañeros. She was completely clear about the *why* of the struggle.

They left me there about a month. Not in the house but in the brush, in the woods, about 600 yards from the house. At first I got lost every time I went to the house; I never did get my bearings in the country, in the brush. I had a terrible time finding the house. I always got lost. I remember once I was returning from Apolonio's—I went over to the house in the early evening—but I couldn't find my way back to my little camp at the base of a tree, and ended up sleeping on the ground under buckets of rain.

They left me alone there to set up a network of collaborators in the zone, to form a chain from there all the way up to Tello's group in Zinica.

When I arrived, they introduced me to Martha, Apolonio's compañera; I met the little kids; well, I hardly knew where to begin. Because I didn't have any experience in that sort of work. My experience was with the construction workers in León, with our supporters in León, barrio work, but never with campesinos where I hadn't mastered the terrain, in the sense of knowing how to get from one place to another on my own. It scared me a little, but I knew I was going to do it. I had learned it was possible to do anything; one way or the other I was going to bring it off. I knew I was going to do it. But I was also very lonely in that place.

Can you imagine staying like that in a certain spot all by yourself in the woods? With no radio, no watch, no books, no food? You couldn't kill time cooking, because you couldn't build a fire; they might see the smoke from the houses in the area. I didn't have anything, only paper and pencil. I remember I wrote a poem once, a little poem, or maybe it was less a poem than a state of mind, I don't know, but it's now like an epitaph on the grave of my brothers, whom I recruited:

> *One day I put it to all of you:*
> *Let's fight together for a better world.*
> *You agreed,*
> *And from that day on,*
> *We were brothers.*

I never saw Apolonio except at night when I studied with him and explained how to go about getting more collaborators, where we might get our foot in the door, in what zones we were most likely to make headway. I coached him on how to gather information, since one of my missions was to study the operations of the Waslala barracks. It was through this collaborator that we got the information Rodrigo needed to carry out his attack on the barracks at Waslala on January 6, 1975, following the attack on Chema Castillo's house in Managua by the Juan José Quezada commando.

So every night I came to talk with Apolonio about all these things—the barracks operations, whom to recruit and how to go about it. I wanted to raise his consciousness and keep him solid so he wouldn't back off or run out on me. Every night at about 6:30 he came to take me to supper at his little farmhouse. We would listen to Pancho Madrigal and talk, then about 9:30 I would go back down. Remember, the campesinos went to bed early. But the thing is, I spent the whole day doing nothing, just thinking, thinking. There in that loneliness I turned twenty-three; I was twenty-two when I went into the mountains, and in Waslala I turned twenty-three. The day of my birthday was a day like any other: I had a hammock to sleep in; if I had a cigarette I'd smoke that before turning in; I started thinking about my girl, about the compañeros, the university, Subtiava, wondering how the Frente was doing in different parts of the country, what the plans were for the guerrilla war, because I didn't know the plans. And at night when I went up to the farmhouse the compañeros had cooked a hen for my birthday. I came to love them very much, and they loved me too. When a campesino starts to care for you, when he starts to love you, it's something extraordinary; they are still half-savages because of that environment, so they love not just with their reason, but with all the force of their instinct. Martha ended up loving me, caring for me very much, and I felt the same for her.

Once when we were outside the farmhouse, there was a dazzling moon. We looked up at the sky, which was full of stars, and started talking about the stars, the life of the stars. And I started telling them some of the things they say about other galaxies. How there wasn't just the sun, but other stars bigger than the sun, and so on. I don't know how it came out: "Hombre, compa, it can't be true, can it, that the earth is round and revolves?" Which was what I had said to her innocently. She just stared at me, unbelieving, then burst out laughing in my face. "Of course it's true," I repeated. "The earth is round and revolves." She just stared; she really didn't know the earth was round and revolved. Then she turned serious. "Seriously, compa," I said, "the earth is round and revolves." "Compa, you're not making fun of me, are you?" Since I'd been talking so much about the stars, the planets, the Big Dipper and the Little Dipper, the constellations and this, that and the other thing, theories of space and so on, she could see I was superknowledgeable, supereducated compared to her. So when I told her the earth was round, she thought I was taking advantage, using my knowledge to make fun of her. I realized that in fact she didn't know the earth was round or that it turned in space, good God in heaven! How could I explain to this compañera? She would think I was making fun and be resentful. So I said, "Look, compa, it's really true, the earth is round and revolves." "But if that's true, the water would flow into the air, the trees would send up roots to the sky, rivers would lose their waters, we'd all fly off." "No, compa, the earth turns so fast that nothing happens." And I picked up and whirled a jug of water to demonstrate. "See, the water doesn't run out. See, I'm turning it over." Well, I managed to convince the compañera that I wasn't trying to fool her or make fun of her. But she wasn't, as they say, totally satisfied, since I couldn't go any deeper at that time into a scientific explanation of the earth.

Anyway, I went back down to my spot in the woods; spent the whole day there; I watched the sun rise and set, with no watch. I never felt more like an animal than in that spot, a contemplative animal, observing nature, its full cycle. I thought plenty there; I thought until I was sick of thinking. Night came, and I couldn't sleep, from thinking so much. I spent over a month like that. I remember one night some erotic thoughts came over me: I started thinking of my girl, of making love to her; I was starting to get a hard-on; I thought of movies with beautiful women, and my mind started galloping, it had been so long since I'd had room for thoughts like that; I was getting excited and starting to stroke my cock, to stroke my cock and dream, and pretty soon I was supererect; I went on stroking . . . and before I knew it, I had finished masturbating. I'd been in the mountains about six months and that was the first time I masturbated.

I remember I slept deeply. After a number of days of being a little nervous, thinking about death, about the work—how slow it seemed to be going—I felt a little desperate. And all by myself, not being able to go where I wanted—I wanted to go out and talk to the campesinos in the area—all alone, half-tense, half-pressured. Who knows how it came about, but tension is a spur, an incitement, and all of a sudden that surge of erotic thoughts, sexual ideas, then sexual images flooded my brain. And when I realized it, I had already finished masturbating and felt calm, easy, relaxed.

And in fact that's how it was with the guerrillas; after a little while without doing it, you masturbated and felt calmer. Though most of the time you forgot all about the problem of women; you forgot and never thought about women or any of that. And sometimes, if it did come up, you tried to repress it right away, so as not to torture yourself. Because it's hopeless. And nevertheless, even though you didn't think about women, the sexual tension would mount up. Though you didn't want a woman every day, when you had a certain amount of tension stored up, that moment came when just for a second you thought of it, and that was it: you masturbated and felt peaceful again. I'm not saying if they put a naked woman in front of you you wouldn't do anything, don't kid yourself. But that's how it was, for me anyway. That's what sex was like.

Well, the sun rose and another day began. I used that month to store up a great deal of patience, and it helped me to sharpen my senses even more. Since the only sounds I heard were the sounds of the mountain, I couldn't help but learn to distinguish things very clearly: the sound of a fruit falling, the sound of a tree crashing to the ground, the noise of the wind coming from far off and drawing nearer, then passing over and moving away. When the wind is rising it sounds different from when it's drawing near or going by. Or the sound of a woodpecker, the patter of a squirrel, the tread of an ox. Or when a bird is startled by another animal, or the sound of water when it's raining in the distance, or the rumble of distant thunder.

Day by day you make out the sounds of nature with more clarity and precision, all kinds of sounds. When you hear a

101

noise, whatever it is, you know right away if people are coming, though maybe you don't know it in a straightforward way. More than anything you know your own sound, the sound you make yourself, and the sound of nature. So, when you hear a different noise, I tell you, you know that sound's not right, there are people coming, and you're on your guard. You hear all those sounds; they register in your brain, from the slightest, the tiniest, to the most unlikely sound you can imagine.

The same thing happens with your eyesight. From seeing the same thing over and over you know the trees by heart, their forms and shadows, the different effect of light at different hours in the mountains, the changing tints of shade in the afternoon, by day, and at night; you know how what you see in the morning or at dawn will look later on in the day—different silhouettes, forms.

The same with your sense of smell. You learn to smell everything: the smell of nature and your own smell as one more element of nature; the smell of my blanket, my jug, my hammock, my pack, my boots; the smell of my skin, my spit. Because your phlegm has an odor; when you have a cold there's an odor. The smell of food, of food scraps, different kinds of scraps, the smell of sweat, of semen. You know the smell of the brush, of the dirt, of the different grasses; the smell of the animals that come near. Because when you introduce a new smell, the smell of a cigarette, you smell it very precisely, because it's not mixed with any other smells like in the city. In the city there are hundreds of smells all around, but if I take away every smell and leave you just the smell of the cigarette, you'll know all there is to know about that smell. That's what happened in the mountains. If you introduced a strange smell, when that smell was gone, only the smells of the mountain remained.

A Soldier's Christmas

I didn't waste my time during the days that month I was alone. I did exercises in the morning; in the afternoon I wrote reports or I would write a poem, or walk a little. I practiced my eyesight: I scanned out to one side, then to the other. And though I kept busy, even though I was by myself, there was almost always time to think about all sorts of things. One night a campesino we knew named Margarito showed up with a new compañero who was being sent to Tello; he was passing by me on his way up. It was about 4:00 A.M. when I saw a great big boy coming toward me. He was tall and powerfully built, with big, bulging eyes and short curly hair. The minute he got to me, *pom!* the poor guy plopped himself down as if he was taking a tremendous load off his feet. I could see he was up to his ears in mud, with mud on his face, in his hair, on his rifle up to the hilt. "Omar Cabezas," he said, "I know it's you, my brother." And he started asking me questions, the same questions I'd asked Tello and Silvestre when I saw them for the first time: about what it was like, how many guys were there, where would he be going next, were there lots of camps, did they cook, would they always have to march as he had marched up to there, did I have any salve or alcohol for his blisters? And he pulled off his boots, the poor guy—he had a deep gash on his hand from when he'd fallen and reached out to keep from smashing his face against a rock; he was holding a muddy kerchief wadded up in his hand. That was Casimo, who knew me because he'd also been a student at the university. His real name was Orlando Castellón Silva. He was another one who died in the guerrilla war.

Later on I gave military training to hundreds of men. I led about forty guerrilla schools in my five years or so of life in the underground. I tried to teach the compañeros with real affection, real fraternity, keeping the training tough but always trying to treat them like brothers, to put an end once and for all to the prejudice that existed against students in the mountains. I understand that later this was corrected.

In Waslala there are mosquitos all day long, mosquitos everywhere, and it's ten times worse at night—gnats, bocones, all kinds of mosquitos and insects. You can't sleep because they get in your blanket, and you have to make a bed of embers under your hammock, a little fire of smoldering sticks to create smoke. You're in your hammock with that constant *bbzzzzzzzz* in your ears. There's a tiny insect that harasses you all day, then at night it slips through the weave of your hammock or blanket and keeps right on biting you when you're lying down. It's a nightmare; it's horrible; you can't sleep in peace.

That's why your face becomes lined in the mountains—your expression is always pained. When you take a shit you wet your ass on the icy brush; the food's awful—there's nothing appealing, no sugar; you hardly ever smile; every few minutes you get scratched; you're always burdened down, always wet. So your face is constantly expressing pain. And as days pass, and weeks, and months, and years, your face becomes set in that expression, the muscles clenched; your face hardens into a grimace, as if your muscles could not relax into their normal state; your face has changed.

Over the years the faces of the guerrillas change, and that

change reveals the new tempering. The changed face tells you that you are not the same, and naturally the same thing happens to the look in your eyes. Then, since you can't sleep either, with all those damn insects bothering you, you are always frowning and keep slapping yourself in the face. There's not a pleasant moment, except when there's a decent meal, or a compañero arrives, or when you masturbate, or when you hear some fantastic news, or when we listened to Carlos Mejía Godoy's "Our Daily Music" on the radio. That was like a cool drink of water, because we knew we weren't alone when we heard Carlos singing. That was a steady diet, "Our Daily Music" every day at 6:00 P.M. in camp. We crowded around the different radios; we came together to hear "Our Daily Music" and the mazurka ballads and Carlos talking. We could always look forward to that—it helped us endure that existence.

We sent Casimiro off, on toward Tello. One day, in November, a courier arrived at dawn, a campesino who had come to get me. Modesto had sent for me so we could talk. I still hadn't met him and didn't know yet that his real name was Henry Ruiz. Okay, I figured that after meeting with Modesto I would return to my spot. So I went with the compañero to Modesto's camp, where I found everybody who had come out with me from the center, plus some new people, and some campesinos I didn't know and some other collaborators, about thirty or forty men. Shit, I thought, there are quite a few of us; I hadn't known they had other combat units there.

So I arrived at Modesto's camp. In the month or two we had been separated, the other compañeros had been through a lot, many new experiences, and so had I. Anyway, I entered Modesto's camp. They were eating breakfast when we got there, since we had started out at night. They were finished for the time being with Rodrigo's exercises. He'd been working their asses off; I'm not shitting you, that Rodrigo was tough, exercises every day at the crack of dawn, in formation for exercises at 4:00 A.M. By the time it was light you were finishing your exercises, with your pack on, and immediately after that there was personal hygiene—everybody off to wash up, to brush your teeth, wash your face; if you wanted to take a bath you took a bath, with permission, if you were in charge of something. Then breakfast—a handful of hard corn, boiled until the kernels burst, or maybe just boiled and not burst. The usual amount was a half-cup of boiled, hard-kernel corn. That was our breakfast for years. We hated it, since we were sick to death of it. But when we were suffering from hunger, when we didn't have even that, how we longed for that little cup of corn.

Modesto was eating from his little pail, I remember, when the campesino took me over to him. "Pleased to meet you, compañero," I greeted him. "You Eugenio?" "That's right, Eugenio." "Ah, I'm glad we have a chance to talk." I went and got my food and started eating; you could say there was a bit of a chill between us, in spite of the fact that Modesto was the symbol; it was a cold business, I guess because of that same old problem—a sort of contempt they had for students. By that time I was very clear on this, because I was a guy who was constantly analyzing everything.

I should mention that in Waslala about fifteen days before we got to Modesto's camp, I had noticed a small white spot on the calf of my right foot, and on the calf of my left foot another tiny white spot, a tiny dot, like a mosquito bite. But since your hands are all covered with mosquito bites and gashes, with hundreds and thousands of bites that go away, then you're bitten again and it's bite on bite, gash on gash, scratch on scratch, that's normal—and sometimes the bites get a bit infected, so you go around with your hands all bitten up and oozing with pus. You apply alcohol if you have it, or Merthiolate. The bites heal and you're bitten again, and so on. But I noticed that these little bites were turning into little white dots on both calves, and around the white dot it was red, red, red. A deep, deep scarlet on both calves, and slowly, as days passed, it grew to the size of a 10-centavo piece. I squeezed it, then it was like a shilling piece, then a 50-centavo piece. Then it started to hurt. It hurt like hell. I could see it was oozing pus, and I figured that when we got to Modesto they would give me a shot to knock it out, because they had a fair supply of medicine.

I said to Flavio, our guerrilla doctor, "I'm all screwed up— here, on my calves." "What you've got there's an infection." This so-called infection started growing then like crazy; it was as big as a córdoba piece. It hurt so much I couldn't sleep. I had to fold over the top of my rubber boot, since if it even touched my skin it about killed me. They had given me some antibiotic capsules to knock it out, but I said to Flavio, "This bullshit isn't going away. Flavio, I'm starting to smell something bad, this shit's really starting to stink." Flavio leaned over for a whiff. "You're right, brother, this is putrid." He smelled the other one. "Ugh . . . I'm going to give you a shot of benzetacil." That was my first shot of benzetacil, 2,400,-000 units of penicillin in my hip.

I spent four days crippled, off my feet. We were all of us weak, just skin and bones; a shot like that just wiped me out. Four days passed and they began my treatments. It was horrible, because they stuck pincers wrapped in cotton right in the open sore and dug down into it with the cotton swab. Then the other one. I gritted my teeth and clenched my fists . . . *aiii, brother!* I yanked back my foot, and Flavio sat down on it and kept hold of me.

Finally, when all the pus was out, there was a huge ulcer, and that stench . . . They bandaged up both the lesions where you could see the raw flesh. Forget walking—I had to sit all the time. Since it still didn't heal, he gave me another shot of benzetacil. Remember, that kills your red blood cells. We were undernourished and reduced to shit. I had to stay off my feet, and the treatments continued every day because every day there was pus, and the ulcer got bigger and bigger. He gave me three benzetacil shots, and the thing was getting worse; it was eating me alive, and that pain . . . I couldn't get

up, not even to go get my food. It was all I could do to get up
and go shit, or take a bath. That was a real sacrifice, because I
took a bath every day. Do you know what that's like to strip
naked in a stream, in the iciest, iciest water, every morning
and sometimes twice a day, so I could wash? And still the thing
wasn't clearing up. I could see that Flavio was worried, because other compañeros were starting to get the same thing on
different parts of their bodies, tiny spots. Mine were the biggest. Flavio was worried; he could see it was no infection. I'd
already been flat on my back for a month, full of antibiotics,
and they were still growing. Huge, round ulcers. Growing and
eating away from inside; you could see the bone.

It took three people for my treatment. A compañero would
cut a couple of branches. They put one in each of my hands
and another in my mouth so I wouldn't yell out when they
started swabbing out the holes in my legs with gauze. I could
feel them digging right down to the quick. A hideous, indescribable pain shot to my brain. I snapped the sticks in my
mouth, it hurt so much. I was like an animal. It tore me completely apart. I would not wish that pain on anybody except
Somoza. I almost fainted when that guy dug down with those
gauzes, and what a stench! The gauze came out all covered
with pus and blood and chunks of flesh a bit bigger than a
bean or a kernel of corn. I was losing little chunks of flesh.
Now I just have the scars, but the lesions were much bigger,
about 5 inches in diameter, the size of your hand, and all eaten
out inside.

To top it off, in Waslala I had started having pains in my
appendix. So the appendicitis was all mixed up with the other
trouble. Poor Flavio was always in his hammock, depressed
because he couldn't figure out what it was. One afternoon he
came running up: "It's lesymaniasis, lesymaniasis!" Like
somebody crying out, "Land, land!" "What's lesymaniasis?"
"Brother, it's what you've got, it's mountain leprosy, that's
lesymaniasis." I remembered in a course I had taken before
coming to the mountains we had studied tropical medicine:

"That's . . . that's . . . Repodral, Repodral! That's the cure, Repodral!" "Let's hope so, brother." "Okay, then, they have to send down for Repodral." Do you know what it means to send down to the city for Repodral? When would it come, would it even get past the roadblocks of the Guard? I went five months like that. I kept putting on more and more bandages; sometimes I got up to go get firewood, or they put me on sentry duty.

The thing is, I asked for work, so as not to be doing nothing. Anyway, that leprosy was toughening me up; I was getting hardened. Maybe that's why we were so demanding, since if you don't have convictions, if you don't have pride, you get out; you ask to be sent down. I never once asked Modesto to send me back, and they knew the shitty shape I was in. Then one day it was Christmas, Christmas of 1974.

I didn't like Christmas in the mountains. I remember some of them more than others. I spent five in different places, in different camps, in different zones, and with different people. It wasn't always the same guerrilla column. There were new attachments, new groups coming in, new compañeros. I would tell them where we spent the last Christmas, the one the year before, since it's usually easier to remember the most recent Christmas.

I get Christmas mixed up with New Year's, because both are traditional holidays, but the campesino celebrates New Year's more than Christmas. Christmas in the mountains is a common, ordinary day, barely observed; since there aren't any toys, even silly toys; there's no fiesta. There's no Christmas in the mountains, but New Year's is a different story. I remember one New Year's I had a few drinks with some campesinos.

The first Christmas I spent in the mountains was in 1974. That same month Carlos Agüero, René Vivas, Nelson Suárez (Evelio), Aurelio Carrasco, and some other compañeros had gone to do a holdup. We were in camp when Rodrigo left. We knew he was off on something, but he didn't tell us what. Later we heard all the uproar over a robbery in Abisinia.

"That son of a bitch was Rodrigo," we said, and we sweated it out until he got back to camp.

They made it back in time for Christmas. We were in our hammocks, those of us who had come in that year, thinking of Christmas, the colored lights, the presents, the supermarkets . . . Naturally, I thought of Christmas in León, where they put all sorts of makeshift booths in the front of the cathedral—dolls, strings of lights. And on the corner of Sesteo, near the university, on the corner of Chinchunte coming into León—where the pool hall is, and an old guy called Taponcito—on that corner they always hung a beautiful display of Christmas lights. So many memories . . .

We were in our hammocks listening to music, to a song that went, "If you're far from friends, come to my house for Christmas." So we started singing, "Come to my rain cover for Christmas." We didn't want to go to sleep. So there we were. That was the twenty-third. Rodrigo turned up on the twenty-fourth. We were happy, since we were going to be together on Christmas, even if we did feel like shit. We had the idea that with Rodrigo there it would be different. Besides, though he wasn't religious in a traditional way, he was a guy who understood human nature, and he understood us. We were fairly used to the problems. Because sometimes we spent Christmas in the cathedral on strike for the political prisoners. What I'm saying is, in a way we were already used to it, from the time we'd been students, used to spending Holy Week or Christmas or New Year's shut up in churches for political campaigns.

Rodrigo turned up with a couple of turkeys. Those screwballs, after pulling off the job in Abisinia, had thought about bringing us things from town, since they had gone there. We had been in the mountains for months. I remember when he got back we asked René Vivas, "Brother, were you right in town? Did you see the electric lights and cars and people?" It had been so long since we'd seen any of that. Rodrigo said, "We're going to have a fantastic Christmas, because guess what"—Rodrigo loved to cook—"we've got butter, *petit pois,* catsup, Worcestershire sauce . . ." They had lugged it all in their packs for about twenty days to get it to us by the twenty-fourth. In some situations that might not mean much, but the fact of weighing down your bag or your pack with even four additional ounces of extra weight, and of marching with that, when marching was the rule and resting was the exception—that was really something!

So Luciano got busy cooking. It was his turn that day. But Rodrigo cooked, too—he said he was going to cook a turkey the way they did in the city. And he had all he needed to do it right. We were going to have a dynamite feast! After all those months of boiled corn, burst-kernel corn. But in spite of all the gaiety over the food and Rodrigo's return, you wondered sometimes where your girl might be, or your mom, or your friends, or your compañeros in the city who were better off right then, in the yard of some underground house; they would surely have been having a few drinks, and surely they were thinking of us. It was a permanent human solidarity. We were always united wherever we happened to be, at whatever moment, always thinking of one another.

Rodrigo returned in the late afternoon, totally drenched. We knew he was back when we heard the sentry's shout. We saw Evelio, stocky as ever, with his pack on, soaked, the usual expression on his face. And then Rodrigo with his cap and blond hair, coming behind Evelio as usual. He came in smiling. Rodrigo had a tiny smile, not broad at all. A radiant smile, because he had come from Abisinia, and he was coming to be with us for Christmas. Surely he must have missed us as we missed him. I remember it was afternoon and sort of misty, since up there December is the middle of winter. Luciano, who was acting as kitchen aid to Rodrigo, took the turkeys— it was almost dark—salted them, and gave them back to Rodrigo, who put them on to cook—an aroma I can still remember. The rest of the troop—in camp we put the rain covers up in a circle—sat down in the center to talk and joke around, in the same place where we always stood in formation. What are they doing in the city? we wondered. Rodrigo said we could sing, and we did.

After singing awhile we had to go pee. When you left the group to go to pee, you thought immediately of the city, your family, your mom, your girl, our chances for victory. How many more Christmases, how long would this all go on, when could we go back home? All that in the instant you went off to pee. But back in the group again and singing and kidding around, you forgot all about it. While we were chatting Rodrigo was cooking. Aroma after aroma began to float out from the kitchen area as one by one Rodrigo tossed in seasonings. And one by one the familiar smells came back to us—capers, catsup, Worcestershire sauce, mustard. We were 20 yards from the kitchen, but the wind was blowing, and these were such familiar smells. Our senses, our sense perceptions, had grown sharper, and we recognized the spices. "What was that one?" we asked. "That's it!" And so on.

When it was time to eat, the aroma was almost too much for us. We could hardly wait. They had brought us two extra cigarettes apiece. The ration was six per day, under optimal conditions. They had brought us two more, and also three candies per person. That was a windfall, a real fiesta: extra cigarettes, extra sweets, the turkey, the aroma of the turkey. Nevertheless, when you went off from the group, the magic evaporated. That was why I almost hated to go pee, because sometimes it's better to be dreaming.

Finally, the call we'd all been waiting for, in that usual tone between firm and noncommittal, firm and mechanical, firm and dry: "Time to eat, compañeros!" We all got in line. And that mouth-watering smell! First, I touched the food with my fingers, in the dark, not with my spoon but with my fingers. I remember I touched the olives, the capers. In the dark by touch you recognize all the different ingredients. I took an olive and chomped into it. It made me think of the olives in the city—the olive juice or your saliva mixed with the olive produces an ecstatic sensation that takes you back to the city. And there you were: the capers, the scent of catsup. If you eat in the dark and close your eyes, you can do wonders with a little imagination.

But then came the great tragedy, with a whole shitload of curses flung at Luciano, and Rodrigo's fury, and the demoralization of everybody: the meat had come already salted, but Luciano had put more salt on top of that, and it was inedible! I bit into it, not out of hunger but just to savor it in my imagination. All the seasonings were there—I sucked around the edge of the meat; I ate all the seasonings. Finally, I ended up eating most of the meat. That night after supper we all went to bed thinking, thinking about fighting . . . about life . . . about the struggle.

I also spent one Christmas in Tegucigalpa before the victory. In a safe house. It was a very urban Christmas. I remember I was in charge in Honduras. I had finished, but my stay had dragged on. I was in charge there with Rafael Mairena. We got together with some compañeros and compañeras. The situation was less tense, so we danced, had dinner, and remembered our compañeros. The compañeros I thought of were the ones in my combat unit. I imagined them in different situations in the mountains according to how it had been on past Christmases. I remember we spent some of them marching all night. Marching, marching, you forgot all about it, but when you sat down to rest you said to the guy beside you, "Look, brother, this is outrageous. Who knows what's going on in the world—we're here while people God knows where are drinking rum, doing who knows how many things." It hits you hard, and if you don't have solid principles you become demoralized. Because these are such traditional holidays, so rooted in the people. You march along remembering the city, the cars. I drifted off sometimes, and I was the one in charge. I was distracted by my thoughts. Though a person has mental resources—and I had them—you have to apply imagination to your fatigue to avoid exhaustion. I decided that every step I took was a glass bulb on a Christmas tree in the house of a rich man. One bulb, another bulb . . . until every bulb on the tree was smashed.

In those first years, out of curiosity, we always observed the life of the campesinos. To see if their shacks had a festive air about them. To see if we could smell the fragrance of Christmas in the mountains. In the city it's completely different. The lights, the billboards, the streams of presents, cards, parties—Christmas has a very unique fragrance. The last days of December are special. Around Christmas and New Year's people are more cheerful, nicer. The houses . . . even your own house is different, though it's the same old house. We wanted to see if in the mountains, moving out of the brush toward a little shack, we could breathe the fragrance of December, if we would feel that emotion that blossoms in December. In the city, people always buy something, even if it's just a little thing. And if not that, they create something, but it's the children who celebrate Christmas; they have their toys. It's got to be a very desperate poverty for Christmas not to come, the way it is in the mountains.

The Mountain Mourns a Son

A few days after Christmas a great thing happened. Because I was sick they put me in charge of the radio, responsible for listening to all the news programs and at the end of the day reporting back on the most important developments to the whole troop in formation. To keep them informed. And I gave a brief analysis of what seemed to me the most important things in the news. I was happy to be doing something.

Suddenly I heard that something unusual was happening on the highway to Masaya, that you couldn't get through to Masaya, that the Guard had been called out. I realized it was something serious and went to Modesto. I remember he was in the cooking area. "Brother, brother, something awful's going on in Managua. They say the road to Masaya is blocked and the Guard's been called out!" Of course they knew in advance that the Frente was going to strike in the city, but we didn't know shit. They knew exactly what was going on—it was an attack on a house party to capture hostages. I'm talking about the big action of December 27, 1974.

What houses, what embassies were on the road to Masaya? I don't know, I'm not from Managua. It was the attack on

Chema Castillo's house. In the mountains we always looked forward to listening to the news. A bit later when we were listening to the communiqué from the Guard the radios went dead; they had cut them off. Here it was, the big hit, but what was happening, what? A tremendous anxiety set in. Good God in heaven, let those sons-of-bitch boys come out of this alive. What could be going on? We knew it was an action. In a little while: "General Headquarters: The General Headquarters of the National Guard informs you that the house of Chema Castillo has been taken. . . . The Archbishop is mediating. . . . One of the assailants inside has been identified as Carlos Agüero. . . ." So that's it! I suddenly realized it couldn't have been Carlos Agüero, because I saw that Rodrigo had burst out laughing maliciously with René Vivas, and I knew right away who he was. I already knew that Carlos was tall and had light skin and blue eyes. Aha! So this joker is Carlos Agüero! It's him all right. I started putting together a whole bunch of things he had told me before. I hadn't placed him, but it hit me then—Rodrigo and Carlos Agüero were one and the same guy.

All day long we speculated about what was happening in Managua. And since I was in charge of the news, I stayed glued to the radio. "Is there any news . . . any news?" "Negotiations are continuing . . . they're going to broadcast some communiqués from the Frente . . ." And our communiqués came on! Son of a bitch! we said. We stuck that to 'em, those bastards, now we've got them where we want them. An incredible gaiety filled the camp. The poor sentries, when you came with their food: "What is it, brother, tell me." And you started blurting it all out, but that was against the rules so you went back. "But tell me more, more." "No, I'll tell you tonight."

Finally the compañeros came out of the house. I don't remember if we did any shooting, if there was rifle or machine-gun fire. The fact is that December 27 was an extraordinary boost for our morale. Shit, we were ecstatic, because the whole country heard our denunciation of the murder of cam-

116

pesinos in the mountains, and the names of the places we had marched—Zinica, Waslala. We felt that we weren't alone anymore, that the places where the guerrillas had been active were becoming famous, that the repression in the mountains was being denounced.

About four days later we noticed a commotion in the bull-pen—under Modesto and Rodrigo's rain cover—meetings with Arcadio and others. The upshot of this was that Rodrigo took off with five men. About six days later a campesino arrived in camp: "They're saying they've attacked the Waslala barracks, there was a gun battle, a lot of Guardsmen have been killed!" Rodrigo had gone out to attack the Waslala barracks. That was the plan. They say the Guard lost eleven men. The Guard never imagined that such a fortress of a headquarters would be attacked. They'd never been attacked in the mountains; now all of a sudden the bullets were flying. It was chaos inside; they were killing each other in the confusion, and the compas beat an orderly retreat, victorious. They executed several local judges. It was a fantastic moment for the guerrillas, which was clouded only by the death of Tello.

About three days after Rodrigo's return to camp the Guard broadcast a communiqué announcing that in the zone of Zinica or of Cusulí a Guard patrol in pursuit of the attacking band had encountered the resistance of an armed man; the man, who had died in the clash, had been identified as René Tejada Peralta. The Guard had captured one of our collaborators who had confessed that in such and such a house a guerrilla was hiding. Tello was with another compañero who had managed to get out alive, barefoot. About six in the evening, thinking it was the collaborator bringing him food, because they gave the signal and everything, he opened the door. The Guard opened fire, and since it was dusk and the light was dim, they got him with the first bullet, a man like Tello, who was always on his guard, they got him with a bullet from a Garand rifle right in the forehead.

I'll tell you what I felt when I heard of Tello's death: I felt fear when Tello died. I felt fear, since in a way I had modeled myself on Tello. He had taught me how to fall and the various positions for lying on the ground. He had taught me what to do if the Guard came, what to do if they were getting near. Tello taught me what to do in battle, or in a retreat, and how to give orders in combat. And just like that it's Tello who's killed, the guy who taught me everything. I thought sometimes, everything he taught me is useless, because if he didn't apply it, if he didn't use it, it was all pure theory and not worth shit.

Nothing was sure anymore. What kind of guerrilla force is it anyhow when the best man of all, your teacher, is the first to die? By the time of Tello's death I was beginning to feel as if I had some balls; I was a bit tougher, more capable, superior to the student, the politico, I'd been before, the student leader in the university; I was beyond that. I was a guerrilla now and could manage the weight, I could march, I could handle a rifle, I could handle heavy weapons—and suddenly Tello was dead. So what the fuck was the point of all he had taught us? What good were his lessons if they could kill him first, before any of us? If they had killed a compañero we had trained with, at least we could have said he hadn't absorbed Tello's lessons. But no, it's Tello who dies, Tello first, and you felt superfragile, as if the Guard was invincible, and what we had was nothing but a caricature of a guerrilla army, nothing but good intentions, a pathetic dream, a joke of a guerrilla effort. That was how you felt.

I remember a helicopter flew over our camp that afternoon. The helicopter that was going to take Tello's body to be identified in Waslala. And we didn't even know he had been killed. We rushed to put out our fire, thinking they had spotted our position. We were ready for a fight. We doubled the watch, got our packs together . . . and nothing happened. "If those sons of bitches had shown up here, we would've wiped them out," we said. And later we found out that Tello was dead. I never forgave Tello for being killed by one bullet, just one bullet. That afternoon when the news came I went to my hammock, to my rain cover, to think about everything. And I thought of León and of the barrios and the university, and I also thought that the whole guerrilla war was one big piece of shit. I could not come to grips with Tello's death. The students threw stones, but what did students know about real combat, about the Guard? I had been one of the main student leaders and now I was a trained soldier, and I felt it, deep in my gut, that the guy who had trained me had been the first to die, somebody who knew more than me and by extension more than Subtiava about military matters, and more than the university, and more than all the compañeros underground and aboveground in the Frente Sandinista.

It was as if the mountain, too, felt fear. The wind dropped and the trees stopped swaying. There was a quiet, an overwhelming calm. Maybe it was just my own enormous fear, but I remember the trees drew apart, not a leaf stirred, and the tall trees, the towering trees were still, and the trampled brush; not a leaf stirred, as if the shell of the mountain had fallen away. All was quiet, unlike before when you felt a violence in the sway of the trees, as if they were defending themselves against the wind or hurling who knows what with their branches, as if warding off death or danger with their flailing branches. And the birds stopped singing as if frightened into flight. All froze in terror, awaiting that moment when the Guard would come and slaughter us all. I don't know, I can't explain what happened there. The compañeros were all talking about it. I wonder if the compañeros who had trained along with me were afraid, too. I know some of them didn't feel Tello's death very much. Or maybe it wasn't so much that they didn't feel it, but that he'd been so hard on us, and they were wondering why he hadn't shown more balls when the moment came. As he always had with us. It was like a reproach—where were all the things he had taught us? Even the constant murmur of the stream had stopped, as if its time had come and something was going to happen to that rippling sound—it had joined with the trees that had stopped swaying and the animals that had fled and the songless birds; all was silent, even the movements of the compañeros; there was no laughter drifting from the cooking area where they were grinding corn or preparing food.

I couldn't believe that Tello was really dead. What I mean is, it wasn't certain anymore that the position of your knee on the ground should be as he said it was; it wasn't certain you should move this or that way in battle. It was all pure theory and the Guard with its strength, with its power, canceled it all out. Were the lessons he had given us correct or not? They didn't matter shit to the Guard. Although the Guard didn't know half what Tello knew, they pumped that bullet into him right at the start. So the Guard was a thousand times superior; the Guard was just laughing at all this shit, or not even noticing it. You may know plenty but they kill you just the same. So was it all worthless, all we knew? It was no good against the Guard. But if that was so, how could we hope to defeat them, how could we hope to wipe them out? How were we going to put an end to the dictatorship if it was neither here nor there to the Guard whether we knew how to shoot in a certain way, or to fight in a certain way?

I felt impotent. Not because of the weight of the pack—I could deal with that now, I could march, I could climb, I could stand the hunger, I could stand the loneliness. But the bottom had dropped out, out of my confidence about taking on and destroying the enemy, the most important thing of all. And I had felt I was representative of so many people, of the barrios, of the university, I had thought I was prepared.

Tello's death was incomprehensible to me, even though from the beginning I'd had his words ringing in my ears: if he should die he would be leaving behind people who could carry on the guerrilla war. I thought: if that joker has prepared us the way he prepared himself, if we're going to be like him and fight as he fought, if the lessons we've learned aren't worth a chickpea to the Guard, have no power to neutralize the

Guard, if they're not good for anything, well, they're going to slaughter us all. And Tello admired Carlos Fonseca, too. Probably the only reason Carlos Fonseca is still alive, I thought, is that he hasn't come up here. It's hopeless, a half-assed guerrilla army against an enemy so incredibly powerful.

And what chance did Che have if the Rangers who killed him were trained by the same people who trained Tello's killers? Maybe if Che had not been a Quixote like Tello, or like us—the whole Frente Sandinista was probably a Quixote—maybe then he would have survived. And the student movement, the movement in the barrios, were these nothing but a couple of movements more, like so many others that have sprung up in different countries in Latin America, especially in the southern cone, that blaze for a moment and then are snuffed out? Cuba must have been an exception, because they had Fidel, Raúl, Camilo; they were able to bring it off because the enemy was inexperienced, because imperialism still had its gloves on.

It seemed as if all the songs, all the revolutionary literature coming out of Latin America was nothing but window dressing, an intellectual veneer on a shaky theory of revolution that would never, in practice, succeed. And that Latin America had no prospects, that we were going to fail, to be defeated, as the Colombians had been defeated, and the Venezuelans, and the Guatemalans.

And what saves you then? Because eventually your head stops spinning. Those feelings subside and you start to reflect maturely, calmly. You are saved by the fact that the FSLN inculcated in us a historical will, an infinite, boundless stubbornness. And all at once your brain starts to function. Okay, thousands of people may die, but you have to keep on fighting to bring down the enemy. Because to be against the Guard, even though you may die—to be a guerrilla fighter—is an absolutely honorable stance. If you die, you die with honor. Your death is in itself a protest. So Tello's death was a protest. And we were going to die protesting. Even if the Frente Sandinista was just another guerrilla movement that imperialism would crush, that Somoza's dictatorship would crush, as they had crushed so many movements all over the continent. The important thing was not whether Tello applied what he knew, or whether or not what he taught was correct; what mattered was we had to die for an ideal. We had to put aside our dreams, hopes, and ambitions and break through the mountains, break through all that was unknown, break through everything, but finally and above all, break through!

The important thing was to fight, even though to do that we would have to give up making jokes about our military training or casting doubt on our own capacity as an army. We would have to die, and we would have to store up and keep tightly shrouded within us all our doubts and frustrations about our capacity; we would have to pool all these things and hurl them against the enemy and against the mountain and force the trees to sway again and bring sound back to the river.

A sense of pride emerged. From deep within rose the spirit of struggle, of never giving in, even though you might die. Your destiny had to be to rise to your death, to raise it up, to transform it into a standard and to thrust it on ahead, to forge ahead together with your own death and with your compañeros, and with the animals, to force the mountain to take our side, to force the trees to sway again.

From thinking so much, and since it was night, I fell asleep in a rage. And the next day I woke up in a rage, longing to fight, longing to test myself against the enemy, to test all of us, and longing to die, so that our deaths might stand as an affront to the enemy.

What I mean is, I woke up with an intense desire to live so that I could die and to die so that I could live. I wanted to die in order to live, to struggle in order to live for Latin America, to live and die for the Indians, to live and die for the blacks, to live and die for the animals, to live and die for my dad, who was a son of a bitch but a very nice guy. For the students, for

Subtiava, for everything. These were the ideals I cherished and kept with me, in a private way, from the time I came up from the city to the mountains, and that I never talked about to anyone.

I tramped through the mud, I was glutted with mud, spattered with mud; I shat in mud, cried in mud, sloshed through mud, sunk my head in mud; there was mud in every crevice of my body, my cock was caked with mud; but I had something with me in the mountains that I never talked about, that nobody knew about. I think I only confessed it once to a compañero over some drinks, but that was later, in 1978. I kept that secret and held it tight for four years. You see, I wanted to live, because I went into the mountains with a fistful of ideals tight in my hand; I never let go of them or got them dirty; and if I fell flat in the mud, when I pulled out my hand, there, tight in my fist, were those ideals.

I remember about three days after Tello's death we thought the Guard was going to come after our camp. So we retreated upstream. We were right in the middle of eating a cow—superdelicious—when all of a sudden a compañero named Evelio rushed in. "Compañeros!" he said, "the Guard's coming, over there, somebody's guiding them!" It was a campesino from nearby that the Guard had got hold of and taken along by force. The order went out: vanguard, center, rearguard, and me with that shitty mess of mountain leprosy on my legs, and we had to retreat. They instructed Flavio to layer me up with more bandages. I could barely get on my boot. I was raging to fight and to die fighting the Guard. We started upstream, which means against the current. It was a stream about 15 yards wide, full of stones, and winding through a rugged mountain wilderness, on top of which now the mountain was an ally of the Guard. It had fallen silent, it no longer swayed; for three days it had stood stock still awaiting the moment when the Guard would come and the horrendous battle would begin.

We fell into formation—vanguard, center, rearguard—and

123

started marching. It was as though the mountain realized that what was happening was no joke and began to sway. You see, the mountain had been holding back because Tello had been killed. She wouldn't sway; it was as though she had gone over to the side of the Guard. She was unbending, watchful, waiting to see what would happen, and when we started to march in full battle readiness, retreating upstream but expecting to clash with the Guard, she came to herself, she shook herself to life. It was as if we had shaken the mountain as you would shake a woman, taking hold of her and saying, "Okay, bitch, what's going on," but with affection.

We started to march, with Rodrigo heading up the vanguard, Modesto in the center, and Aurelio Carrasco in the rearguard. A campesino marched in the center, and Modesto, since he was the leader, and me, since I was sick, since if you're fucked up physically you go in the center. The river was loaded with stones; the water was crystal-clear; as you went along you could see the stones, and you stepped between them. You kept falling down, and right at the outset all my bandages got wet; water seeped into the open sores, and with water in leprosy sores, you're wide open, as if the water was in league with the Guard.

The sores started stinging, to hurt me as if on purpose, for no good reason, as if purely to harass me, and my flesh fought back as if it, too, was fighting the water. But as I warmed up, the sores warmed up and didn't hurt so bad; I was stumbling against stones but it hurt less.

By that time I didn't give a damn whether I lived or died, because Tello was dead and we were going to find out right there who knew more—those bastard sons of bitches—we would see who would die. My rifle was loaded, and the longer I marched the more furious I was to fight, to have done with the Guard and everything else—to have done with the leprosy and the hunger and with everything they had forced us to give up, meat, everything. And Tello's death—dammit—we would see who knew how to fight, we would see who had reason on his side. It was a challenge flung down to history. I felt a rage that was like a million tiny atomic explosions through my pores. My brain was tight with rage. And my water-creased hands were fingering the trigger, wanting the Guard to appear and knowing I was going to die because I would never be able to get across that river. But I was going to let loose a storm of bullets . . .

At one point in the climb we had to scale about 30 yards of steep stone, a waterfall in that stream, which wound through the heart of the mountain. I said to Modesto, who was climbing up ahead of me, "Hey, Modesto, you forgot to tell me to bring along my mountain-climbing manual!" since it was 30 yards up and I could see that Modesto was having a hard time climbing. But we came out of it and continued to march.

The sun on the water burned us, even in the shade; through the foliage. I said to Modesto, "Look, Modesto, if I die, tell my son"—I knew then I had a baby—"that his father was a revolutionary, that he did what he had to do, and that all his life he should be proud of his father." Do you know what Modesto did when I said that, right on the march? He said, "I'll tell him, I'll tell him." And he touched me, brushing my wet face with his hand, which was so out of context because each of us had always to be covering our flank, because even though the mountain had started moving, she might still hold back—the mountain that had been our protectress, that had helped us, hidden us, kept us in her womb. But she had been still for so long when Tello died, I didn't trust her anymore; she might have gone over to the Guard. But when she started swaying, when she saw us in combat gear, "She's coming alive," I said, "she's returning to normal." But I thought: watch out for that mountain, that she doesn't go over to the Guard. I told Modesto that. We continued on, and the Guard didn't come.

When we emerged from the stream the mountain became composed, as if her confidence in us had been restored, as if she had been waiting to see who could do more, or who was right, or had the strength. But I ended up suspecting that the mountain was not wondering about who had the strength or the power to destroy. I ended up thinking that the mountain leaned toward whoever kept a hundred years of life in his pack, or in his hands. Sometimes I wanted to say, Look, mountain, if you are stone or inanimate vegetable you have nothing to do with this, you have no power to judge anything, okay? I had the impression that the mountain was starting to discern, starting to think, as if an inner force was leading her to think and take sides and judge. Who the hell does this bitch think she is? I wanted to say to her, Look, you have no business here. You are vegetable, you are rock, you protect whoever seeks your protection. Because I had started to think she was protecting the Guard, that she had something to do with changes in the weather, and that the changes in the weather were all in favor of the Guard, in favor of the status quo. Probably since she was scared they would clear her forests, for the mountain's own survival. Okay, here you are, an inanimate being, but we are humans, rational creatures with soul and consciousness. We command you, rule and govern you, since you are nature. You give no orders.

I knew that as for discernment, reason, and intelligence we were more intelligent, more educated, more discerning than the Guard. So she had no right to strike those attitudes. As if she were swayed by what I said, or by what I thought, or by our readiness to fight after Tello's death. Because Tello was probably a symbol not just for me but for the mountain, too. He must have been a symbol since he had lived with her; I'm sure that he lived with her, that he had relations with her; she bore him sons.

So the mountain held fast to Tello as to the measure of all things. And when Tello died she felt that all was over, that her commitment was gone, that what was left was foolishness. But when she saw the readiness to fight of the group of men there marching over her, through her heart, she realized that Tello was not the beginning and end of the world, but had been her son. That Tello had been her son, though he may have been her life, her secret lover, her brother, her creature, her stone, though Tello may have been her river; she had to realize that Tello was not the end of the world. She had to realize that Tello was the beginning of the world, because after him came all of us with our teeth clenched and our feet bound up with mountain leprosy, with our wet fingers on the trigger, with our heavy packs—we had the power to light a fire in her heart.

As if she knew she had in fact screwed up, that she ought never to have fallen silent that afternoon when Tello died; she ought to have continued rocking, if only as a show of neutrality. But we bent her over; we shattered the neutrality of the rivers and gigantic trees; we brought her back to herself; the sound of the river changed as we passed, for we possessed the river, had impressed our own sound upon it, which was different from the sound it had taken upon itself when I was listening in my hammock and when it seemed the river sound was dropping down on purpose to meet the silence of the leaves on the silent trees. So, when she saw she had screwed up, there was nothing else to do—we brought her around by force. When the Guard came she realized her mistake.

At last we emerged from the stream. My legs were screwed, all cut up by the stones, and dammit was I sorry that the Guard had not appeared; we were almost sure we were going to clash with the Guard, that we'd be ambushed, and we had marched with the highest spirits, almost wanting to clash with the Guard. Because of Tello's death, and all the other deaths. So when we emerged from the stream we were happy, especially me because of my legs—we were going to rest. At the same time we were sad in a way, since that had been our chance once and for all to avenge Tello, to humble the mountain, the river, the stones—our chance to show who was who or to die protesting in the river, protesting with bullets over the river, as so many guerrillas all over Latin America had died in streams, in battles.

But the Guard was not there; it was off somewhere else searching for us. Or it had followed us but lost our trail, since we had gone through the stream. The point is that we came out of the stream without having fought. It was wonderful, because we were going to rest. I remember that the compañero who shared my rain cover helped me put up the hammock. In the mountains when the column was very long we usually slept in pairs so as to leave fewer tracks. So the compañero who was with me helped me put up the hammock. I remember that no order to change our clothes was given; we were on alert.

Reunion and Departure

The next day we moved into another region; we came to a ridge, a mountain crest, toward the top; but instead of climbing all the way up, since it's easier to march along the top, we marched "sloping," as we called it. Because the Guard usually patrolled the crests looking for our tracks; they assumed the guerrillas always marched on the higher ground. But that time we all marched on the slopes of the range, which of course was the hardest possible place to march, since you have to put one foot lower and the other higher up on the slope. And you come across drop-offs, ravines, ditches, hanging vines, and huge fallen trees that are very tricky to get around, since you can't climb over them. You have to find the edge of the downed branches and cross over there, over all the leaves and a whole mess of branches. Your pack gets caught and your rifle gets snagged; it's a battle every inch of the way. And since you're tired and walking on a slant, you slip and fall, and you leave tracks. You have to pick yourself up and erase the signs of your fall.

It was freezing cold along that ridge. We set up camp in a cachimbero, which is a dense jungle full of hundreds of varieties of brush and grasses and vegetation of all kinds—shrubs, trees, little creeping plants, vines. We made camp on that slope, which was very steep. Just tying our hammocks to a tree was a major effort, and when you were lying in your hammock, if you leaned to one side you could touch the ground with your hand, and if you leaned to the other you could look out over a huge precipice. To go from one rain cover to another you had to be very careful, or you'd fall, and the rain covers were about 15 or 20 yards apart. I'm not sure how many we had, ten, twenty, I can't remember now. We made camp there for a number of days, maybe fifteen. I figured we were waiting for the Guard to finish combing the area. That must have been what Modesto and Rodrigo had decided, because there was no order to move to the guerrilla offensive. For the moment we were strictly in a defensive position.

When we broke camp in such a hurry, each of us threw some salted meat into his pack, and we were carrying powdered milk. It was just a scrap of meat, a little piece, about 2 inches wide and 8 or 9 inches long. We cut the meat into strips, narrow strips. We started in first on the meat, since it was going bad, and we didn't know how long we were going to be there, how much time we would have to spend in isolation from the population, which by that time the Guard must have really come down on hard. We ate the meat almost raw; we put it on a little stand and salted it, then to eat it we tossed it onto the fire, not to cook it, but just to sear it, to smoke it a little.

At night we built a fire to sear the meat. We had to get water from about a half mile away down the cliff. We took our little pails, and coming back, to keep them from spilling on that steep ground, we had to be real jugglers. We were expert jugglers; it was a real balancing act—tightrope walkers were nothing compared to us.

The water that remained after washing the meat we drank as a sort of broth, which seemed delicious to us. It was bitter cold, and the "soup" was hot. We couldn't warm ourselves by the fire, because the fire was on a little plateau about a yard across, and we couldn't all gather around it. Besides, it would have been dangerous. Lying in your hammock, when it wasn't your turn to cook, you could see the fire where they were cooking way down in the distance. After a while you heard a voice call out in the dark: "Time to eat, compañeros!" An almost guttural sound. And very slowly each of us groped our way down to get his food. On that ridge we knew the worst hunger we had known. I remember after about four or five days our meat had rotted. Our hunger was getting worse and our rations were shrinking. The meat was starting to get wormy; it was starting to stink and to rot. But we were so hungry that even the stench smelled good to us. By that time we were like animals; we pulled the stench of that meat into our lungs—delicious!—because even if it was rotten it was food; and even the stench was appetizing. Naturally the farts afterward stunk like hell. It made us want to throw up

When the meat was gone we started in on the powdered milk. At first the ration was three little spoonfuls, which we ate as it was, as powder. We couldn't go down in the daytime to bring back water from below because of the clatter of our pails and the noise of the branches scratching against the metal. So you got in line with your little pail, which by that time was all battered up; you got your three little spoonfuls and went back to your rain cover. It was almost a ritual. You went to your rain cover and withdrew into yourself to eat your milk. It was also something to do, an activity, and all the more wonderful because it was food. You took your spoon and dipped it into the little pail—just the tip of the spoon—to get a few grains of milk. You started eating with the tip of your tongue and your teeth. With only three spoonfuls, believe me, you were left with a horrible hunger. Three for breakfast, three for lunch, in that freezing cold. It was forbidden to get our blankets out and cover up, because if we had to fight on the spur of the moment we would lose our blankets. The cold was unbearable. It made me think of those Mexican films where a couple of Indians would be huddled in their ponchos looking very sad because of the cold—beggars with sad, expressionless faces, as if resigned somehow, I can't describe it exactly. The same for supper, then it was two spoonfuls, then only one. You accomplished wonders; since the spoon wasn't flat but had a rounded tip, it wouldn't fit into all the corners of the battered pails; it wasn't easy getting out all that milk. You used your fingernails. You scraped it out, then used your teeth to get it out from under your nails, dissolved in a bit of saliva. The final part of the operation involved sliding your tongue over your teeth and gums to get at anything there, then sucking on that.

There's one image I'll never forget. At the end of the day, after not having fought the Guard, waiting for God knows what, without much knowledge of the tactics or strategy of war, freezing cold, in the shittiest kind of shape and all of that—there was Modesto reading Ernst Mandel's *Political Economy*. If somebody had a book floating around up there it would never occur to us to get it out and read. We didn't feel up to dealing with that foolishness. Maybe it wasn't foolishness, but we weren't capable of reading a book on the theory of revolution. So that was the sort of stuff Modesto was made of: he passed the time reading, studying.

Sometimes, there on the ridge, we got together in the afternoon under Rodrigo's rain cover. Rodrigo was a good talker, and he was always teaching. We talked less to Modesto. Modesto was more complicated—his vocabulary more complex. Modesto was an extraordinary compañero, but dammit, he was so quick, so intelligent, that sometimes you couldn't figure out what the hell he was talking about. I understand him a little better now. In those days I couldn't make fuck-all of what he was saying. But we always knew he was right, what he said was correct. I didn't understand it, but I always felt it was correct. Rodrigo understood Modesto. I think Nelson Suárez was more intelligent than any of us, because he understood Modesto; he was a campesino, and they always got along very well. Rodrigo was completely under-standable when he talked. So we would sit around talking when it seemed that the danger had subsided. We were always talking about Vietnam, about international politics, or telling stories and kidding around. Rodrigo was always teaching us, until finally we left that area.

We moved into another zone, a distant zone, and if I'm not mistaken, we marched for several weeks. When we got to the new place, I remember, there was a meeting of the General Staff of the guerrilla forces operating in the zone. We started marching toward Yaosca, Cuscawas, El Chile, in that di-rection, coming from Las Bayas and Waslala.

One day on the march, I'm not sure when, Modesto broke the news that they were going to send me down to the city to have my leprosy taken care of and my appendix looked at. I think it was somewhere along that march, which went on for several weeks heading into that new zone, that the Repodral medicine turned up. It seems they had sent down for it, and suddenly it was there, in the hands of a contact. I only have foggy images, I can't remember much about it. The thing was that the Repodral had to be injected three times a day for I can't remember how many days, I think three. It was laugh-able—because at that time we hardly had hygienic conditions, on top of which we were marching through very dangerous zones. So they gave me my first shot before starting out in the morning, lying down; then, when we stopped to rest on the march, I'm not shitting you, I'd get another shot. "Eugenio, your shot!" Our little doc came over, Edwin Cordero, and I unbuckled my belt, and with my pack on and everything, my rifle on my back, I'd drop my pants just like that, standing up. The little doc, with his pack on, too, and his rifle on his back, would take the syringe, with no alcohol or cotton or anything, and *jaa!* he jabbed it in, like a savage. Fortunately the doc had a good hand and it hardly hurt at all the first couple of days. But after a number of shots, when we got into camp at night . . . You can imagine how it hurt to march, to march with my ass sore as hell, and with the pain of that leprosy, which was indescribable. And the hunger, and on top of everything, Tello's death—we couldn't get Tello's death out of our minds. The way you felt when they gave you that shot, it was as if you were an animal, since you don't lie down, there's no cotton with alcohol . . . only a rush of memories. I could see myself going to my Uncle Victor's little farm for vacations. He always injected his cows when they were on the run; he chased after them to inject them when they were running loose. Or sometimes they were tied up.

So I remembered that and felt like a cow or like a horse, and with Tello's death on top of everything. The doc told me to relax my ass, and when he stuck in the needle I made it go slack so it wouldn't hurt. But the minute the needle was in, I tightened the gluteus muscle, as if out of spite or out of anger against that shot. To receive a shot under those conditions was like the consecration of my own animality. I was just like my Uncle Victor's cow. When they jabbed in the needle I bridled a bit, the way that cow used to bridle. Then Uncle Victor's cow would amble off with her little calf and be fine. The cows in the pasture were happy; they couldn't care less that they'd been jabbed. But the trouble with me was they jabbed me every ten minutes, then I had to march, and I couldn't come to grips with Tello's death, and the last straw was that I didn't know if Claudia had had a boy or a girl. They had told me I had a baby, but I didn't know which, and it was always on my mind.

We finally got to a place that wasn't a proper camp. You could see it was more on the outskirts, I mean a zone on the edge of the mountains. Not completely jungly. But it wasn't like the country in the west of Nicaragua either, because the north country is different. It was there that I experienced one of the greatest satisfactions of my life, one that I'll never forget. We were approaching the camp when they told me El Gato Munguía was there. Son of a bitch! It was more or less our great reunion. I don't know if it was his return, or my return, or our coming together—I suppose it was neither his return nor mine, but our reunion. El Gato! I said, and El Gato knew that I was coming, too. El Gato for me had been something so extraordinary, as I told you before. There were five of us bosom friends—Leonel, Juan José, El Gato, Camilo Ortega, and me. I thought in my gut, Son of a bitch, Camilo, El Gato, Leonel, Juan José, and me in the mountains! If someday we are all in the mountains, I thought, Camilo and El Gato in the mountains and me and Juan José in the mountains, that will be a guerrilla force to reckon with! That damn Camilo's skinny, I thought, and zoom he'll jump, and if there's a tree trunk he'll jump right over it. And El Gato had those green eyes that I imagined would be able to see better and to shoot better. It seemed to me that the five of us together would be indestructible. And they said El Gato was going to be there! I wondered, what would he be like, would El Gato be the head of a squad? He could be, he had the background for it. He had been in Cuba, and if El Gato had been in Cuba and was a student leader, now after two years in the mountains, El Gato had to be the head of a squad.

That was my reunion with El Gato, a reunion with mystery or a reunion with certainty, one or the other, but my reunion with El Gato was an encounter! I remembered every shirt El Gato owned and every pair of slacks; I remembered all his shoes and all his girl friends. I remembered his face from every possible angle and all his facial expressions. I especially remembered his eyes and all the things he used to say.

Finally we arrived in camp; it was night. In the dark I could make out four or five guerrilla soldiers. I knew that El Gato went by the name Ventura. "Where's Ventura?" I asked. They told me Ventura was sleeping. "Where's he sleeping?" They took me to a spot in the camp, and there was Ventura, asleep. He was in a hammock. It was summer by then, because I remember there were dry leaves. I approached very slowly on tiptoe, though I intended to wake him. But I came up slowly so he wouldn't know we had finally arrived. You walk

135

slowly on dry leaves because they crack like thunderbolts and can give you away. It was about three in the morning when I came to El Gato's hammock, which hung very low, almost down to the ground, about a hand's breadth off the ground. He was asleep. No rain cover, since it was summer. There was a moon, and moonlight filtered through the scraggly trees that grew in that area. Then I saw El Gato's rifle, an AR-15. El Gato's weapon was a better weapon than my M-1 carbine, which made sense, since he was better than me, and older. I knelt beside El Gato and breathed in the same odor I had myself, the same odor my pack had, and my hammock and my blanket. Because El Gato was wrapped up in his hammock. But he also had a slightly different odor; El Gato's odor was different, and let me tell you I was nervous. I didn't know if El Gato would be happy to see me. I didn't know if he would feel what I was feeling. I was nervous, because I didn't know how he would react. What if El Gato only said, "Hey, how's it going?" How did I know what El Gato would say?

So, after staring at him in the hammock for a little while and breathing in the smells and remembering a thousand things and saying to him in my mind, So this is what it's come to, so this is where we've ended up, I nudged him and said, "Ventura . . . Ventura . . . Ventura," and El Gato woke up. "Aaaah?" he mumbled. "Ventura, it's me, Eugenio." When I said "Eugenio," El Gato sat straight up with a jerk; he just sat there in the hammock as if half-awake. When he heard "Eugenio" he must have thought he was dreaming. He was soaked with sweat. Then, "Gato," I said, "it's me, Eugenio," and I took his head in the moonlight. "Skinny!" he cried, and took me in his arms, and I hugged him, and El Gato slipped down out of the hammock and the two of us fell onto the ground embracing. And we stayed like that, the two of us there on the ground. Because I was crouching beside him, observing him, and the two of us stayed like that on the ground, and I could smell the whole odor of El Gato. "How are you?" he said as if saying to me, "How have you been since I left, how have you been since you did all those things back there, and all those things up here, and how are you now that we're together again, after so much has happened?"

And we stayed like that a while, sort of fallen onto the ground and embracing. Then we got up, and El Gato sat in his hammock, and I sat in front of him. There were so many things to say that we didn't know where to begin. I saw in the moonlight that El Gato had a beard; I had one, too, but mine was thinner. El Gato's was a bit thicker, a red beard, and it made his mouth (the same old watermelon mouth) less noticeable, and I saw he had the same green eyes. He asked about Claudia. "And Claudia?" he said. "I don't know, they say I have a baby. And you, what about Susy?" I asked. "Hombre," he said, "that's all over." "What do you mean, it's all over?" I asked. "Well," he said, "she's there and I'm here and it's over." "But you're wearing the ring," I pointed out, because Susy had given him a ring. She had bought two rings, and hers had "Susy" engraved inside and the date when they started going together, and Edgard's said "Edgard." "I know, it's just that I'm here and she's there," he said. "She's with somebody else . . . she's married, I don't know . . ." "No shit! But why are you wearing the ring?" "It's just that I can't get it off, even though she's with someone else."

Well, we just sat in silence, then burst out laughing and talking a mile a minute, about all sorts of things, disjointed, unconnected things—not unconnected, but we were talking in such a crazy way, a whole jumble of little things spilled out. Then we tried to get some sleep, and the next day dawned. We were the first ones up. It was as if we couldn't sleep because we wanted so much to talk and to see each other. The next day we were together again, and I started telling him my story. Later he said to me, "They told me you had problems when you first came in, that the mountain gave you a rough time, or maybe they just told me you had problems. It was very tough for me in the beginning, too." And he told me how hard it had been for him. Now our conversation was smoother, more fluid, calmer. "It looks as if they're going to send you back to the city," he said. "Who?" I asked. "You, they're going to send you down." Then he said, "I think it's a good thing, that you could do more in the city than up here." "No, hombre," I answered, "I'm in good shape now." "I know that," he said, "but now it's no longer a question of physical condition, it's a question of seeing where we can contribute the most from a political-military standpoint. I think they need you in the city. And I think it's a good decision to send you down." "Well, if they send me down, fine, they send me down, I go where they want me to go, but for some time now I've been in good enough shape to deal with the mountains. I've shown that." "No, hombre," he said, "don't keep talking about physical condition when it's not about that; it's a question of where it's best for us to be."

The upshot of all this was that the next day they called me to a meeting with Modesto, Rodrigo, and El Gato. El Gato didn't say anything. They chose Rodrigo to tell me. When it was all over I still didn't know if they were going to send me down because of the mountain leprosy or because of the appendicitis—sometimes I had attacks of appendicitis—or because they wanted to reorganize the cadres, or because they wanted me in the city, or what. The thing is, I was summoned, and Modesto didn't say anything, Edgard didn't say anything, and Rodrigo opened the meeting. "Look, Eugenio, we've been thinking this over, we've been observing you. We've seen your ability, your morale, we've seen how quickly you've been able to adapt, but the mountain is only a school where many compañeros from the city will come for their formation, then they will have to go back down. In that sense the mountain is a great school where we also form men, then inject them back into the city—solid men who can help develop the work there. Because the mountain isn't everything. We need work in both city and country." He said a whole lot of things, then added, "We have something we want to tell you, which is this—the Eugenio that came up here is not the same Eugenio

138

who is going back down; you're going to go back to the city, and the compañeros will place you where they see fit." Many things ran through my mind at that moment. I thought, Well, if they're sending me back to the city, will it be to León? Okay, but I'm known in León. I wouldn't be able to walk a single block in León, or three blocks. I wouldn't be able to stop at a stoplight in León, because a policeman would recognize me, he would know me right away. Or a Guardsman. Okay then, I wasn't going to ask them not to send me down, because I would go wherever they told me I ought to be.

So, they informed me I was going down. And let me tell you, I felt depressed, because I had come to care for that environment, to feel affection for the people; I had gained self-confidence, I had learned so many things in the mountains. I said to myself, I can't abandon the boys. I can't go down. I can't leave them in the mud, or on these trails. I can't leave them in this loneliness. Well, that was the decision of the High Command and down I went. It was summer, the middle of April, 1975.

Return to the Past

I started down with Juan de Dios Muñoz and Valdivia, José Dolores Valdivia, who went by the name of Faustino (or Silvestre). Faustino came along up to a point, then I continued on down alone. Faustino was going on to Cuá, to open up a new zone, or a new route, I'm not sure exactly what. We marched for several days until we came one night to a little shack. That was where I met Francisco Rivera. I already knew Juan de Dios, who had been with El Gato in that camp; I knew him since he had taken me into the mountains in '74. So we came to a shack, gave the signal, they signaled back, and we went in.

It was a tiny shack about 5 square yards with a kitchen area, some three-legged stools, a little rough-hewn table, a hammock, a cot, the cookstove, and another three-legged stool by the fire where a man was sitting, waiting for the black coffee to be ready. A handsome man, light-skinned, with blue eyes, wearing a hat. He didn't blink when we came in. When Juan de Dios said, "Rómulo, this is Eugenio," he answered, "You're Eugenio? Glad to meet you, compañero," and he held out his hand. That was it, nothing more; he remained seated. "And how was your trip?" he asked. "Fine, compañero."

"Compita," he turned to his wife, "it looks like it's about to boil." He busied himself with the black coffee, putting it in, stoking the fire, and smoking a cigarette. "How are the boys?" he asked. "Fine, compa." He had the campesino way of talking, but he looked just like a city man. With his blue eyes, light skin, and fine features, in the glow of the stove he looked just like a cowboy out of the Wild West. A Texas-style hat. Shit, I thought, this guy looks like a Texan and talks like a campesino. We chatted awhile, he with his campesino manner, asking us things and talking. Then we all went off to sleep outside the shack, in some hammocks about 500 yards away.

We talked a little more the next day, then took off, continuing on down and down. And all the way, as I realized it was no joke, that really I was going back to the city, my head was spinning as I tried to make some sense of it. On the one hand I was leaving behind what I loved more than anything else at the time, my brothers in the mountains, but at the same time I was approaching what I also loved, the city and my brothers in the city. And that tremendous uncertainty—where were they going to send me? And the city with its electric lights and colors again, and the cars and the blare of radios and watching TV and sugar—there would always be sugar, three times a day—and ice cream and sodas and chips and now and then a movie. And all the cars.

I never did figure out if I loved the mountains or not. Because it hurt me to leave them. But I also hated them; I came to hate the mountains. But I loved them too—who knows what the fuck was going on inside of me. The thing is I was thinking about the city again. First, there was my operation. And after that? Would they send me to another city or back to the mountains? I would either go to the country or stay in town, and there would be girls. I would see Claudia. And yes, I was going to make love, and the idea of making love with Claudia, or with any other woman, thrilled me, the sensation of kissing a woman again, of caressing a woman, of running my hand all over a woman's body, of being on top of

141

a woman, of coming on top of a woman. And I thought of the women who were in the underground at that time, I went over them all; which one did I want most to see, if Claudia wasn't there, or if Claudia didn't want me anymore, which one would it be? What women were there, what were they like, these women I didn't know? It had been exactly a year since I had touched a woman's face or brushed back a woman's hair. A year with nobody to give me even a little kiss on the cheek, nobody to be naked with, no skin to feel next to mine. My head was spinning.

The university again, would I go by the university? What people would be there? And if they put me back in the student movement? What people were in it now, what new girls had come in? Would one of them be the girl I'd be with? Or maybe they would send me to another city where there wouldn't be any girls. I hoped to God there would be a compañera, but who knows? That was how I daydreamed along the way. And the minute I quit thinking of that, I would think of the mountains. And if they kill me in the city, I thought, what if they recognize me and kill me, or take me alive? But they'd take me dead. Until it was finally time to put on different clothes. We took off our guerrilla outfits and I shaved; I only left my mustache, that was all. Before, aboveground, I never had a beard or a mustache.

And we continued going down until we got to a place that I think was Cuá, in the area around Cuá, and we caught a group-transport truck. It had been so long since I'd heard that sound, the distant rumble of a truck. I know that sound, I said, it's a truck. I said this with absolute confidence: it's a truck; I know that sound. I was so curious to see if I'd remember the sound of cars. And how would I eat, could I manage, would I be able to use a spoon, or a knife and fork, after eating for so long with my fingers—shoving in food like a savage, looking at things like a savage. Anyway, we caught the truck and climbed into the open back, which was packed solid with people, passengers going to a little town in the area. I was looking around at everyone, trying to act natural but drinking it all in—the city men dressed in every possible color. The people in the truck were a combination of city and country.

We were not yet in the city, but somewhere between the mountains and the open fields. And all the while I was thinking about these things I've been telling you. Remembering how we used to demonstrate with pitch-pine torches and with candles. And how, in Chile I'd heard a slogan that went like this, "If you don't jump you're a mummy!" (a "mummy" in Chile during Allende's time was a member of the reaction, of the bourgeoisie). Anyway that slogan popped into my mind in the middle of a demonstration back home, and I yelled out, "If you don't jump you're a toad!" Because in Nicaragua the Somocistas were called toads, and everybody, about three-quarters of the people in the demo, started jumping up and down: "If you don't jump you're a toad, if you don't jump you're a toad! *El que no brinque es sapo, el que no brinque es sapo!*" Everybody jumping up and down, and that same night the Guard came looking for me at my house.

I remembered that and wondered if I was still the same guy who had organized those demonstrations and jumped up and down like that, who had been in the mountains and was now returning, with no idea what was going to happen next. That great uncertainty—what would they decide down there?

And the truck drove on; it was one long lurch and bump, stirring up those typical clouds of dust that go with cars on dirt roads in the summer. We were far from León, but León was in the air. The dust got in my nostrils and ears and throat; my hair was turning a chalky brown; the hair on my arms was turning blond; my mustache was almost white—which reminded me of León. It was hundreds of miles away, but I was breathing León. This feeling grew stronger as the sun beat down harder and it got hotter and the terrain opened out, and there were fewer and fewer trees. I could smell León when people in the truck started putting kerchiefs over their heads and faces to keep out the dust. We did that in León when the

Cerro Negro volcano blew its stack in 1971, and whirlwinds of ash whipped through the city.

Like everything else in those days we made use of it against Somoza. In the darkness brought on by the clouds of ash that were sifting down over León, El Gato and I took advantage of everybody going around with kerchiefs over their faces to go out to the Central Market with our faces covered. As we made our way among the baskets of crabs and clams and green vegetables, we'd moan: "It's terrible, terrible, it's the wrath of God, the wrath of God, God is punishing us for not kicking Somoza out! And He'll keep right on punishing us because Somoza is still in power!" We walked by the meatsellers and soft-drink vendors: "Wrath of God, wrath of God!" And past booths of clothing: "Wrath of God!" Past shoemakers and itinerant repairmen and people selling rice and beans: "If we don't kick Somoza out this will go on forever!" And people were pissed off because the dust was ruining everything and sales had fallen off. Naturally they were looking for somebody to vent their anger on. They listened to us because we gave them somebody to blame. And people started saying: "That son of a bitch is bringing down curses on us. That mistress of his, Dinora, is bad luck." So we made use of the circumstance to make propaganda against Somoza and the Guard.

Riding on that truck was like being on a time machine that was racing backward through time. As you rode along, the topography you had been used to seeing in recent months gave way to the topography you grew up with. The same madroño trees, the gnarled jinocuago, the same stones, the lizards, the iguanas, the hot dirt. As you went back over the road, this time going down, things came back to you from the past. Not just from the recent past, when you went up to the mountains, but from the past of your childhood. When I saw the madroño trees, or the calabash for example, I remembered the calabashes in the backyard of our house and how my dad used to cut switches from them to whip us with when we got out of hand. So when you saw the calabash you flew backward at an incredible speed toward your childhood.

In the late afternoon, after traveling for about eight hours, we came into El Sauce, where we were going to take the train. I remembered the railroad in León, when I took the train for the first time, and the thought of the train also brought back my childhood; coming down from the mountains in the truck was a continual coming and going over my own past, with the velocity, the agility, of a monkey, the way they swing through the branches at a breakneck speed. That was how you went from your childhood to the mountains, from the mountains to the city, and so on—in a rapid-fire juggling, a sort of mental trapeze act over little bits of your life—going farther and farther back in time.

There weren't many people in the streets in El Sauce, and we started walking toward the station. It wasn't long before we turned the corner and saw the huge train standing in the station, with lots of cars—long, black, and old, the very same train, of my childhood. It was as if the dialectic had come to a halt, because it was the same train, with the same railings, the same people, the same voices. "Ice water . . . ice water, pork and yucca . . . pork and yucca." The same women selling things with their big tin bowls, the porters hoisting up bags to be weighed on the scale, then throwing them on carts to take to the train. Men sloshing down rum, and here and there drunks scattered about the station, and innocent young girls begging, with whores on one corner and a pool hall on the other. It was all the uproar of the station I had known in the past: people clutching hens, loaded down with bags, fruit, all sorts of stuff; and campesinas in from the hills with their cheeks rouged for coming to town, with fresh lipstick on, that bright, bright red they always wear; and swarms of fat old ladies in aprons shooing away dogs and a drunk falling down off his horse and pigs in the street eating the little kids' shit; and pigsellers herding pigs onto the train, and women with food to sell shooing away pigs—squat pigs, snubtails, black pigs, barrow pigs, pigs fattened up for market. And some damn fool of a gypsy telling fortunes with parrots, and campesinos milling around looking amazed, while a loudspeaker on a parked car was hawking a salve that was good for all that ailed you, including your griefs. And the same old Guardsman on the corner, minding his own business. . . .

We went in to buy our tickets: the heavy stench of piss in the corridor with the ticket window, and the ticket seller the same dog-faced guy you could tell from a mile off was a spy for the Guard, pushing the same old tickets toward us, with that little puncher that poked out a tiny hole. Then, in a while, that familiar whistle *whiiiiii* that meant the train was leaving, and everybody rushing to wind up their purchases, and the conductor chasing the little tykes off the train and "Just a minute!" from a woman still buying something, and "Quick, ice water!" or "Tortilla with pork and yucca!" And a guy racing along the platform because somebody had forgotten his change, and the guy on the train with his hand stuck out yelling, "Brother, my change, my change!" And the guy with the change still not catching up, and the other guy yelling, "Son of a bitch, my change!" Until he finally got it to him, a little scene that's played out a million times. And the train began to pull out of the station.

At last we were on our way to León, and the time machine raced even faster. Now the dust was behind us; we were starting to see something I hadn't seen in a long time: fields of white cotton. Cotton and again a flood of memories: the trailer trucks rolling out at dawn before the light, full of cotton pickers with the women in men's shirts. Everybody went to pick cotton, which always used to piss off my dad, because the workers in his business always took off to pick cotton, where the pay was better. The whirling cotton gins of León—I could almost feel the cotton fluff in my nostrils. And the train sped on with that same sound and pulled into a station, and the whistle blew and again the ice water and lottery tickets and dogs and the people climbing aboard and the conductor scrambling. Then the bell in the new station, and the train pulling out.

As it hurtled on, I'm not sure why, but I began to feel more distressed. When the train neared Malpaisillo I was really beginning to feel uncomfortable, more and more uneasy. You see, it was gradually hitting me that I was going to have to face León again, to deal with a past I felt uncertain of. I became more and more nervous, skittish, restless—the pressure intensified. I didn't understand what was happening to me. I felt I was going to be hurled out of the train. So when the train started whistling, coming into Malpaisillo, I don't know why but I clung to the window with my hands, with my arms. I was sitting on the outside, by the window. I held on for dear life; I grabbed hold of the seat, feeling I might be catapulted forward. It wasn't that I wanted to go back—absolutely not. But I felt that something beyond my control was rocketing me toward León.

When the train came to a stop in the Malpaisillo station we didn't get off right away but waited for a bottleneck of people. We wanted to sort of blend into the uproar of all the people selling ice water and vegetables and clothes and every possible thing. A feeling of nakedness came over me in that station. We'd been in the mountains for so long with no contact with people, keeping out of sight, seeing only each other, not even going up to the shacks—because not all of us were authorized to approach the little shacks—we weren't used to being seen by people. Deep in the brush, we didn't let ourselves be seen. It hit me then that you get used not only to never seeing anybody, but also to nobody seeing you. You get used to being alone, right? I felt naked in Malpaisillo, in the sense that everybody was looking at you, in the sense that when you walked along you didn't stumble against any obstacle. You felt naked, with no protective shell. It was like being in an open field, on a beach—I don't know, but completely exposed. You don't have to keep picking up your feet to avoid the obstacles of the terrain. You walk normally, without pushing aside branches all the time. That's how you discover that the trees in the mountains and the topography of the mountains have come in a way to be your clothing, a protective dress.

Walking through the streets I was filled with fear, because being from León I had taken a number of trips to Malpaisillo. So there were people who knew me, school friends, people from Malpaisillo who used to live in León. The fact of being known made me feel naked; anybody at all might see and recognize me. This feeling of nakedness was all the stronger since in the mountains you always carry a pistol or a heavy weapon like a rifle, a submachine gun, or a carbine. And your rifle was always loaded, and your clips full, too. And sometimes you had reserves of food in your pack—so you were self-sufficient in the environment. You felt the protection of that heavy weapon, which in the mountains is like a part of your flesh. Your rifle is part of you in the mountains. You slept with your gun, marched with it, bathed with it right beside you, did exercises with it. Icy gun, greasy gun, gun on your shoulder, in your hand, rusted gun, stalwart gun, whistle-clean or rain-wet gun—you always had that gun at your neck, on your shoulder, or in your hand. In the mountains your weapon is like a part of you, like one more member, one of the most important. When you fall down you try harder to protect your gun than you do your own hand. And you start to feel affection for that gun. You always nickname your guns. For example, Aurelio Carrasco called his Garand "El Garañon" (The Stud). Another compañero had a black-stocked carbine that he called "Black Lady." I had an M-1 carbine, and since I always slept with it beside me, sometimes right in the hammock with me, I called it my "Teddy Bear." In Malpaisillo I felt unprotected without my Teddy Bear, because it guaranteed me the opportunity to die fighting, a chance to defend myself.

I was tense, but I did my best to look like a normal run-of-the-mill guy; I wore a little hat, low boots, blue jeans, and an ordinary shirt. I had kept my mustache, but my great fear was that somebody would recognize me. I acted normal, but I was watching people's reactions as they went by. Not letting on, but I was observing people to see if anybody recognized me, and unfortunately, somebody did.

At that instant of recognition an electric current ran through my body, like a jolt in my stomach—I almost bolted. I wanted like hell to run. Was he going to say hello? Or call out my name? I decided I had better just walk faster and try to reach the highway to León. I remember we hid for about an hour, waiting for him to go for the Guard, but nothing happened. In a little while we decided to start walking along the highway toward León. Nobody had recognized me, nor Juan de Dios Muñoz either, who was with me. Or if they did they didn't dare turn us in.

As we went on foot down the highway I was filled with a tremendous curiosity that was like joy, because I was going to see my companeros. Though really I wasn't that enthusiastic; too many things had happened for me to be carried away with enthusiasm. But it made me happy to think I was about to see my compañeros in the city, especially Iván Montenegro. But the magic was gone; it wasn't that thrill I felt when I left for the mountains. It was different now. People had died. We had learned that some die and others live; we had learned about suffering, that there was sadness as well as happiness.

I guess what thrilled me the most was the chance to see my daughters, or my sons. I remember now, before we started down, that son-of-a-bitch Rodrigo had said to me, "By the way, congratulations on those twins." Claudia's belly had been huge, and it seems that a courier or somebody somewhere along the line had mentioned that she was huge and probably was going to have twins. So by word of mouth it had traveled all the way up to the mountains, and somebody had told Modesto and Rodrigo that I had twins. And the joking started in. "Hot stuff, eh Eugenio, you must really be something!" All that ribbing you get when you have twins.

It was only when we got in on foot to a place near Telica, a

149

little shack, that I ran into a compañero named Francisco Lacayo who put me straight. "Eugenio, do you know you have a little girl?" "No, hombre," I answered, "not twins?" "No, hombre, it's a little girl and she looks like you." What a fantastic feeling! When they told me it wasn't twin boys but a little girl, well, an incredible tenderness filled me. It had never occurred to me I would have a girl, a little woman. When they told me that, I don't know, a very special tenderness came over me, I felt so delicate, so gentle. And naturally I'd been thinking for a long time of requesting a meeting with Claudia and the little girl, to see the baby.

Well, they came to get us; we sent a courier to León, and they came for us. They told us that the Regional would be coming in person to take us as far as the highway. The head of the Regional was Iván Montenegro. One night Iván Montenegro turned up in a taxi that belonged to a compañero. I guess you can imagine my joy at seeing Fat Man, who said to me a little nervously, "Get in, get in, get in." And we got in and started driving toward León.

Coming into León I felt—you know what I felt?—it was like one of those nightmares of being in León; it was like dreaming I was suddenly in León and that everybody was staring at me. And I was unarmed and the Guard was chasing me, or I was shooting but my gun wasn't working, I was firing but the bullets weren't hitting, or they were hitting but the Guardsmen weren't falling, they weren't dying. Or the barrel of my rifle would drop off; that was the nightmare when I thought of León. So entering León in a car at night, about eight at night ... Blood of Christ! the same boulevard, the same Debayle Avenue from before, the hospital, the same drive-in, the train station. We turned at the station and ran into San Juan Park. They gave me some of those dark glasses, can you imagine, so nobody would recognize me. I looked out at the people—it was awful. It wasn't just that I felt naked; it was more than that, do you know how I felt? I felt, I'm in the underground entering León. What I mean is, the unthinkable,

150

the unimaginable was happening, the thing I had feared the most. It meant the greatest possible physical danger, the most real possibility of being killed or captured. Really, it meant being totally exposed, totally in the open.

It was crazy in a way, but it had to be done—I entered León. We tried to keep to the barrios, skirting the main part of the city until we came to the safe house. It was in Subtiava, the house of a tailor, a compañero whose name I've forgotten. I don't remember the address very well, but it was in Subtiava, about a block or so from the Calle Real. Then—the fantastic joy—I got out of the car and there were "El Chiricuto," Luis Guzmán, Quincho Ibarro, Jorge Sinforoso Bravo, whom I knew from before. "Soup's on," somebody said. I took a bath; they gave me civilian clothes. I wanted everything—chocolate, an ice pop; I wanted a "burro's milk" candy from Prío's. What didn't I want? I wanted everything. It didn't seem possible that I was there, once again in the heart of León, and neither the Guard, nor Somoza's Security, nor my friends, nor my family knew anything about it.

Doctors and Nurses

After I'd been in León about four days, an order came from Pedro Aráuz, member of the National Directorate: I was to leave for Ocotal, where first they were going to operate on me, then put me in the Northern Regional. At that time the head of the Regional was "Pelota" (Pudge), also known as Manuel Morales Fonseca. Bayardo Arce was there, too. We set out on foot as it was starting to get light, about 5:30 A.M. They were going to pick us up about two blocks from the house. Can you imagine, Iván Montenegro, Quincho Ibarra, who used to be President of CUUN, and me, the three of us walking down the street at that hour, when houses were already open and the bakers were out with their bread, and people were out selling fresh butter. They walked on the outside, since they were less notorious, with me in the middle, to hide me a little from people's eyes. We were walking right down the middle of the street, a dirt street, with stone pavings.

I said to myself, This is insane, this is really the limit! and sure enough, people recognized me right off the bat. I saw how their eyes widened, and some of them even said hello. But Subtiava was a militant sector; politically it was more or less completely liberated territory. So they put me in a car—I don't remember who was driving—and we took the León–San Isidro Highway.

At the San Isidro junction another car was waiting, and I got in. I wasn't carrying anything, just my .45 with one magazine and a few extra bullets. I recognized the guy at the wheel—fantastic! it was Toño Jarquín, Doctor Antonio Jarquín Toledo, favorite son of Nueva Segovia. "Hey!" he said, very surprised, because he thought I was in the mountains. "Skinny, how are you? Son of a bitch, you're fatter!" "You're shitting me, how could I be fatter?" I answered. "It's just that you look fatter to me," he said. It had been so long since we'd seen each other that I seemed fatter, you might say swollen from all that corn. You see, corn swells you up. I was swollen from eating pozol (ground red corn). And he thought I looked pale, which made sense, since I never saw the sun; I was definitely pale. So they took me to Ocotal and started setting things up for my operation. The whole thing scared the hell out of me—I thought they were going to operate on me in some underground hideout or something like that, with some doctor who was a friend, in some tiny guerrilla "hospital." I'd heard talk of the Tupamaros who had clinics disguised as beauty parlors, and I figured by this time we had all that, too.

"When's the operation?" I asked him. "Hold on," he said. "First we have to check out the hospital in Somoto, because that's where I have to do the operation." "What, I'm going to be operated on in the hospital in Somoto?" I asked. "Sure, of course, and where did you think we were going to do it?" "Uh, I was just asking, that's all," I said, "just curious. I only wanted to know what hospital it was." No shit, my heart dropped to the floor. And we started for Somoto.

The next day I asked Toño, "Hey, what's happening with the hospital?" "Hombre," he said, "the thing is, you see we're working on it. We have to see which of the nurses can be with you, and we have to find an anesthetist." "And the anesthetist and the nurse will be compañeras?" I asked. "No, neither one, but the doctors will be Saul and me—there's no problem. Besides, don't worry, I'm going to say you're my cousin and that you're only going to be there the minimum amount of time, say three days, then we'll get you out of there." "Okay then," I said, never thinking that what was going to happen to me would ever happen.

The next day: "Okay, brother, let's go." And about five o'clock in the afternoon he checked me into the hospital. I was carrying a grenade. I said to myself, Good God in heaven, what a disaster if they discover me, and the Guard comes and drags me bareass out of bed and starts beating me with their rifle butts. They could beat me shitless and I wouldn't be able to move after that operation. I wouldn't be able to defend myself. If I fell, my incision would rip open; they would beat me right in the open wound and my guts would spill out. And the worst of it wasn't thinking what they might do to me, but the idea of being powerless in front of those sons of bitches. I said to myself, if the Guard bursts in here, what I'll do is have the grenade and pistol under my pillow. And I undid those two little clips on the grenade; I put them straight up; all I had to do was pull the pin, and I kept it right beside me. If the Guard comes, I thought, I'll take the grenade and explode it right in the room, and that will be the end of the Guard and of me, too. But those dogs were not going to fuck me over. They were not going to murder me when I'd just been operated on. All I could think of was Enrique Lorete, who was an epileptic, and how they beat him over the head when he was in prison to bring on one of his fits. And when the fit came they really started beating the shit out of him; and when the fit passed they kept right on beating and torturing him until they brought on another one.

That horrible sensation, knowing they could fuck you over in a situation like that, it was awful. I had got Toño to promise that after the operation he would stay with me while I slept, and that a car would be there at all times, ready for anything.

154

Well, the nurse came. "Take off your clothes," she said. "We've got to clean you up." So I took off my socks, my shoes, my pants, my shirt, and there I was. "Take off your shorts. We've got to shave you." "Won't the doctor be doing that?" I asked, taken aback. "No, no," she said. "I do it, and hurry it up." Son of a bitch, I'm screwed! Because if this woman touches me, I'll get an erection, and she's going to think I'm a crude, dirty-minded person. How could she know it had been a year since I had touched a woman, since a woman had laid a hand on me; and on top of everything she was a gorgeous brunette. Just looking at her is a hard-on, I thought; what humiliation. But what could I do? I took off my shorts, and she was serious as she could be, all busy about her utensils, the boxes of instruments, trays, with all sorts of colored jars, Merthiolate, alcohol, iodine, who knows what all, scissors, gauze, cotton. I was totally naked on the cot with my hands behind my head. I'll shut my eyes, I thought. But right away I thought better of it—if I shut my eyes this woman's going to think I'm imagining something off-color. But maybe it was better to close them, since that way I wouldn't be able to see her, and the risk of an erection would be less. I just couldn't decide.

The woman came up, took a shaving blade, and started in, *ra, ra, ra, ra, ra.* She took hold of my testicles and lifted them up, touching me underneath; then she took my cock and moved it to the side. Good God! I felt a hard-on coming. What I did then was to concentrate my mind on the mud in the mountains, remembering what it was like to march through the mud and to keep falling down, or to go for firewood, or be exhausted and have to climb a steep hill. I imagined my first step, then the next step and the next and the next, slogging through the mud. But the woman was holding my cock with her fingers, her delicate, feminine hand, and moving my cock, then slipping her hand underneath, under my testicles with a damp wad of cotton. She started swabbing Merthiolate all over me. It felt icy, delicious, and I couldn't stand it anymore; I couldn't stand it. I gave up counting and let myself feel everything she was doing. I felt her hands and imagined her hands with their polished fingernails, and I felt her skin on my flesh, on my cock, kneading it, scrubbing it, moving it back and forth. Then my mind flew back to the mountains, and I took hold of my head and pulled my hair; I shut my eyes tight, then opened them. It was asking the impossible. There it was, rising up, up—and I could see she was finished washing me. She threw away the cotton, but now she was starting to pull on my cock. Finally I had to say to myself, Hey, I'm a fool, I'm getting a hard-on, and what can I do about it? If I can't stand it anymore, if I'm just a normal, red-blooded Christian, then I'll have a hard-on, and I mean hard, hard, *hard*. But how humiliating: there was nowhere to turn there on that cot, naked and totally erect, nervous and embarrassed. The woman started laughing. "Don't worry, young man," she said, "we're quite used to this sort of thing." No shit you are, I thought, this son-of-a-bitch woman has excited me on purpose. Because I could feel she was washing me and everything, but I suspected there was something else going on. She was caressing me when she was soaping me up, and you can't imagine what it's like when they rub soap and water on your cock when you haven't made love for a long time, when a woman comes with her pretty hands, with her pretty nails, her lovely, gentle hands, and starts stroking your cock and your genitals and all around the pubic area—it's enough to kill you.

Pretty soon Toño Jarquín showed up; he came into the room laughing like a hyena. "Ha, ha, ha, you got a hard-on, Skinny, you son of a bitch, right?" "Right, brother," I said, "I've fucked up . . . it's embarrassing. What did the compañera tell you?" "Never mind, brother, forget that shit," he said. "You've just lost me fifty pesos." "What?" I said. "What is this shit?" "That's right. I bet with the nurse that you wouldn't get a hard-on, and she said she was sure she could make you have one." Can you believe it? That son-of-a-bitch Toño Jarquín had bet I wouldn't get a hard-on. And naturally the woman won—she excited me to win her bet. I was right to think she was touching me a bit more than necessary.

They put the operating gown on me, and with real dread I left my pistol and grenade under the pillow at the head of my bed. They took me to the operating room. I'd never been operated on before for anything. They poked a needle into me and told me to start counting: one, two . . . I got to three and *ping!* I was out. When I woke up again I was back in my room, covered up, in my hospital gown, half out of it and talking nonsense. I sat up a little in bed and saw a huge pile of gauze. Okay, kid, this is it. Good God in heaven, don't let that mother-fucking son-of-a-bitch Guard burst in here or we're all dead. They'll never take me alive. But if they come when I'm sleeping, they'll murder me. My incision hurt so much I couldn't get up. I asked Toño, "How's it going? Is everything okay?" "All okay, don't worry," he said. "There's no problem, brother, it's all under control." "But watch out," I said. "Anything goes wrong in this place and we're in deep shit, and I mean deep." "No, no, don't worry, there's nothing happening. You know what, Skinny," he added, "I think I'll go over to Estelí—I'll go see Luisa. We've had a fight," he told me. "But you'll be back in time to sleep here, won't you?" "Sure, I'll be back, don't worry."

And Toño took off, but he didn't make up with Luisa at all. Instead that idiot got mad and started sloshing down cheap rum in Estelí, and they had another fight. He started back to Somoto, but he was so drunk he didn't want to keep driving and pulled off along the highway to sleep. Sure enough, he forgot to look where he was stopping, which was right outside of Condega. Naturally the Guard noticed the car and went to check it out. After banging and banging on the windshield they woke him up and asked him what the hell he was doing there; they started searching the car and found a pistol he had with the serial numbers filed off, plus a whole shitload of revolutionary literature—and they carted him straight off to jail.

And I didn't know about any of this until the next day when a compañera came with two compañeros, about six in the evening. "Get dressed, hurry," they said. "We're getting out of here." "What's wrong?" I asked. "They captured Toño Jarquín last night. We don't know what he might have said because he was drunk as a skunk."

What next? I thought. I put on my shirt; they helped me get on my pants and put my shoes on for me, since I couldn't bend over. "And what cover are we going to use to get out of here?" I asked. They didn't have one. "Okay," I said, "this will be our cover: once we get into the corridor I'm going to hang on to the two of you like this, on your shoulders, like I was drunk. And you're going to drag me along holding me by the waist, like I was falling down drunk. I'll be mumbling like a drunk."

Which is what we did. They swung me to the side of the bed; I sat on the edge, then took hold of them, hanging around the neck of one guy with my other arm around the other guy's waist. And we started walking. They half-dragged, half-carried me, and that was how we got out of the hospital.

They packed me into a Willys jeep, and we started for Ocotal. They took me to a house in Ocotal, then at night, as soon as it got dark, they whisked me out of town, because the repression in Ocotal was intense. That was the start of a hideous torture. They took me to a little farm in the brush, right? A terrible road, with the jeep lurching around, a bumpy road, full of stones, awful—the car, no matter how slow you went, every pebble hit right to the quick, in the incision, sweetheart; every tiny pebble registered as pain in that wound. I would have had to fly through the air to avoid that pain. Even on a smooth road and in a good car it would have been hell. You can imagine what it was like in a Willys jeep with no shock absorbers, that piece-of-shit relic of a Willys jeep that was driven by another relic, an old guy named Guillermo Cáceres Vaungh who I now remember had been nicknamed "Fitipaldi" by that joker Pelota. He was Pelota's driver, and since the jeep could go up to 35 but the old guy never drove much over 20, Pelota dubbed him Fitipaldi, after the race car driver.

So there I was, in Fitipaldi's jeep, with Fitipaldi at the wheel, and really, that trip was long. I felt every stone right in the incision. It was as if it first hit the incision, then ricocheted back and hit it again. "My God!" I said. "All we need now is to run into a roadblock, and I won't even be able to get out of the jeep!" If we got stopped and a Guardsman ordered me out, I planned to pull my gun and shoot, and I also had the grenade all set to throw. That was my consolation. I could hurl that grenade and take some Guardsmen with me. I wasn't going down alone. Those bastards would not get my life for nothing.

It took us a good two hours to get there, maybe three. We got in late at night, to a place in Macuelizo not far from the town, a little farm that belonged to a compañero named Teofilo Cáceres; his nickname was Fidel because he looked like Fidel Castro—tall, with a powerful build and a huge nose. And there my nightmare began. I still had not had a bowel movement, and it was already fourteen hours since the operation. There at Fidel's little farm I had to go, but there were no toilets, no outhouses, no latrines; to obey the call of nature the campesinos of the house had to walk about 150 yards over to a ditch. It was all I could do to walk a few steps, so that's how it was the first time. Two compañeros had to hold me up between them; they pulled down my pants, and hanging onto their shoulders I had to shit half-standing up. It was the most awkward and embarrassing thing. I felt like an animal; you could not feel human under those conditions.

Another thing was the daily dressing of the incision and my shots. Pelota and another campesino named Manuel Mairena, who was from the area, and his mom, a campesina, took care of me; every day they changed the dressings and gave me shots of antibiotics to keep the incision from getting infected. And on top of the pain of the incision and feeling so incredibly fragile, my ass couldn't handle all those shots, because they shot me up to the limit with antibiotics—they really let me have it.

After about eight days, when it was already past the time to take out the stitches, we were finally able to return to Ocotal, since the worst of the repression seemed to be over. They took me to a safe house to remove the stitches. Saul, the other doctor who had operated on me with Toño, had to cut into me about an inch with a sterile shaving blade to get them out. The little bit of thread on the surface had rotted away from so much swabbing with cotton and alcohol around the scar, and it was a newfangled sort of stitch job they had done on me, with the stitches under the skin. That was a bonus—a pain I hadn't counted on.

We became very attached to the people in the house where they took me. Those two houses, I should say, since there were two families living across the street from each other. It was a little complex, a "safe complex." Because the two families worked together, and there were underground people in both houses, or maybe just in one. But the two families saw each other all the time. Three old ladies lived in one house, and they could not have been nicer. The youngest was about sixty, and all three were couriers for the Frente. They were never arrested because never in a million years could the Guard have guessed that those little old ladies could be couriers for the Frente.

They had that traditional aura of conspiracy about them that people from the north country have, going back to the time of Sandino. They always talked to you in a whisper or a low voice, and that's how they would tell you all the stories about Sandino's war. No shit, it was as if they were talking about the last contact they had made just the night before; for them what we were doing was a continuation. It was like old times when they conspired with their husbands and brothers on their farms. Now it was continuing with us in the city. Those old ladies loved us like sons, like revolutionaries; it was

160

a very spiritual affection, very open. They were always coming into our room to leave us something. One of them brought hog plums, another came with mangoes, another with corn swirls, and whenever they came it cheered us up. Also, we kidded them and played practical jokes, silly things. They adored us. We nicknamed them the Three Wise Men because whenever they came they brought gifts.

The other family was made up of the wife, the husband, who was an old revolutionary, an old Sandinista from the early days, and two or three daughters. He bet on cockfights. We also kidded the young girls who were in the house. The oldest had a crush on Leonel Espinoza (Marino), so Pelota called her "Marina." They were all very nice people. A girl was supposed to come there from the Pacific coast to make contact with Pelota. I didn't know who; I suspected it was Luisa, Toño's Luisa, but I didn't get to see her. I wanted to but couldn't; I wanted to call out to her, "Luisa, Luisa, Luisa, we're here!" She was so good-natured and such a good friend, we would really have enjoyed seeing each other, but it didn't work out. After that I spent several days in another house, the home of a woman teacher, a compañera. She also took care of my incision. A very heroic woman; I have fond memories of her—Rosario Antúñez. She was captured several times and tortured by the Guard. They murdered her fifteen-year-old daughter in Nueva Guinea. She's still alive and works with the Frente in Ocotal.

Lessons from the Mountain

While I was still at the teacher's house, about twenty or thirty days after my operation, the National Leadership decided to set up two big guerrilla schools; the idea was to beef up our military training and strengthen the various sectors of the work with both more and better men, including those in the mountains. So one of these schools was set up in Macuelizo, just beyond the little farm where they took me after the operation. It was called Julio Buitrago and had thirty students. This was in June 1975. They notified me that I was now part of the Regional, and that we were going to operate a school for guys who would also be going into the mountains. I was to be assigned to the school, to help with the training and to teach the basics of the guerrilla struggle, in light of my own experience and the training I had received.

They named me military director of the school; Manuel Morales and Bayardo Arce were first and second in command, and Augusto Salinas Pinell was director of logistics, since he'd been working in that zone as underground organizer of the compañeros in the sector. That school was a tremendous experience for me, because I began to see my own experience reflected on a mass level, a collective level, in thirty compañeros.

Jorge Matus was there, who later died in the war; Marcelino Guido, who is now a captain and second in command in the Domestic Order Unit of the Second Military Region of the Ministry of the Interior; and other compañeros whose names I've forgotten, but whose faces I can still see. Some were killed; others survived; all sorts of people were there—students, workers, campesinos.

As the first day of the school progressed and I noted the limitations of the compañeros, I realized that what I had gone through in the mountains was not a unique experience—all the compañeros went through the same thing. Of course, the conditions in the school were somewhat different; it wasn't jungle, but pine forest, brakes of pine trees, which had already been fairly devastated by the North American lumber companies. The vegetation was not thick and overgrown, but very low and sparse. It was almost like holding classes in a park or an open field. It was so bare of trees that we had to camouflage our rain covers and camp utensils, so they couldn't be seen from the air.

There was a hill called "El Copetudo," which was quite deep in, and on top of that hill we made our camp. It was there that I started seeing the compañeros fall down, get frustrated, then push on ahead. I saw their problems and weaknesses emerge and start to be corrected. I saw the uneven development of the men, the different levels of ability. You can bet I busted my ass to teach them the very best I knew, and in that sense René Tejada was always present in me. He had died, but I was imparting Tello's spirit to the school. The course ended July 14, 1975. It began around June 14.

About ten days into the training, bits of news started coming in about strange people in the area. It seems officials of the Guard's military intelligence had detected traffic, comings and goings in the area at night, signs and more signs of our presence. The Guard didn't come for a long time, and we were able to finish our course. But one day we got word that the Guard had finally arrived. And there we were with thirty boys who had never fired a shot in their lives and had no experience

163

marching. Just marching up to the camp had made their feet a swollen mess, and that was only eight hours. A march of eight hours, no more. But for them it was a big deal; they felt like hot-shot guerrillas when they managed that. So with guys who had never seen battle, who weren't used to marching or lugging packs, with hardly any weapons, just hunting rifles, with only two or three heavy weapons in the whole camp, a meager supply of ammunition, on a treeless, well-populated terrain—one thing was clear, if the Guard came, we were screwed.

We had set up the school there because we didn't have anyplace better to do it. And now the Guard was coming! It was decided that Manuel and Bayardo should go down to the city. We couldn't take on the Guard, not with just one contingent, and we had to get those guys back to the city. So later on they could be sent to the mountains. Pelota and Bayardo were supposed to arrange some way to get them out of there fast, in order to avoid a confrontation. We needed cars sent up to us, and houses where they could stay in the city, or be leap-frogged into other provinces; they were supposed to check out the highways, to see what roadblocks had been set up in town, what kind of surveillance was in force, so the operation could be carried out.

But dammit, the only thing we managed to do was get Bayardo and Manuel out. After they left, nobody else could get through. The Guard had encircled us. I was military head of the school, and Augusto Salinas Pinell was responsible overall, and now school was over. It ended the day the Guard came in.

We started down. When we had gone some distance we stopped near the shack of a collaborator to wait for our contact from the city to take people back, first through the brush, then along the highway.

This was where I put Tello's lessons to use. Tello lost his life because he was hiding about 500 yards from a collaborator's house; the Guard came, arrested the collaborator, and the

164

collaborator led the Guard right to him. So I posted a sentry to watch the collaborator's house. If the Guard arrived, we'd retreat before the collaborator had a chance to turn us in. Even if he didn't turn us in, we had to take security measures.

In a little while the guy on watch informed us that about forty or fifty Guardsmen were in the collaborator's shack and had taken him prisoner. Immediately I gave the order for retreat, but by that time the whole area was crawling with patrols. The zone was completely surrounded; they were coming in after us. The Guard had helicopters, planes . . . the usual shitload of equipment. They had intelligence on the school, and they were going to bust it up. I decided to send Heriberto Rodríguez, a compañero who was a veteran of Raiti and Bocay, to head up the retreat into a different sector where we had another collaborator, where Augusto Salinas Pinell had just gone. He had left me in camp while he went to try to make contact with other collaborators who could help get us out of there. While the guys prepared to retreat, I stayed behind with some other compañeros; we had decided to hold off the Guard with an ambush, because if the Guard got to where we were, in a ravine, a dry stream bed, like a little canyon, we could gain time with an ambush.

But we managed to retreat with no problems; and once we got to another spot I went looking for contacts to help in getting out, since it was obvious no help was coming from the city. There we were—a whole bunch of armed men, and our only way out was to fight our way out. We would have to bust our balls against the Guard in an unequal battle. The truth is, we didn't know what to do; we were in a tight spot. We had to figure out how to make it to the city; we needed cars, even if just to go a short way; we needed houses in the city to put up all those guys.

I started out with Manuel Mairena, in civilian clothes, carrying just a pistol. We were going to Fidel's to try to make contact, where I'd been before, after my operation. I left instructions for Heriberto Rodríguez to take the compañeros

165

and head for another spot where we would link up with them later. We marched the whole day. When we were getting near Fidel's, we started marching in a dry stream bed with a sandy bottom. At about four in the afternoon we emerged from the stream bed. I said to Manuel, "You go on ahead and try to make contact, since you're from this area. I'll be right behind you. If anything goes wrong, we'll hightail it out back the way we came." I'm not sure how it came about, but we were marching along when all of a sudden we heard a voice: "There goes one of those sons of bitches!" "Brother," Manuel whispered, "let's get out of here. We've been spotted." We backed off, firing two shots, and started running like hell.

The Guard was in the shack now, lying in wait for us. Those sons of bitches, they had some guys standing around outside dressed like campesinos but who were Guardsmen; there was also a traitor, a spy from the area who knew Manuel Mairena, who knew he was in the underground with us. They let loose a hail of bullets in our direction, and we just had pistols, and one extra magazine. We were running as fast as we could in tactical zigzags through the stream bed until we came to a spot where we saw we could come out. We did, but other groups of Guardsmen had come running up from the other side—the hunt was on.

There was no brush, hardly any trees, just low plants and shrubs, little bushes, some charralitos. The Guard split up into groups of five, eight, or ten men, with machine guns and Garands and more rifles, with all their modern weaponry, and for sure they had grenades. We came out of the bushes, they saw us, and we shot off running again. It was one big rabbit hunt. As if you had turned loose a couple of rabbits and started tracking them down. We were scared shitless, but I was also in a rage. It wasn't so much that I minded dying, but I was furious that they might wipe us out like that.

Finally they had us cornered, but they didn't know it. I whispered to Manuel, "Cock your gun with the safety off, but don't shoot unless I do." The whole sector was crawling with

Guardsmen. We were crouching down between four little trees, those low ones, tiny trees, crouching on our haunches, because on our haunches at least we'd have a chance to jump up. In that precarious position we watched the Guardsmen, who were right on top of us but didn't see us. We decided that each of us should pick a Guardsman out of the group, get the drop on him down the barrel of our gun and follow his movements from the underbrush. If they spotted us, we would open fire from the bushes and run for our lives—I mean if they hadn't already pumped us full of bullets.

"Those fuckers are in here!" they were saying. "Where are those sons of bitches? They can't have gone far." They referred in their talk to other patrols in the area, in the stream bed or alongside of it. "They're in here," they said. "They've got to be right under our noses! Let's go straight ahead." And they came up and passed right in front of us, right near the bushes where we were hiding.

By that time it was getting to be six o'clock; dusk was settling in; it was almost dark. My God, did I want it to get dark! And finally it did. But they didn't go; they knew we were there, but they didn't know where. About seven or eight I whispered to Manuel, "Let's make a move. But listen, first put your hand on the ground and very quietly in slow motion push back the leaves until you've got bare dirt. Get rid of all the little twigs. Then, when you've got rid of the little leaves and twigs, take a step. Then with your other hand, a bit farther on, do the same thing, and take another step. That way you'll be sure not to make any noise—but watch out for the twigs, because in this quiet a cruuuunch could kill us. They'll start shooting indiscriminately in the dark and with machine guns. It'll be all over."

That was the plan. We had just started clearing away the twigs and the leaves when we heard a cough. I whispered to Manuel, "Let's hang on a bit longer. The later it gets the more likely they will go, and even if they don't go, they'll get so tired, they'll fall asleep."

We were still crouching on our haunches; our legs were numb; we shifted our weight from one leg to the other; then both legs were asleep, then just one—it was awful, can you imagine? We didn't dare move and were almost embracing.

At 3:00 A.M. we made our move, but we didn't go by way of the stream bed—we knew we'd be ambushed there—but through the brush, and we made it. We finally came out near the city. I arrived in a town under siege, but managed to get to the house of a guy who bet on cockfights. When I came in about 5:00 A.M. he jumped in surprise. "Child!" he said. "What are you doing out in the street?" "Looking for help, that's all," I answered. "Because, listen, we're stuck up there in the hills. The Guard has got us surrounded. The compañeros are waiting for us to come and get them out." "Ah, my boy, you'd better get going. Everybody in Ocotal's in jail," he said. "They've captured all the collaborators."

The situation in Ocotal was really bad; the Guard had occupied the city and made mass arrests. The old compañero who drove that car—whom we affectionately called Fitipaldi—they had hung him by his toes and beat the shit out of him in the barracks. All our structures, our safe houses, the whole network of collaborators had been destroyed, the people terrorized. That stunned me. It made me feel like shit, because these poor people were just getting going and now it was all ruined. But we also knew we had to forge ahead.

We went to another house and managed to make contact with Bayardo and Pelota. "Our hands are tied," they told me. "We're screwed, totally fucked. The Regional here has hit rock bottom; we can't make a move. Get one person out of this town and you've accomplished something major, really major! You go back up there, and you, Omar, you and Salinas take charge of those guys," they said. "Find a way to get them out, by the highway or whatever—just get them out. Here's some money and some cans of food." The guys up there were dying of hunger.

We started out again at night, skirting the town, scared of

running into the patrols that were combing the area, and lugging big sacks full of canned food. No car. All we need now is not to be able to find them, I thought, since there was a possibility the Guard might have arrested our remaining collaborators and we wouldn't be able to reestablish contact with the compañeros. We managed to reach Don Bonifacio Montoya's little shack; he was one of the first guides for the FSLN; he told us he'd been a guide for Carlos Fonseca. He was a wonderful old man—tall, fine-boned, light-skinned, with blue eyes, sort of brownish-blond hair, very good-looking. He was eighty-two and as pure as a child. He lived in a miserable little shack with his old wife, whose name I've forgotten. She was light-skinned, too, with blue eyes; they were campesinos from the north country, Sandinistas from Sandino's day, both of them.

We met them as they were coming from the stream, hauling water in a pail. We ran to them. "Don Bacho, Don Bacho!" "Boys! Over there. Get in the house!" he said. He could barely hear us calling out to him. "Careful they don't see you outside. The Guard is everywhere." "Have you seen the boys?" I asked him. "Of course. I've got them up on a hill," he said. It was a bare peak that only goats could climb, billygoats. He gave us black coffee. "The Guard hasn't been to your house?" we asked. "No," the old woman said, "and if they come, even if I've only got hot water I'll throw it in their faces."

That little old man, Don Bacho, was a page out of history. Salinas Pinell told me that the first time he came to Don Bacho's on behalf of the Frente the old guy was overjoyed to see him. "You see," he said, "you see, I knew you would come again! The fact is I have some things of yours buried here, that you left a long time ago." "But what?" Augusto asked him. "It's something the gringos had, that's what, something you left the last time you were through here." And he started digging under a tree trunk and brought up a little military pouch that dated back to the Yankee occupation. It fell apart when you took it in your hand. Inside was a pile of Enfield bullets, can you believe it? The old man had kept them, can you imagine that? —the old man had kept them, and every day he had brought them out to air in the sun. Because he knew that someday the Sandinistas would come again.

"If you help me along, I'll take you to where I've got the boys," said Don Bacho. And we took hold of him—he was so old he could barely walk. We started climbing, almost carrying him between Mairena and myself. We found only some of our compañeros, and they were nearly dying of hunger. On one of the marches, since there were so many people and with only Heriberto Rodríguez to head the column, the line had broken along the way. And with only one guide—or no guide, I'm not sure—some of the boys fell behind and got separated. Because if you lose sight of the compañero in front of you, and you don't know the terrain, you can lose your bearings and wander off. From then on you're on your own to find your way out.

They killed three or four compañeros like that; the others managed to reach the highway. Of the ones who managed to get to the highway, they captured one or two in Estelí. One was an extraordinary boy, one of the best students in the school. Salinas, Mairena, and I were responsible for getting the rest down.

Once we reached the hill, we parceled out the food to the compañeros. The canned stuff plus some mangoes we had picked at Don Bacho's; for eight days Don Bacho had had nothing to eat but mangoes. The compañeros were at their posts all along the steep cliffs, fifteen or eighteen compañeros in all. As you climbed, you found them staked out one after another with their shotguns, their .22's, their Enfields, or whatever else—posted on the hill, on the steep pass. To have gotten them out of there the Guard would have needed planes. And it was no joke getting them down. We were inside the Guard's encirclement; we could move inside that circle. The problem was to break out of it. The Guard was starting to send out patrols, up and down the area, trying to engage us in combat, and then tighten the circle. Salinas told me that they were able to get to the hill because Don Bacho had led them along a stretch where there weren't any Guardsmen. There were gaps between one patrol and the other, and Don Bacho knew all about how to move very close to one patrol and not be seen by the other.

We finally arrived, and I saw those hopeful, impatient faces, all thinking we had the magic key to getting them out. We ate a little something, then started to mull over the problem. Okay, we said, we have two choices: we either try to break through the ring or we wait for the Guard to find us and all die on that hill. That was the dilemma. But if we decided to leave, which way would we go? The farther out you went, the fewer the trees. There were pastures, completely open areas, corn-fields, a few bushes, with here and there a scraggly stand of little pines. Getting through that area wouldn't be easy. We finally decided to head for the Pan-American Highway, and from there each of us would try to get some civilian clothes from our collaborators along the highway, then catch a group-transport truck and get on out. There was no other way. The mission was to rescue the guys and get them back to the cities. Some of them were destined for the fronts in the mountains; others would be part of the networks in the city; others would go home and continue working aboveground.

So we planned with Don Bacho and his son—since Don Bacho also had his sons involved as collaborators—the best way to get out of there at night. With no flashlight, can you imagine, with all those cliffs. Luckily there was a good moon, which was both an advantage and a disadvantage. An advantage because you could see where you were going, and it helped the guides; it helped Don Bacho to get oriented. But a disadvantage because the Guard might see you. We started down. I put myself in the vanguard and Augusto moved me to the center. I remember that in the afternoon, before we started to march, we changed our aliases. I was called Eugenio, but I took the name Juan José because the enemy knew some of our aliases. It was important to deny the enemy that sort of operational information.

We put our marching rules in force and headed out, no flashlights, each of us with a nylon cord attached in back. I was afraid that we might get separated along the way and they would murder the boys as they did the other guys that had gotten lost. So we tied a little nylon cord to each guy, right on the belt loop in back, so the guy behind could hang on to the little cord and not get lost. We had already practiced night marching in the school. They more or less knew the rules for marching at night. We made them even stricter, because this was a night march with real and immediate possibilities of a confrontation. I proposed that I should cover the retreat if a fight broke out, so that Augusto, who knew the area, could retreat with the guys. That's when we had an argument over who would go in the vanguard and who would cover the retreat. Augusto insisted that he, not I, should go in the vanguard, since in any case he had to cover the retreat because he knew the terrain, and besides we had another guide, Manuel Mairena. So I should go in the body of march.

In the end I think he was trying to keep me from getting killed—he was to die himself—because of the affection we had come to feel for each other in the course of running the school.

Augusto was an extraordinary fellow; he was a teacher in Somoto, a rural schoolteacher who had gone to the Estelí normal school. And his teaching experience had left a deep mark on his personality. He was a calm compañero, very brotherly and sweet. He had leadership ability, but in the style of a teacher to his students. He used to teach the campesinos how to read, using the underside of platanillo leaves; you could scratch letters onto the back of those leaves. He never lost his enthusiasm for teaching. I always put him in charge of teaching the campesinos to read wherever we were, because I knew

172

he was most fulfilled as a teacher. That was Mauricio, incapable of hurting you, always selfless in everything and constantly teaching one thing or another. Very brave. He didn't smoke and had a terrible sweet tooth. Sometimes he was inspired to write; he wrote little poems that he showed me. He was always talking about his little girl—he had a daughter; he didn't say much about his wife; mainly he spoke of his daughter. I even remember what size pants he wore—size 32.

We started down the cliffs in the dark, not carrying much weight, but very weak physically. For ten or fifteen days we had eaten nothing but brown sugar bars, some canned food, and mangoes. There was no water on that hill. You had to bring it in at night; a half-cup a day and a slice of mango or something like that was the daily ration. So the compañeros were weak; we were all weak, but I was more used to it than the others who had just come from the city to the school. And the guys started falling, tumbling down the steep pass. It was a very tense descent, because if you slipped you could kill yourself, and if the Guard was anywhere near they might hear us; you might even set off an avalanche or a rock slide.

Finally we managed to get down from the hill and start marching through a treeless area. I could hardly believe we had marched for three hours tied together like that. The guys rose to the occasion there; we couldn't fault our progress; the compañeros had grown tremendously. Of course, at the same time our lives were at stake. Augusto said that the idea was to get out of there and live to fight another day under better conditions. So on and on we trudged, through one place after another, marching all night. Don Bacho went with us up to a certain point, then we continued on with his son Pastor. Never have I seen men who were that hungry march that fast at night, or, as I was saying, who had grown so much. I remember that about twice we crossed a dirt road that went from Ocotal to Macuelizo; we went in a spearhead formation that we had recently practiced, with our weapons ready to fire. You see, we had morale; our morale was tremendous, in spite

173

of the difficult situation. We never let up on the process of political education. It was a constant, double-barreled thing, and you better believe it made a difference.

At five in the morning, exhausted, we came at last to a hill with the peculiar name of "La Señorita," a stony hill but covered with a dense vegetation. A tiny peak, some 200 yards from the Pan-American Highway near the town of Totogalpa, to the south of Ocotal, toward Estelí.

Another dilemma: whether or not to push the guys onto the highway in twos to try to hitchhike or catch a bus or just start walking. We had gotten through the worst of it; we were outside the encirclement. How awful it would be, we thought, to push those boys and ourselves, too, onto the highway and end up getting killed. With the experience we had accumulated in aboveground work and in that incredibly rich year in the mountains in my case, it was my feeling that to toss them overboard like that was too big a risk. Boys so newly trained would end up getting killed. We went over and over it and finally decided that they should hang on there a little longer while Manuel Mairena and I slipped back into Ocotal to try to get hold of a car to take them to Estelí. Once they were in Estelí, each of them could find his own way down to Managua.

Our collaborators in Totogalpa were bringing the boys a little food, mangoes and stuff like that, one hen for fifteen men, a hen per day, ten tortillas for fifteen men for a whole day. But they couldn't keep running up to that hill—the repression throughout the zone was too great.

We left them on "La Señorita" and once again slipped into Ocotal at dawn. I remembered a man I'd met before; he wasn't a compañero yet, but I went to him, since there was nowhere else to turn. He was a carpenter with a tiny shop, and Manuel Mairena and I hid under a table; he piled up some boxes at the end of the table so nobody could see us; customers came and went, but nobody knew we were there. We didn't dare fart, we couldn't do anything, least of all smoke. And on top of everything I wasn't sure that the carpenter wasn't going to turn us in, he was so scared. I sent him out to make a contact for us; the guy, to get rid of us, went and found Señora Antúnez, the teacher, who got busy and came up with something.

The trouble was that our networks were so fragile that all the houses had been evacuated; the collaborators were all being arrested. There was only one house left that we hadn't used before. Mónica Baltodano had arranged for it; she was already in the Regional at that time. The collaborator was a very nervous guy, but there was nothing to be done. We had to make the risky decision for all of us to stay in the only place we had, which was his house. Can you imagine the guy's fright when in the middle of the night Bayardo Arce, Manuel Morales, Mónica Baltodano, Manuel Mairena, and I—the entire Northern Regional—turned up at his door? He wanted to chuck us out on the spot, but we had no intention of leaving.

I don't remember exactly, but I guess it was proposed that Bayardo go to Estelí. I don't know if the idea was to try to get hold of a car, or because it was necessary to clear out Ocotal, which had become one gigantic rat trap. Anyway, Bayardo took off with a guy in a truck—God knows how he got hold of a truck; he talked the owner into it, I guess—and Bayardo took off for Estelí. This was the plan: if they were stopped at the roadblock on the bridge the driver was going to crash through the Guardsmen in the truck, and they would shoot their way out. But the guy—who knows why, maybe he lost his nerve, I don't know—when they ordered them to halt and get out of the truck, obeyed. So Bayardo had to get out, and they started searching him. When they found his pistol, Bayardo grabbed the Guardsman's Garand, leaving the Guardsmen with the pistol and Bayardo with the rifle. The other guy opened fire on the Guard, jumped off the bridge, and Bayardo took off running toward Ocotal in a hail of bullets. As soon as he had a chance he dove off the highway into the brush.

The Guard started looking for him; they rounded up all the

jeeps they had—one or two, I'm not sure, but all they had—
and surrounded the place where Bayardo went in. They
started to hunt for him, but they were such cowards, seeing
how Bayardo had acted, that they moved very cautiously, reminding each other, "Remember, he's got a Garand, that
fucker has a Garand." It terrified them to go into the brush
with Bayardo in there. The first guy who went in came right
back out. Bayardo sat tight, he hung on, and at dawn we heard
a knock at the door, *bam, bam, bam, bam.* It's the Guard! we
thought, since patrols of the Guard had just gone by in jeeps
on the street and on foot along the sidewalk, banging on doors
and harassing. So when a knock came three or four minutes
after the last patrol had passed, we were on the alert. We
sprang to our positions, but it was Bayardo who entered. I can
still see the horrified face of the poor man who owned the
house, shitting green at the sight of Bayardo's swollen face.
He was all beaten up, his whole face and mouth, his lips were
all swollen, from the fall he took in that run-in with the Guard.

Sanctuary

Manuel Mairena and I went back to "La Señorita," with money for the compañeros to buy food. Now we could plan how to get them out of there. They had managed, they told us, through a collaborator in Totogalpa to send word to Salinas Pinell to get us a car, and he had succeeded. He'd been a student there and had some contacts, and he turned up with a truck. He made about three trips down and back, leaving some of the guys on the highway in civilian clothes. I remember that two compañeros, two of our best people, were caught right off the bat. It seems they were captured on a bus in Estelí. The authorities saw their military boots, hauled them off the bus, and murdered them. One of them was a strong, dark-skinned fellow, a high school student whose name I don't remember.

Augusto was to set things up for us to stay in Estelí. Mairena and I were the last to leave the hill, in the truck of a collaborator from Palacagüinca. They dropped us at Tobías Gadea's house in Estelí—but can you imagine our surprise when we ran smack into a huge party? I was dressed like a cowboy, in leather boots and blue jeans, carrying a bag and lariat, that leather cord they use to tie up cattle, plus my gre-

177

nade and my pistol. Tobías was shocked to see us because the radios were all full of news about the battles of Ocotal, which in fact never happened. But since they had brought out helicopters and planes and everything, plus the huge mobilization of the Guard and the beep-beep of their communiqués with the names of the dead from these battles—who were none other than the compañeros they had murdered—the guy was surprised. But he took it like a man. "You can't stay here," he said, "but we'll find somebody, a contact, who can take you in."

He put us in the backyard of the house. We dove over a hedge and headed for a little ravine at the rear of the yard, a ditch that ran around the far edge of the yard and was filled with low brush. Mairena and I crouched down in the middle of the ditch, where it was darkest and there were bushes. After every dance set the party guests wandered out to the yard and walked back to the edge of the ditch. And sure enough, about two hours into the dance, the drunks were starting to moan and vomit. Can you imagine my horror when I saw some son of a bitch at the top of the ditch with his cock out all ready to pee on my head! Manuel and I didn't dare make a sound, and we were pelted with at least four arcs of piss—I'm not exaggerating. Plus two blasts of vomit. After the first spray of piss we took the burlap bag we had with us and put it over our heads and managed to survive the remaining blasts.

The atmosphere in Estelí was incredibly tense, but it wasn't like the military occupation that was going on in Ocotal. Our contact came for us in the tiny hours of the morning. No car. So we went on foot from the outskirts of Estelí to Calvario Church; it was Juan Alberto Blandón who came for us, a compañero who later died in the insurrection in '78. It was 1:00 A.M. and the blocks were dragging on. I remember at one point we heard a jeep coming toward us, going in the opposite direction; we leapt for cover. Peeking out a little, we could see it was the Guard. Luckily they didn't see us—you can imagine what a sight we were! Mónica always said that I looked exactly like what I was. "You poor guy," she said, "you've got the face of a guerrilla. You couldn't look more like one if you tried."

We arrived at Rosario Church. All of Estelí was quiet, asleep, in silence. When I entered the church, the silence was intensified by the quietude, the sacredness of the shrine, by any number of things, by the frozen images, by being enclosed, by the motionless curtains, the white of the walls, by the pecos—it was more than a year since I'd set foot in a church. It was like an echo chamber, because the cupolas were soundless, the windowpanes were motionless and chill. And suddenly I was inside—and it seemed that time stood still. Because this was a calm foreign to the tension of Estelí, a calm that had nothing to do with "El Copetudo," nor with our march, nor with "La Señorita," nor with anything—as if time had been suspended there, as if everything was bare, voiceless. You could hear your own breathing, your own presence. A young parish priest received us, whose name, if I'm not mistaken, was Julio López. He was a very much loved priest in Estelí, very revolutionary; he put us in the priest's quarters. Mauricio and Heriberto Rodríguez were already there. Only Bayardo, Pelota, and Mónica were missing, in another house in Estelí.

We were so excited we couldn't sleep. I remember we got cleaned up and the padre opened up some wine; I felt like a savage because his room was so monastically clean—a bed with two mattresses—and his chests of drawers were so nice, and his books, the missal, a little carpet, his closets with his cassocks, all of them clean, the pretty bathroom, so neatly arranged. We felt, there in that room, like strange animals. "Get cleaned up, have some food, here's a little wine," he said. And we started rehashing with Mauricio and Heriberto the whole story of what had happened—had there or had there not been an informer, did they or did they not have information, had we been infiltrated, how did they crack our Regional and massacre so many of our people? And we grieved for the loss of our compañeros.

The padre's room was an extension of the tranquility of the

179

church; the same cleanliness, the same chill. You could feel those cool drafts of air; and it was part of the church, because it, too, had a Christ, the classic Christ with the crown of thorns, the face turned to the side, with several drops of red blood on the forehead, dripping down—that image that always fills you with a sense of peace.

The churches with all their saints have an aura of peace, and the padre's room had that aura, too, a sort of peace of the centuries, as if the churches had pooled that vast absence of sound, the extinction of millions of voices, of millions of sleeping souls, resting, dead, quiet. A peace of extinguished spirits, of sleeping passion. There in the padre's room I absorbed that absence of sound, of voices—what a great contrast with the situation I had just come from, with everything that had happened, being hunted with Manuel Mairena by the Guard, that hellish night march, the flight of the boys from the school, the military occupation of Ocotal.

I don't know why, but on entering the church and the padre's room, the little church of Calvario in Estelí, the roar of what we had lived through on "El Copetudo" and "La Señorita" was suddenly hushed. Or was it only the peace of underground protection that I felt, concentrated there in the padre's room? It was as if you didn't want to speak out loud; you didn't want to violate that silence, the silence of the centuries, of everything that had happened before you; you didn't want to disturb the emptiness with the absurdity of your stubborn solitude, your conscious, necessary solitude. And all this stirs you, quite apart from whether or not you believe in God; it's something so personal, so intimate, like the padre's slippers at the edge of the carpet, furry slippers that said nothing but only figured as mute witnesses to the weight of a man who lived in that world.

We made contact with Bayardo in the padre's house. He came to see us with Pelota. It was decided that we couldn't all stay there, besides which the work had to continue; there wasn't a moment to lose. Pelota and Bayardo in coordination with Pedro Aráuz, who was a member of the National Directorate, decided that I should go to the countryside to kick off the work there, to carry on the war, purely and simply to begin—with no point of departure, not knowing where in the country or if I'd find anything there at all.

Anyway, it turned out that a boy named Andrés Aguilera was in hot water; he was originally from Somoto and a teacher at an institute in Condega; his involvement had become known, and they decided to send him underground. They had found him a place to stay, in the little house of a man named Zavala, who was a sort of Christian; they asked him if he could put somebody up for a couple of days, and the man agreed out of a sense of charity. He lived by the road that goes from Condega to Yalí, in a little settlement of five or six houses called San Diego, near the cattle ranch of René Molino, one of Somoza's henchmen. So they took me to that guy's house, by myself—Salinas Pinell was staying in Estelí, and Manuel too. They sent me on alone to Aguilera in San Diego. The owner of the house was horrified to see another person, but Aguilera was delighted. He had a pistol, a .38 I think, with the magazine and an extra. I always carried the .45 I'd had for several years, and an extra magazine.

The following day the owner of the house asked us when we were leaving. We weren't in the house proper, but about 30 yards away in another little shack that was empty. The next day when I saw him he asked me again when we intended to leave; I answered that we hadn't come there just to turn around and go, but to stay and work with him for the revolutionary struggle and to make the war and overthrow the dictatorship of Somoza.

His eyes widened. "No, no, no," he said, "they told me the Guard was after a boy, and being a Christian I took you both in. But what you're talking about now is a commitment. And I've got a wife, kids, my job. I can't go getting mixed up in these things, because these things lead nowhere but . . . and I advise you to get out of it yourselves, because they're going to come down on you. Look what happened over in Ocotal, by Macuelizo." He had no idea that was where we had just been. But for that man, just having taken in the compañero Aguilera was a tremendous step. Because the whole region was being terrorized.

Bayardo sent us a courier, a little girl related to that guy who worked with FER in Condega; she took a message back in which I told Bayardo that the house wasn't a safe house, that the owner didn't go beyond his Christian sentiments and was pressuring us to get out. Bayardo shot back a reply. "Look," he said, "don't go bringing me problems, bring me solutions, but in any case what you've got to do is build on what you've got and open up a route to link up with Henry Ruiz in the mountains, because some other compañeros are working to link up with you from the other side." A route of more than 180 miles. The guy is fucking crazy, I thought. He doesn't realize what he's saying to me.

Even though what Bayardo was saying seemed absurd, I was absolutely clear and convinced that it had to be done to continue the war, which was the whole reason I was underground, and why it was necessary to come up with even the impossible in order to get rid of Somoza and liberate Nicaragua.

So I went to work on that man; I told him I wanted to talk to him, that we were just going to study, and when we had finished a little pamphlet, then we would go. "No, compa," he said, "I already know more or less what's in the pamphlet, so don't worry, I'm with you, I understand, I agree with everything—you want justice," he said. "But please, go, because this is a serious commitment; they've come down on so many people already." Then he said, "My wife's sick; the poor woman is going to be sick again." Which meant she was going to have a baby.

But we didn't go. "Well, compa," I said to him, "let's do this: if you want us to go, find us a house to go to." "What?" he said. "Come up with a house," I repeated, "because where are we going to go? Who will give us food?" "The trouble is," he said, "everybody around here is a Somocista, and they all drink like fish; it's nothing but cheap booze and informers around here, so what's the point of bringing the Guard down on your head, and on mine? It's better if you go." "No, compa," I insisted. "Let's talk a bit, let's see who these fellows are." And I started drawing out of him the names of the people who lived in the area. "And what kind of a guy is this one?" "He's a good man but he drinks." "Well, it's no sin to have a few drinks," I said. "Just because a guy drinks doesn't mean he's no good. Go talk to that guy, then." "Well, okay, we'll go feel him out."

One day he came in to tell me, "I'm here to inform you that you are going to be out of here today, this afternoon." "What?" I answered, surprised, and putting on a fierce look. Then, in an authoritative tone, to try to get him to accept my authority: "But didn't I tell you to go talk to that guy? And now you're saying we have to be out by this afternoon! Oh, no, I don't go along with that sort of thing. Go talk to him. You can't throw us out in the road, because if they pick us up in front of your house they're going to say we were here and they're going to kill you. Besides, how can you be a Christian and want to kick us out?" I poured it on and managed to placate him, to recharge his batteries.

But it was very upsetting, because we weren't making any progress. We weren't getting anywhere, all holed up in that one house we had in the area. So during all this time, since Aguilera, my compañero, had never had any military training, I started teaching him in that tiny room. We started by loading and unloading the .45. Using a pole for a rifle, I taught him the knee-on-the-ground position and how to crawl on your belly. Vanguard, rearguard. All day long, grilling poor Aguilera on that dirt floor; it was a total dust pit; we were powdery-white with dust.

The owner of the house came back to us there to say, "Look, I couldn't talk to him, because the guy's an informer, and now I'm really telling you to go—you've abused my hospitality for too long as it is." And he got angry at me. So I got even angrier: "Here we are, a couple of human sacks; you're such a damn Christian, why don't you just take these sacks and throw them out on the road, so when you throw them out you can send us to our deaths like a good Christian? Because the minute we set foot on the road we're dead." "Oh, no," he said, "it won't be my fault if you two get killed." "Yes it will, because you're going to take these sacks and throw them out. Unless you don't, and let us stay on here." "Oh, but you see, it's my wife who made me; she's nervous, it's not me. If it were up to me . . . look, if it weren't for my wife and the kids . . ."

Well, that's how it stood. But unfortunately one day Aguilera started fooling around with his gun and it went off, *bang!* the huge blast of a .45. And in those little shacks everybody knows who's got a pistol and who doesn't, especially one of that caliber. So we realized we had to pack up and get out. We decided to go on foot to Condega—to the great joy of our host—to stay with a family named Espinosa. I'm talking now about August of 1975.

There we made contact again with Bayardo. "Look, brother," he said, "we're in deep shit. The problem is, you can't stay here. We don't have safe houses, and we have to push on with the work." "No," I said, "I didn't come to propose that I stay in Estelí or in Condega. I'm a man of the brush. I can't get used anymore to being underground in the city." "Look," he said, "we have Toño, Antonio Centeno, a guy who used to be foreman of an estate between Condega and Yalí, the San Gerónimo plantation. It belonged to Luisa Molina's dad. This foreman is very much loved by the field workers. You guys are going to tour that area with him, so he can point out to you the houses of those field hands, and see if you can stay with any of them."

The plan was ridiculous, but we had to do it—we had to take the plunge. We got to work the next day. We got to

Yalí, coming in from the Los Terreros side, through several valleys that are in that region. We stashed the vehicle somewhere and went in on foot. We went disguised as medicine peddlers. We each carried a bag with a blanket and hammock, and on top of that a whole shitload of pills, and we each had our little hat, and a lariat, too, as if along the way we'd be buying cattle, or pigs—whatever! After walking for about six hours we came to the shack of one of the workers that Toño the foreman knew. He pretended he was just out paying calls on his old acquaintances. Aguilera and I stayed in the brush about 400 yards from the shack.

He came up. "How's it going, how are you?" "Toñito, what a miracle, what a miracle that you are here." "Yes, you see, I'm going around seeing people, just saying hello, because you shouldn't lose track of your old friends." "Ah, Toñito! come in." There was a scorching bitch of a drought that year. The food was all gone, even the corn, and people had eaten all their hens. There were no beans, only tortillas made of poor-quality wheat, horrible, hideous tortillas such as I'd never eaten before. "Don Toñito, this drought has hit us hard, there's no beans, no rice, nothing. We've eaten the last one of our little chickens. Oh, it's too bad, but let's go get a bit of wheat to make some tortillas." So, after chatting for a while, Toño said, "Look, I've got a couple of friends that I'd like you to meet." "You do? Hey, and where are they, in town?" "No, they're traveling with me and are right out here." "And who are they?" "They're good boys, good people, I want you to meet them. I want you to come with me. You've always had confidence in me, right?"

The name of the man we were going to see was Don Pedro Ochoa. "You've always believed in me, Don Pedro." "Of course, yes, sure." "Come along then." In those parts friendship has more weight; a man's word means something. Pedro Ochoa knew something odd was up; he guessed that something peculiar was going on, but since they were friends and Toño had done him favors when he was foreman, he was ready to trust him. He led him to us. Naturally the fellow about fell over when he saw us. It was written all over us—city men who had taken to the brush, armed with pistols, and with a couple of bags spilling over with stuff from town, and on the ground an open tin of sardines. "These are my friends." "Pleased to meet you," he greeted us. "So you see, uh, compañero," I said, "we're in the FSLN . . ."

Brother, let me tell you, that poor guy just about died when we told him that, because the Guard had just been murdering people in the mountains, and the repression in Macuelizo and the battles were all very recent; so our presence there spelled disaster for them. From the beginning in some zones our presence meant commitment and misfortune and death. "So, we're going around meeting people," I told him, "because if someday we pass through here again and need a tortilla, now we know we've met you, and we'll come by like this, hidden, like we are now, and you'll give us a bit of tortilla, and we'll eat it and pack up and be on our way. We have collaborators like this everywhere. But we're going around, you see, getting to know this zone, because you have to know about short-cuts—do you know what I mean? To be able to deal with whatever might come up, the Guard . . . and now I know that these routes exist and that you live here."

I didn't dare tell him we had nowhere to go, no roof, and were bluffing like crazy, can you imagine? And on we went, from one person to the next, from shack to shack, all through those valleys. And the campesinos with always the same terror when we spoke to them, and the same humble way of welcoming us, and that hideous poverty. They were all half-naked, and skin and bone from hunger. And terribly sad. We covered the whole area from Los Terreros to the San Gerónimo estate.

On one of our many stops Toño introduced me to a campesino named Moisés Córdoba, a guy about thirty years old. "Ah, you're Sandinistas," he whispered, as if afraid, but also like somebody who was in the know. "Watch out they don't

see you or they'll kill us all; my dad was a Sandinista." The
light dawned! "And is your dad still alive?" I asked. "Sure,"
he said, "he's alive. He lives over there in a house with my
mother. And I live in a separate little house that I put up with
my wife and our kids." "And could we talk with your dad?" I
asked. "I'll see if he would like to. I'll ask him. Perhaps the
next time you come back through you can talk to him." So we
went on, sleeping where night overtook us, all through those
valleys.

We started out for Buena Vista, through the whole sector
of Canto Gallo. In Buena Vista we spoke with another compañero who was a member of the Conservative Party, Gilberto Zavala, who was also a field worker at the estate and a
relative of the Zavala who was so scared, and also of another
Zavala who lived across from him; the two of them had a dispute going over some land, and they didn't get along. Don
Gilberto said to me, "Ah, you can't stay here." "No, we're
not here to stay," I told him. "We're just passing through." I
told him our usual story. "You see," he said, "there's bad
blood between me and those people over there; they're nothing but . . ." "Ah!" I interrupted. "Does that mean you don't
like the Zavalas from over in San Diego either?" "It's the
same family," he said, "and they don't like me because we're a
bit better off than they are, because we have struggled. That's
why they envy us." He mentioned some lady or other who
had left him some lands that the Zavalas wanted to take away
from him. "Ah, of course," I said, "yes, they told me about
you." "And what did they say? Did they say bad things about
me?" "Oh, no!" I said. "But I think I might be able to resolve
that problem, because they have a lot of confidence in me.
And probably talking it over can resolve it, because it
shouldn't go any further, you have your children; they
shouldn't be at each other's throats—that brings disgrace on
the whole family. I know him, and I know that you, too, are a
good man. So let's sit down someday when I'm passing
through and look at things calmly. I'm going to see if we can't

straighten it all out." The man seemed to want to do that; he was enthusiastic about the idea, but at the same time our presence scared the hell out of him.

Once again we went to try to buy some food, and without realizing it, we stumbled into the house of a local judge. His name was Presentación Laguna—I think he was executed later on. The man looked at us in a funny way, and it was only after we were there that the compañero told me that the guy was a local judge—he had only just found out. He sold us beans with curds and tortillas, and when we'd finished eating I said to him, "Well, my friend, we have eaten now, we've bought something from you. Now you, sir, may buy from us." It was just bullshit, so he'd think we were peddlers. I opened my bag and started pulling out cans of sardines, juices, Alka-Seltzers, Bufferins, aspirins, Milk of Magnesia. I took out a couple of new batteries; I had a blanket, a brand-new one, as if everything were for sale, but it was all my personal property. "And those hogs, are you selling those?" I asked, and on I went, like a real trader. "And how many head of cattle do you have? Do you sell on the hoof or on the rack?" We had practiced all this, all the lingo, and the man swallowed it. That son of a bitch really believed I was a peddler. And his wife chimed in, too. "Don't you have any clothes for children?" she wanted to know.

After that we returned on foot to the Zavala house in San Diego, to the house of that Christian who was so nervous. We dropped in on him again and came straight to the point; it had been eight days since we had been there. "Let us in. We're just passing through," we called out to him. "We're hungry. Don't be afraid." He finally opened the door. Once inside we sent for the little girl courier and gave her a letter for Bayardo, informing him that our tour had been a success, that possibilities existed for advancing our work. He answered that we should forge on ahead. My plan was to continue going around visiting people until one by one they were solid supporters. And that old Sandinista was never out of my mind.

Nor the man with the dispute over land, whom I hoped to win over by helping him solve that problem.

Bayardo sent us money, and we started off on the tour again. But this time we went in from the opposite direction. The first shack we came to belonged to a man named Juan Canales, the foreman of another estate, the Daraili. (Four years later we would be back there meeting with about a thousand men.) We got to the house of that first collaborator and banged on his door. It was already dark. "Who's there?" we could hear from inside. "It's Juan José," I answered, "the pill peddler." Because I looked like a medicine peddler. So he opened the door, and can you imagine my surprise when I saw the whole house crammed with people—sprawled on the floor, sitting, standing—because only the day before his wife had been killed; she had been run over by a car in town. Now the wake and the burial were over, and everybody was in the house. We were tired from our walk and just turning to go, but he took it like a man. "Well then, when will you be heading on?" "Tomorrow," I said. "We need some tortillas for the road." So he put us in an empty shack that was like a tiny granary for drying corn. He brought us food, and the next day we were ready to be on our way.

The house was still overflowing with people. "Hombre, don't you have any friends you could introduce us to, people who could help?" I asked. "You've got to be kidding, my friend," he said. "The people around here are all terrible gossips. They can't keep their big mouths shut. It's not possible." "I understand that, hombre," I said, but kept insisting until he started to loosen up. "Okay," he said, "I'm going to check out a guy who's a field hand at the estate where I work." And he spoke with this fellow, who agreed to put us up. But not in his house, which was very tiny and right by a local trail which led to another trail which went to the Daraili estate. But we could stay in a cornfield. It was hard enough to talk him into that: "We'll stay right in the cornfield, compa. We'll be quiet as mice—we won't make a sound." "But what if people come

189

into the cornfield and find you?" he said. "But hombre, doesn't that field belong to you? Who would be coming?"

Anyway, we spent about three days there; he brought us food, and it was a victory that he didn't turn us in. As long as they didn't turn us in, there was the possibility of doing political work. And as long as he kept coming to bring us food it was possible to talk with him for half an hour and to raise his consciousness. He had three sick kids, and since we were loaded with medicines and had some money, too, we gave him money to buy medicine for his kids and some little things for us. It was a whole shitload of things—we helped him solve the problem with his kids and we heightened his awareness. He was living in dire poverty, so we gave him 100 pesos to buy some cream. That was how we did our political work with this man. Anyway, he eventually agreed to leapfrog us on ahead into the valleys of Buena Vista, Robledal, to "La Montañita" and "Los Planes." We had already talked with Juan Flores in "La Montañita" and with Laureano Flores, and Concho, his son, who had lost an arm—I nicknamed him "The One-Armed Swordsman."

One day the owner of the cornfield didn't come; he didn't show up when he had promised he would guide us through the brush. He had abandoned us, and there was no more food. The bastard's backed out on us, I thought. He's going to turn us in, or he's staying away so we'll leave. So one foggy morning, when it was so foggy you could barely see in front of you, Andrés, who was adventurous and glad to be with me—because he felt very secure, knowing I was a man of the mountains and burning with the will to work and make war and be a guerrilla and kick out Somoza and the Guard, all in the struggle for justice—said to me, "Let's go, Juan José, let's strike out through the brush; we've got to get to those shacks." "Hombre, let's go," I agreed.

And we started out walking in the morning. We had a compass; it seemed to us that the needle was pointing north. "Let's go this way"—but son of a bitch, can you believe it, by noon we were completely lost. Shit! We looked around and saw a main road, but which one was it? There were local trails; this one, where does it go? And we looked around and climbed up to the top of hills to try to get our bearings. Where the hell were we? Well, dawn came, and we were sound asleep by a stream. We ate some cornmeal. That was the first time Andrés had slept out in a hammock or any of that. We were lost, but it didn't matter. We felt that we were looking history straight in the eye; we were meeting it head-on, in order to win the future, the world to come. Our morale was fantastic. I'd been in the mountains a year, right? Was I going to let a thing like this get me down, after all I'd been through up there? That sparse, scraggly vegetation was a joke. Besides, there were shacks where we could buy a bit of food. And if I managed to eat one sardine per day, that was a daily banquet, right? The next day dawned, and we started out again. But we couldn't find anything. We were looking for the Canto Gallo hill, but that son-of-a-bitch shitpile of a hill was nowhere to be seen. First we came to Fraile hill, which was beyond Canto Gallo, and looking for Canto Gallo we got all turned around.

We emerged from the pitch-pine forests of Daraili and Fraile into a mountainous zone with a different type of vegetation, where there were coffee plantations. We had passed near San Gerónimo, but since we were lost we didn't realize it. The next day we woke up drenched to the bone. "Brother," Andrés said, "there's a road over there and a shack in the distance. Let's drop into that shack like we were selling this shit and ask directions to Robledal, and how to get to La Montañita, and we'll find out where we are." We walked right into the house and found a woman alone. It had rained that morning; we came out of the brush supersoaked, about 6:30 A.M., and all of a sudden, not knowing how we got there, the woman saw us in her house. She didn't know where we had come from. We had popped out of the ground, as the campesinos say. "Good morning. How are you, ma'm, how is everything?" "Still here," she answered. "And these children, are they yours, ma'm?" And I'm not sure what else. "You see, we're passing through selling medicine. We have Alka-Seltzers, Bufferin . . . wouldn't you like to buy something? We have batteries, too," dropping the price way down so she would buy. "The problem is we're flat broke," she said. "We've had a drought, you see, and there's no money." "Look, why don't you get us together a bit of a meal," I suggested in a while. "But I haven't a thing to give you. All I've got are those beans over there and some black coffee." But she finally agreed.

After we had eaten, we said to her, "Listen, we have to go over to Robledal, around La Montañita and Buena Vista. Is this the trail that goes there?" "No, this trail goes somewhere else. That one, the one straight ahead, goes to the trail you want. This is a fork in the road." And she started giving us all the typical country directions. Once we were oriented we started out over the trail, in broad daylight, what the hell! We'd had no luck making our way through the brush with the compass because we didn't know how to use it. The compass was good; the problem was that we were such fuck-ups we didn't know how to use it, so our way of getting around had to be by asking questions. We would pass by the shacks, talking and talking. "Halloo, friend, is that pig for sale, friend?" When I offered to buy something I always offered a price way below the proper price so they wouldn't sell, even taking into account their poverty. Because I knew they would give it to me cheap since they needed the money. But I put the price superlow to make sure they would say no, and I didn't buy shit. And on we went, Andrés and I, until we came to Buena Vista.

At night we went to Gilberto Zavala; the guy was finally starting to come through for us, quite apart from his dispute over the land. Gilberto was in the Conservative Party, but since that party didn't represent his interests, he, like a lot of other campesinos, became a Sandinista. We spent about four days at his place, working with him. His wife was a total basket case, constantly praying—out of fear. "You see how it affects her—she doesn't sleep a wink," Gilberto told me. "If a dog barks in the night she just about dies of fright." We were camping out in a little coffee grove that Gilberto had, about 200 yards from his shack. "She's a good woman," he said, meaning his wife. "Listen to what she says about you: 'That poor boy,' she says, 'so young and wandering around in that brush with no food.'" So I realized she had real Christian charity; she was a very noble woman. But of course she was terrified, on top of which she was old, like Gilberto.

I said to him, "I'd like to have a word with her, with your wife." "Oh, no, she would die, she would just die," he said. "Go ahead, tell her I'd like to talk to her." I convinced him, and she agreed to talk to me, more out of fear than anything else. So at night I slipped up to the house, and we started talking about all sorts of things, generalities. "That's a nice statue of the Virgin you have." "Yes," she said, and since she had another Virgin, the Virgin of Fatima I think it was, I asked, "The Virgin with the most miracles is the Virgin of Fatima, isn't it, because she never fails you, isn't that right?" And then she spoke. "And you, sir, do you have a mama?" "Yes," I said, "my mom is at home." "And what job does she have?" "I don't know. I used to support her." "And do you have children?" "Yes, I have a little girl." "And your wife?" "She's back there, the poor girl." "You poor boy," she said, "you don't see your mama, nor your wife, nor your little girl?" "No," I said, "because as Sandinistas we have to leave everything behind, because we want our people to be free." "Ahhhh," she said, "the Guard is very bad, isn't it?" "Look," I said, "this is my little girl." When I was in Ocotal they had given me a color photo of my sweet little girl, a very nice little girl. "Oh, what a lovely little creature. If she only knew her father . . . true? How awful, true? If they kill you she will grow up without her father," she said. "Ah, may God preserve you, may God protect this child from being an orphan," she said.

"And this is my mama, look." I pulled out another photo. "Oh, oh, what a pretty woman. Oh, how awful. Dear God, please take care of yourself, see that nothing happens to you!" "With God's help and the help of all of you, whenever we come by if you could just give us a scrap of tortilla, or make us something to take along, something to send with us. And being careful is a way of life for us; we are always careful. Don't you notice how we never come in the day, only at night, and how we talk very softly and come in without a flashlight? And we move very slowly so the neighbors' dogs won't bark at us; we skirt the yards of the houses—you've seen that already."

The old lady, in time, came to adore us, Andrés as much as me; then, in full confidence, we asked Gilberto to go get Moisés Córdoba for us, in Los Planes, also to find Juan Flores in La Montañita. They took me to them, and I met with each of them separately.

"Hey," said Juan Flores, "you're back." "Right, passing through," I said. "You see, we're going around really getting to know the area, and we'd like to talk with you people. We've already spent about eight days with the compañero Gilberto, and we've had plenty of talks." "Ah, good," he said, "and when are you coming over to us?"

I was still hoping to see the old Sandinista from Los Planes, but the little old man was still sick, so I decided to go on over to Juan Flores in La Montañita. Before leaving, I managed to convince Gilberto to take a letter for me to Bayardo in Condega; in the early days Gilberto was the first courier for what later became "Bonifacio Montoya" Combat Unit.

"Brother," I wrote Bayardo, "we're cutting through this shit, we're moving it on ahead, and the slogan here is Free Homeland or Death." I spent a few days then with Juan Flores. Our situation was complicated because it seems that the local judge Presentación Laguna was suspicious: the Guard had come in and combed the area; some Guardsmen had raided San Gerónimo or something like that, and had gone by the Daraili estate and around there. At Juan Flores's I talked with him and with Laureano and Concho; I met other people, the heroic Mercedes Galeano, who rose to be the head of all our work in those valleys and who later died in combat.

When I finished making these initial contacts I returned to Gilberto's, to the little granary. I remember once I got in about nine at night, and he still had not come back from town with the reply from Bayardo that the courier had brought. I was a little worried about the work—it was showing timid signs of life, and the Guard was already on the scene. So I went to the granary; I lay down and started thinking of the mountains. I wondered how Modesto was, how the Regionals of the Frente were doing in the west, or in the interior of the country. I started thinking about everything that had happened in the north, in Ocotal, in Macuelizo; what had happened in El Sauce, because at the same time the Guard was breaking up our school in Macuelizo, they were also breaking up the school in El Sauce. I thought of Bayardo, of Mónica, of all the compañeros in León; and thinking about León, of course I thought of Claudia.

Reasons for Living

hen I left for the mountains I was in love with
Claudia. Loving her for me was something sub-
lime, something beyond measure and magni-
tudes, as Che once said. I had put into that relationship the
very purest of man's constructive and artistic powers. Out of
that relationship I had built a great city, a very beautiful city.
Let's say that our relationship was the beginning and the end,
the alpha and omega of everything man has ever known about
love. What I mean is, Claudia, or my relationship with Claudia, had become for me a standard in the mountains, a flag
that I held aloft and that never got caught in the vines, that
never fell, that never got wet or splattered with mud. What
I'm saying is, after Claudia, after my love for her, after that
came the jungle and everything that my mind had never
counted on. Before entering the mountains I had no assess-
ment of either the jungle or the forest, no conception of what
the mountain really meant. So I went to bed with that standard beside me; I kept it always with me; I folded it neatly
and put it under my head like a pillow, and went to sleep.
That helped to keep me going; it helped me to live; it helped
me to be better. I felt the pride of being an example for her.
I felt the need to be an example—for her and for our baby

girl. Claudia was my motivating force, my security, my confidence; she meant bullets and being able to see in the dark, and more air in my lungs, more strength in my legs; she was my sense of direction and my fire; our love was warm, dry clothing; it was rain cover, victory, tranquility; it was everything—the future, children—everything my brain could calculate.

So, there I was in the little granary, and since it was winter and raining, it was horribly infested with fleas and mosquitos. And Gilberto arrived from Bayardo with a letter for me. I saw the letter was marked "Personal for Eugenio." I started reading: "Skinny, how are you?" it went, or something like that, I don't remember exactly. "Skinny, I admire you very much. Skinny, I want you to know I have a deep respect for you, that so many of the things I know I have learned from you. You've been one of the people that has most influenced my life. And because of this affection and the respect that I feel for you, I want to be honest—I want you to know that I've fallen in love with another compañero. I don't love you anymore, I now love him. I hope you'll understand. I want you to know I will always love you, or will always respect and admire you. Affectionately," and her alias.

I remember when the letter came I was very hungry, because I hadn't had lunch, or supper either, and the campesinos were afraid, and the Guard was snooping around everywhere, and some damn fleas were biting at my balls, hideous fleas. I had a fungus that made my feet burn. I couldn't remember the last time I'd brushed my teeth; when I ran my tongue over them I could feel a fuzz of built-up and accumulated food; my tongue was like sandpaper on my teeth. I felt really shitty that day. I had missed some contacts I was trying to make in the afternoon, and to top it all off I had lost a couple of bullets on the march. I never lost bullets. And there I was that night, resting, when that letter came. I also got a letter from Bayardo Arce that I didn't read until about two hours later. Because when I started reading Claudia's letter it upset me a lot. It seemed so unfair. This just couldn't be happening. It was not in the cards; it was illogical; it didn't follow. How could she do that to me? I understood that she wasn't going to wait for me forever, like in the Middle Ages when the knight goes off to the Crusades, and after a thousand victorious battles comes galloping back and stops in front of the castle, and the lady appears, smiling, on the balcony, like in a fairy tale. I knew I couldn't demand that. But neither had I imagined that she would abandon me when I was keeping her standard spotless, unmuddied; when I was carrying that flag up all those hills, and every time I came to the top, without saying a word, I drove it into the ground. And at night I folded it and went to sleep with it. I saw it in the leaping flames of our bonfires, and in our victories, our triumphs. I saw it on all our marches. And I could not believe this was happening. Do you understand what I'm saying? I felt my world coming apart.

Have you ever noticed how in an airplane, when the plane turns, when the plane tilts, the surface of the earth is on a huge slant, and the hills are slanted, and when you fly over the sea the water seems about to pour out? And the houses are all askew and the people and the dogs? That was how I felt, as if the ground had shifted. I had lost my sense of space, my equilibrium, all sense of gravity and of inertia, any number of senses. Every physical sense that man has on the earth I had lost, and not only the physical. I had lost my sense of self, my sense of man and of woman, so many, many things.

I remember once, before leaving to go underground, I had said, "Look, Claudia, if they kill me someday—I'm going to tell you something I don't want you to tell anyone—if they kill me someday, it'll only be if I'm in too much pain or if they spray my face with bullets—that's the only way they'll keep me from dying with a smile on my lips, with a smile on my face. So, when you see the paper *Novedades* or *La Prensa* with this caption: 'Unidentified criminal dead,' and you see me and recognize my face and my smile in the newspaper, you'll know, I want you to know, that this smile is for you, that it belongs to you. And when the students march in the streets, when they hold assemblies in the university to protest about my death, I want you to sit in one of those seats in the middle of the auditorium, or in the back. And when they say fine things about me, about how I was a man who did his duty, a man who fought the dictatorship, a brave man, and all that, I want you to sit quietly with that paper in your hand and look down at my face and think how that smile belongs to you, to you alone, and that nobody can ever take it away from you. And when you march in the demonstrations, and are walking or running, with the Guard chasing after you, my smile will be with you, walking or running, and don't let anybody ever take it away. It belongs to you. And nobody will be able to take that smile from me, because I give it to you. But don't tell this to anybody; don't talk about it. And if you have to die, you'll die, too, and before dying, you'll have that smile, but never tell anybody that smile is yours, that I gave it to you."

I thought of all that when I read the letter. Meanwhile, those fucking ticks were biting me like crazy; they were working overtime to really let me have it, biting me not just on my testicles, but all over my chest and my legs. And the fungus wasn't just on my feet anymore—my whole body was on fire. And now the pollen of the corn husks was starting to bother me when I was lying down. I got up. I couldn't sleep, and spent a dog's night tossing and turning. I got up to go pee. I cried that night. And I couldn't get to sleep. Finally, I don't know how, but an evil, Machiavellian thought occurred to me: now I know what I'm going to do. That woman will pay for her injustice. My mind is made up. I'll send her a letter and my revenge will be this—I'm going to tell her in this letter that the day I die, if the Guard doesn't spray my face with bullets, I won't be able to stop laughing, and that the laugh she'll see in the papers will not belong to her. She should know and be absolutely clear that this smile, which is the smile of a protesting man, the smile of a moral man, a consequential man, a man of love, a man of the mountains—that this smile of a dying Sandinista no longer belongs to her. That was my secret revenge, and the great lesson was that this smile was for others, or even if it wasn't for others, it didn't matter. What mattered was that it wouldn't be for her.

Naturally, with everything that happened between the time I opened the letter and when I answered back, it was a very sad period. The tiniest thing made me sad. I was intensely depressed. But nobody realized it. Outwardly I tried to set an example of morale, of enthusiasm, and I managed. But at the same time I felt lonely. For the first time, I felt really alone, deeply alone. Let me tell you, that was loneliness.

When you go into the mountains as we did, it's a violent, even traumatic change. Because just like that, after being in the university leading an organized, disciplined life (after six years in the FSLN), you begin to climb and in twenty-four hours you're on the outskirts of Matagalpa heading into the mountains. In preparation you've bought a dozen Bufferins, a dozen Alka-Seltzers, aspirin tablets, who knows how many Tetracycline capsules, your little bottle of alcohol, your cotton, your sewing needles, thread, buttons, a couple of batteries, a pair of shoes. Besides that you have your driver's license, your wallet, your papers, your notebook, who knows what all. The nail clippers you've had in your room for ages, the pocket knife your brother gave you, the Western belt that was a gift from Luz Marina, your photographs, your old kerchief, the same one she used to wash with, or dry her hands. You take your usual underwear, the same clothes you've put on so many times, worn over and over on so many different occasions, in so many places, always with the same people. You start out with your same hands, your same face, your same eyes and teeth and hair, with the usual expression on your face, with your same old sweater. What I'm saying is, you are leaving the city; you are leaving your world. You are leaving your present, which the moment you start marching is transformed into the past. You take that present with you when you leave for the mountains. But the closer you get, the farther behind that present is; it is becoming past.

200

In fact, what is really happening is that your head is full of the life you've been living all those years, and everything about that life, all incredibly fresh. Everything you used to do—how you stayed up late, made love, fought, slept, ate, what you did for fun—all this is fresh in your mind, in your brain. Your happiest memories, the compañeros, her, your plans, all very fresh. As you approach the mountains, all of this is objectively transformed into the past. As you take all these things, including yourself, into the mountains, including your body, and all the ideas in your brain, these things in large part reaffirm that present in you. That present which is now the past. Am I making myself clear? Why? Because it's all behind you.

When you left for the mountains, you began the process of the forced shedding of your present. Against your will you were hurling that present back into the past, as if bits of your flesh were being left behind. And that hurts. But you have no choice but to go forward in that process of deincarnation, of slowly dying. And each day you are deeper into the mountains. First you stop seeing the type of people you saw before. From then on you won't see the type of people you saw in the city; you won't see the things you used to see every day: the houses, the walls, the glass windows, the pavement. It's all gone; objectively it's behind you, though you have it stored in your brain.

Before long you quit listening for the noise of cars, or of bicycles, or television or radios, or for the shouts of kids hawking newspapers or Chiclets. You quit listening for that typical city tone in the cries of the kids. You no longer see movie houses, or billboards for films. And you keep on going: no electric light. And on. Then no more colors, nothing but green; no colors but what people are wearing, and even those colors are starting to fade. You end up color blind. You won't be experiencing the taste of chocolate anymore, the sensation of rum, or wine, the flavor of Chiclets. Farther in you can forget about hearing music. The popular songs of the day— Camilo Sesto, Julio Iglesias, Leonardo Favio, Nicola Di

Bari—the radios don't come in with you, so the songs must be recorded on your brain.

Deeper in you begin to detach yourself; as you penetrate deeper, you are more and more isolated. Finally the moment comes when nothing is left of your past, in terms of your experience, your senses—I'm not sure how to say it—your immediate, recent past, it no longer exists. You have to resign yourself to never seeing it again, unless someday you come out of there alive, if the revolution triumphs.

About fifteen or twenty compañeros, no more, were up there in the guerrilla movement. How were fifteen or twenty of us in the mountains going to bring down Somoza's powerful armed Guard? Sometimes it seemed it would take years and years for us to triumph. And all those years push your present even farther back into the past, though your mind doesn't want to accept it. The only continuation of your present— your city present, your usual life in the city before leaving for the mountains—all that remains of that present in the mountains are things, the objects you are carrying, which are sensory stimuli to the ideas and memories in your brain. The concrete things that you have in your pack, plus your memories and ideas—there's nothing else to reaffirm your present, which is now the past. So what happens? One day you lose your kerchief, you forget it somewhere . . . son of a bitch, my kerchief! Where did I leave my kerchief? And the kerchief is gone; you'll never see it again. Son of a bitch, you say, she gave me that kerchief . . . the kerchief . . . the kerchief . . . son of a bitch! It's lost. Shit! A little piece of your present is torn out of you, which is how a bit of your identity is torn away, a bit of your flesh, of all you want to hang on to.

Eventually your clothes wear out. Your pants fall apart. You can't wear them, they're in rags, or you need to use them to patch your new pants, which are already full of rips. Then: son of a bitch, my nail clippers! Your nails need clipping and *zing!* that's the end of your clippers. Another piece of your flesh has fallen away.

As things continue to get lost or ruined, the objects that reaffirm your present are disappearing, the objects that confirm your identity, your consciousness of your own existence, your sense that you are not just living on the surface, but have a history. In the end your very sense of time is shot to hell, because as things keep getting lost, time is passing, is drawing on. Okay, would you ever be going back? Maybe you really were going to lose everything—your present, which is the past. And meanwhile the revolution is not triumphing, and the Guard is on top of you, and hunger, and everything else. You can be hungry, but really, if you can hang on to your convictions and an outlook for the future, you can better endure and stand up to the difficulties.

So, when you lose all your things, it's as if that many pieces of your present have broken off from you. It's so extreme that for a moment you don't know if you'll ever go back, if you'll ever return, and each thing that you lose is like a paring away, a whittling down, a falling off of piece after piece of your persona. And in time—unforgiving, unrelenting time that flows on, unchanging—you lose everything, even your mind. You are losing your self; your expression is being transformed, from always wearing long sleeves and never seeing the sun, since the tops of the trees block the sun, and never seeing the sky that could remind you of the sky back there, the sky of León, the sky of the past. And you can't connect the moon on the beaches at Poneloya, the moon you grew up with, with the moon in the mountains, and so associate your old present with your new, and be able to dream and remember and associate ideas, to maintain your sense of historical continuity. Since in the mountains there is no moon, no stars—everything is green. Your body turns a pallid white; your hands no longer look like hands, all covered with sores and scratches from vines and brambles, and filthy from never washing, never taking a bath. And the palms of your hands are thickened from swinging the machete and the ax, from hoisting the straps of your pack, putting up your hammock, and snatching hot things out of the fire. Your fingers grow calloused, your hands; the very body you are master of, which you command, has begun very slowly to change right before your eyes, and you are powerless to prevent it.

And so your very body abandons your present while you look on helplessly; your very body is transformed into a new and different present. And the worst of it is, you never see yourself in a mirror. The first time I saw my face in the mountains was after about five months. Once I didn't see my face for almost a year. And when I finally saw myself again, brother, it wasn't me! I had a mustache, and never in my life had I had a mustache; I'd never let one grow. I was sprouting a beard that I was constantly stroking, but that I'd never seen. The expression in my eyes had changed; my brow was creased from frowning so much because of all the thorns, all the spills you take. The mountains always end up lining your brow, and your jaw widens out a bit. Have you ever noticed in the photographs taken right after the victory? Our brows were all lined, and our jaws set, because you clench your teeth when you march. Your eyebrows are always frowning. And the look in your eyes changes; the expression in your eyes grows sharper, from the effort to see in the dark, the strain of watching for the olive green enemy in the midst of all the green of the jungle—to avoid being ambushed—the strain of trying to see and not being able to see all the things and thoughts that are dissolving before you. All of this changes the look in your eyes, which becomes an aggressive look, but which never stops being clear. So when you see yourself in the mirror, you realize you are not the same. You realize you are someplace else; you are another person.

It's an anguish consciously accepted; you feel you are one more element, one more being in that environment which you have come to grips with and dominate, because you have reason. Because you have intelligence and dominate the environment for a purpose—to use it, in this case for the guerrilla struggle, the revolutionary war. So when you lose all the things you've brought with you, and when your own body, your own substance, has decayed and fallen away from you, your identity has one last refuge: in the ideas and in the memories that are lodged in your brain, which you have guarded and cherished and preserved in the innermost recesses of your brain as the fuel of all your forces, as the core, the pith of your life, the marrow of existence.

Ideas and memories are the most intimate part of man, where nobody can scrutinize, where not even the harshness of the mountain can penetrate—the only thing that nature cannot easily transform. You nourish your memories, and when you lie down in your hammock at night you hold your memories close to you; you bring them out a bit into the world, you turn them over in your head, you parade them a bit, timidly, in front of your eyes, though you never really see them. So you air these memories, and before going to sleep you return them very slowly to your brain, as if back into a spiral shell that is very gradually closing. You wind in your ideas once again, and probably your body curls up, too, I don't know— you start to gather in your ideas, to reel in your memories until they are all covered over and perfectly quiet, in the shelter of your brain, as if resting—and you sleep. You might say that the only umbilical cord, the only thread that still binds you to that past, or to that present which has become the past, is idea, memory.

So when you receive a letter like that, and your memories explode into fragments, it's as if the only thread left to you has been snapped, the invisible thread, the vital link that has bound you to your present, which is now the past, however you might rage against that fact and not want it to be so. When that letter came, it sent shock waves through me, tearing out from the most hidden recesses of my brain, from the most intimate part, a thing I had kept there to fall back on. When that happens, yes, you start to feel the loneliness, the isolation. And that's when, if you don't have a political-ideological mental framework, you desert or go crazy.

205

I remember once I wrote a poem which I also sent to Claudia after that letter, as a final touch, to let her know that what she had done was not going to kill me.

> *Now that I've lost you,*
> *I realize that*
> *Had I not been lead,*
> *I would have been shit.*

I have to explain to you that the word for "lead," in Spanish *"plomo,"* is made up of the initials of *Patria Libre O Morir* (Free Homeland or Death). If I hadn't had a reason for living, another reason for living, namely the struggle to liberate Nicaragua, I would have fallen completely apart—into pure shit.

Legacy of a Sandinista

ut fortunately that did not happen. Early in the morning the next day I left the little granary and went to the coffee field to wash my face in a stream. I think I combed my hair. Then I sat down under an orange tree to suck the juice from some oranges. I started peeling an orange with my pocket knife, and as I separated the rind from the pulp of the orange, as I saw the bits of peeling falling away, separating, giving way to the knife, I felt I was like that orange, and the orange peelings were the things I ought not to think about. When I had finished peeling the orange I felt lighter, not quite so heavy. The orange was now naked, and it was smaller, reduced. I was letting go of my memories in the same way; I let them go as I peeled the rind from the orange. Or more or less, since as the days passed I began to feel lighter; my head did not feel so heavy. And finally, looking back on it, it was as if I had been lugging around a weight that little by little I had let go of. Until the only weight left was the weight of the struggle.

I took a deep breath; I filled my lungs with air; I felt the cool of the morning on my freshly washed face. I set my feet solidly on the ground, and sitting up, I burst out laughing. I knew that a new phase of my life was beginning, there, under that orange tree. I had a sudden intuition that the future was right there, barely visible, like something slippery at the tips of my fingers, and I had only to close my fist to take hold of it. This was October 1975. Now it's all ahead of me, I thought; I'm going to create a life, and I'm going to paint that life; I'm going to paint the story of my life in the color I like the best; let every person paint his life, in whatever colors—and I'll paint mine, and in the finest colors.

So I sent Andrés to Gilberto to tell him to go to Los Planes to tell Moisés Córdoba we would be dropping in at his house that same night. Don Gilberto explained to Moisés that we had stayed with him and had been to La Montañita. It seemed that everybody was getting used to our presence, as if they felt it was no longer so dangerous. Or that it was dangerous, but that they wouldn't be murdered for it that day. Tomorrow maybe, but probably they wouldn't be murdered at all. They were opening up and beginning to become our friends; I was starting to joke around with them, to be accepted, to win their affection. We arrived that night at the crag we had decided earlier would be our campsite. The next day there they were, with hot beans and a tortilla from the town. They came back later with one of their last hens. And of course we had plenty to talk about with Moisés. That was when I suggested to Moisés that he take me to his father, the old Sandinista who was about eighty years old.

So, while he was working on that, I went on to something else, and through him I made contact with some other compañeros. Moisés, because of his dad, wasn't as scared as the others, or was more conscious of who we were, clearer about what it was we were doing. Because his dad had talked to him, before we came, about Sandino's struggle.

I was able to visit three little houses or so in those valleys, and the more people I met the more I was able to advance our political work. You could say the Córdoba family was the most prestigious in the valley; the fact that they were introducing me encouraged the others to be less afraid. If the Córdobas, if Don Leandro's sons, were involved in "that," well, it was okay for them to be in it, too. I spent the day on the rock, by a stream, and when it got dark I went down to their houses. In the little shacks at night, over one black coffee after another, in conversation after conversation, we discussed their financial troubles, and these conversations deepened our friendship. When I became friends with someone I always wanted that relationship to develop into something that had political content, and vice versa—I always tried to build a political connection into a solid personal friendship.

The first thing we would ask was if they owned the land they lived on, and the answer was always no, it belonged to the "rich folk." Or they would laugh, as if making a joke, or they would hang their heads. Because, for the campesinos, the land was a dream. A dream of their fathers, a dream of their fathers' grandfathers. So if you came and asked them if they owned the land, they just laughed. Because the land had never belonged to them, nor to their fathers, nor to their grandfathers. Naturally we steered our political discussions toward the reason the land was not theirs.

The landowners, or the fathers or grandfathers of the landowners, had over a period of years gradually been stripping the campesinos of their land. So the generation of campesinos we knew would tell us about how their great-grandfathers had owned land. And the story of what happened was passed down from great-grandfather to grandfather to father to son. They were now a generation without land. The landowners had appropriated the land through a process of violent evictions, or through legal means.

In the Condega plains, Los Planes, where Moisés lived, there were about one hundred acres and some twenty-five little shacks. They had a good name for that process. "They corralled us," they would say. They had been corralled, cut back, surrounded with barbed wire. And they ended up working the landowner's land and tending his cattle. And the campesinos who had been "corralled" had to grow their crops on land lent them by the local landowners. In the time they had left, they would cultivate a bit of ground they would rent from the landowner. And when the harvest came, they had to sell it to the same owners. And naturally you had to buy your salt, your filing tools, your machetes, your aspirin and other pills from the commissary the landowner operated right there.

We took hold of the campesinos' hands, broad, powerful, roughened hands. "These calluses," we asked, "how did you get them?" And they would tell us how they came from the machetes, from working the land. If they got those calluses from working the land, we asked, why did that land belong to the boss and not to them? We were trying to awaken the campesino to his own dream. We wanted to make him see that though the dream was dangerous—since it implied struggle— the land was their right. And we began to cultivate that dream. Through our political work, many campesinos began partaking of that dream.

Other compañeros did not live right there but were rancheros; people who worked land that was part of the acreage of an estate. A campesino was given a piece of ground on which he would build a shack, which was called a rancho. It went up in two days, just sticks and straw. So this compañero was doubly exploited. It was bad enough to have been "corralled." But the ranchero was worse off still, because he lived right on the landowner's grounds. That is why the land for the campesino was a permanent dream. We kept raising the question of the struggle for the land.

It would break our hearts sometimes, because you came to see how the campesino loves the land and has a richer, deeper sense of the land as an element. Just as a sailor cannot live without the sea, or as a pilot dreams of flying—the campesino has developed a kind of identification with the land, which you aren't likely to find in a man from the city. He has developed a kind of unity with the land, a whole series of special, very characteristic emotions, with respect to the land. And something else—sometimes the campesino will speak of the land as of something sacred, like a mother. Or as if the land were a woman. "I'll make her produce, I tell you, I'll take her in hand, I'll clear her off." Or: "Now I've got her." And of course he begins to feel affection for the tiny piece of land the landowner has given him to work—clearing the brush, removing the trees, planting, harvesting. The campesino clears the brush with a machete to get the ground ready to plant. But you feel that even if it's a violent operation, in the end this clearing of the land is a very tender thing between him and the land, a very special sort of affection. So quite apart from needing the land to produce in order to live from the land, the campesino loves the land, and this is important, as a material element of his existence.

We never promised an agrarian reform to the campesinos, never! We invited them to struggle and to fight for agrarian reform. We invited them to fight for the land. Which was too great a temptation for a campesino to resist! How could they stand by and not fight for what was for them a mother, a wife, a way of living, affection, feeling, secret rapport? It would be very hard for the campesino to refuse to fight, particularly when we were awakening in him the feeling and the idea of class struggle.

The campesino has not only developed, as we said, affective sentiments, but his very sense perceptions have evolved in connection with the land, do you see? He has a greater sense of touch, a finer feel for the land; his sense of smell has evolved in relation to the land. He'll say to you, "Stubble land, sown land, cleared land, wet land," all sorts of land. The greatest crime of the dictatorship was to deny land to the campesino. Because denying the campesino land was like forcing him to wander in a living death. A campesino without land is like a zombie—he is out of his element. Apart from his element he is a broken man. That is why, in the country, animals, wife, children, and land are all one element; to the campesino it is all a whole, his indivisible universe. I'm telling you the campesino without land is an incomplete man, a man without a soul. The soul of the campesino is the land; it is the element that gives him life, that propels him forward. Because he wants land for the harvest, and to be able to live from the land as men of the land must live from the land; apart from all this he is in love with the land and has intimate relations with her. And his wife and children are part of that same bond.

About nine that night after a good long talk, I crept back to my crag to go to bed. Of course, you never fall asleep right away; you are always thinking, hearing the night sounds, dogs barking down by the shack, listening to a little music. You tune in Radio Havana—that little chime that lets you know it's on the air. You hear the "Night Moment" at ten, or tune in a Managua station for a bit of music. I thought of my family in León. I remember that one night on that crag I was remembering my return from the mountains to León. That night in the safe house a flood of sensations overwhelmed me; one of the things I felt most intensely was a sense of the absurd. Distances in the mountains are measured in time: eight days, let's say, or seven days, or a month. It was a minimum of three hours to get from one place to the next, right? To get firewood was an hour, or a half-hour—it wasn't easy! Not just the distance but the terrain. To get anywhere you had to climb, or march for half a day, or a couple of hours. It meant cold, it meant God knows how many scratches on your hands, or how many falls, or how much physical pain. It meant that same awful fatigue in your legs and in your chest and in your lungs. What I'm saying is, going from one place to another meant sacrifice, time; it meant pain.

So, in León, I was filled with curiosity about my family. I asked the compañeros for news of my mother. What did they know about her? Could they tell me anything? How was she? How had she reacted? What was she doing to make ends meet? Because my brothers and I together had supported her, especially my older brother. How did she manage to live? How did she eat? She had no job. Before, she used to take in stu-

dents from out of town who came to study in León. But with
three sons in the guerrilla war, nobody was going to stay
there, to eat there; they would be afraid. Besides which,
as it turned out, every so often the house was broken into
and searched. And there was rent to pay every month, and
sometimes we didn't have any money. How were my little
brothers? And the compañeros started telling me how she
had been.

I thought of going to visit her. Our hideout was only fifteen
blocks from the house; fifteen blocks in a car would be five
minutes or thereabouts, three minutes, ten minutes, and you
wouldn't get wet or be worn out getting there, or scratched to
bits—nothing. You would just sit back comfortably and listen
to the radio. I felt nostalgic for my house; I longed to see my
mom, and the neighbors and Doña Lillian's daughter. I had
fallen in love with her, platonically, but had never told her
how I felt—it was too painful. I felt nostalgic for my room,
my tiny little room, for my bed, for the kitchen, the dining
room, the living room, the wooden chairs, the bathroom, the
yard, the dog. It was all so completely mine, I had preserved
it; it was all so fresh that I couldn't believe I was that close,
that I could actually go. If I asked to go I was sure they
wouldn't say no—they would set it up somehow, to either
take me there at night or to bring my mom to me.

But I also knew that I shouldn't go. Before leaving León I
spent a number of nights like this: as soon as I was lying in bed
I would start going over the blocks in my mind, the number of
blocks, who lived on those blocks. I remembered the street so
well! And it would be so simple to get there! It seemed absurd
not to go! You have a house but you don't have a house; you
have a family, a home, but you don't have a home. Until finally one night when I had gone out on a mission with Iván
Montenegro and Jorge Sinforoso Bravo, I said to Iván, "Fat
Man, Fat Man, let's go by my house." "Okay," he said, "but
in the car you mean ... right? without stopping." God in
heaven! I started shaking like a leaf, can you imagine, it was
too violent. Because the house was so fresh in my memory,

and in the mountains I had lost all hope of ever seeing it again. The mountain was the end of the world—we were like damned men—and then suddenly to be faced with the real and undeniable possibility of going by your house. And probably your mom would be standing in the doorway, or in the living room, or your brothers would be playing in the street with the dog.

A sort of anxiety, a nervousness came over me as we turned into the street. I saw the house with the same peeling yellow walls and the doors, right? My God, I thought, the dialectic has stopped! As if the whole year I had been away was just one second, see? I didn't know if I had really lived it, if I had really been in the mountains, if I had really lived all those days, one after another, until finally I had come back here. Or if, in fact, I had never been anywhere at all. There I was in the underground car, with my two compañeros, armed to the teeth, and we were driving right by the house. I could see the furniture—it was incredible! I had the impression that nothing was real. Sometimes it seems as if the world is turning with you, that you are making it go round; you have the feeling it would all stop if you weren't there.

But one thing was certain—León and my house had continued on quite independently of whether I was there or not. My mother and my brothers had gone on living, eating, sleeping, working, without me—how good that was to see! How alive they were, right? It's not that you think you're the center of the universe, but, well, it's a shock to the mind. Time had passed, a year had passed, and many things had happened, but the house was still the same house!

That confused me. I had lost my bearings in space and time. I looked at myself; I felt the limited and finite space of my body. I was there, materially, in all my finite, bodily dimension. Yet this finite dimension, this material presence, driving by the house—it was as if I could not connect with my own time, could not link up with it, did not fit into my own time and space. I didn't know whether time had passed or not.

There was the house with the same peeling paint, the same furniture, the same people of the barrio. But I could not fit together in my mind the magnitude of time, the year in the mountains, with the finiteness of my physical self. I don't know why, but suddenly I was overwhelmed with the sense that the very inhabitants of my house, or the house itself, were angelic—do you see? As if innocent . . . in another dimension. What did they know of all the things that had happened, of all the suffering, of so much that had been experienced? You think, what do they know?

The yellow walls were pure candidness; the furniture, pure silence. As if my house were a child existing beyond time, or a kind of rarity, a little bird; as if time counted for nothing there. My house had no idea of the war, nor of what was going on in Nicaragua at that time—am I making myself clear? The present and the past were clashing inside me. I wasn't sure where I was; what I mean is, if in my finite world I was in possession of my past or of my present. Or if both were inside me. Or did I inhabit only one, because I couldn't be in the past and present at the same time? If this was the past, I was in front of my house; but if this was the present and I was there—it was impossible. Because I didn't live there. I came from somewhere else, from living something else. Something snapped—my head was a whirl of space and time that I couldn't get straightened out. What I did feel was my own absurdity. Because I couldn't make sense of the two dimensions of time.

The car drove on and on. But I was staying behind, flowing out of myself, letting myself flow back, be pulled backward as if by my hair, until it hit me: no, this wasn't right. That present, though it existed here, did not belong to me. It was the past. I would not be returning there for a long time; it was no longer my world, no longer my life. That hurt it, hurt very much!

And the final, crowning blow, the brutal, harsh slap in the face was this: my whole sense of certainty had shattered back there, the organic unity of my past and present; the measure of my own contradiction had shattered. And it was too late to recover it, since I wasn't going back. I wasn't going to be able to see my mother or my brothers. I would have to see them on down the line, in the future. You accept this emotionally; it's the only rational thing. It's as if someone had hit the little button of history, the little button that sets in motion the film of your life. I never suspected it would be so painful, that violent confrontation between present and past, that rupture through which I became conscious of the new quality of my life.

I remember when we got back to the safe house I was very quiet; I didn't say anything. I felt numb. It was like when a high fever has wrung you out and you're left in a stupor, thoughtful but not sad, more than anything frustrated and annoyed, trying to come to grips with the contradiction, the ridiculousness—I'll say it again—the absurdity of a situation like that. Why you could not go back, could not enter your own house.

As I lay thinking about all this on the crag that night, I felt a great hatred for the bourgeoisie, for North American imperialism, for Somoza's Guard—for they were the cause of this absurdity. We were living in a society of the absurd, and our life was the life of the absurd. We had to do things which in a normal society there would be no reason to do, and we could not do things which in a normal society could easily be done. That's what I mean when I say it was a society of the absurd; it forced us to do or not do absurd things. And I lay thinking so late that night that I fell asleep in the granary with my radio on.

In the morning Moisés appeared with my breakfast. He always came alone, but that day I could hear someone was with him. I knew Moisés's footsteps, the weight of his step, the rhythm of his stride. I recognized Moisés's step but he was walking more slowly than usual; somebody was coming behind him. That alarmed us. We dropped to our knees, Andrés and I, and took cover with our pistols and the grenade. But when I finally got a good look down the little trail that led to the crag, I could see it was a little old man coming behind Moisés. I said to Andrés, "Could that be Moisés's dad?" And sure enough, Moisés himself called out to me, "Juan José, this is my papito," which is a way of saying my papacito, my papa. The little old man started laughing and offered me his hand very shyly in the campesino manner. I could see he was a very thin man, of medium height, with curly black hair and a tanned, wrinkled face. He was like something very old that had been preserved for many years and that suddenly was brought out into the light, a thing that once was new, that once was young, but that had been in storage for so long it had started to deteriorate.

Don Leandro had been young, but so many years had passed—who knows where he had kept himself—and suddenly, *bam!* When I met him he was already an old man, toothless. He was wearing his best clothes; it was very humble, but he came that day dressed in his best. I said to him, "Aha! compañero, sir, how are you?" "Ah, not so good. You see, sir, I'm old," he said, "and you can't imagine how my stomach hurts me. And my eyes are bad. I'm so old I can't see, I'm a miserable man, I can't take a step without this cane; if I start out for the cornfield, in a few minutes I'm so tired I have to turn around and go home. My body is a wreck." And then he asked me, "That gun, what kind is it?" "This is a .45," I answered. "And what did you do with the other weapons?" he asked. When he asked about other weapons I assumed he knew we were guerrillas of the FSLN, that we moved in columns, that he suspected we had been in Macuelizo. I answered that we had to be careful, that we didn't carry heavy weapons since we didn't want people to see them and know that we were in the area. Sometimes we could only carry pistols. "But these are good pistols," I told him.

I did not realize he was connecting me with the old Sandinistas, from his own day, from the time of General Sandino. He was asking me about the other weapons, as somebody might say, you know, the weapons we had in the past, what did they do with those? For him, that moment he had preserved and which had grown old was an instant that lasted forty years. It

was like saying, Where did they leave the Enfield or the
Mauser or the 30 caliber that we had? Then he confided with
an air of wisdom and great confidence, "Those are fine animals, rapid-fire guns, very good. General Sandino once sent
me to get tortillas for them at Yalí." And it all came out. I said
to myself, What a beautiful thing, do you realize you are
touching Sandino, you are touching history! And that very
moment I understood what the Sandinista tradition meant; it
was reaffirmed for me; I saw it in flesh and blood, in practice,
in reality.

And the old man went on talking, and the anecdotes! He
had been Sandino's courier. And he talked about Pablo
Umanzor, with whom he had fought, and General Estrada,
and Pedro Altamirano, José León Díaz, Juan Gregorio Co-
lindres—he fought with all these famous men! He told me he
could see it all; he was in another world; he remembered details. How I wished I had a tape recorder, he was saying such
wonderful things. "Look, Juan José," he said, "I'm going to
tell you something. I can't go with you on this campaign, because look at me, I'm old and what good would I be? I have
the will but I wouldn't last a day, I could never survive another campaign. But I have many, many sons, plus all my
grandsons; here are all these boys." And he motioned toward
his son. "I am giving them to you, to go along with you because we all have to make an effort, we can't let them put an
end to it all." He was saying we can't let them put an end to it
as if it had never been interrupted, as if all this were a continuation of what he had lived through with Sandino.

It made me feel very good, but at the same time, I felt bad.
I was happy, but troubled as well. Because I knew that sometimes things did not work out, that the Guard was repressing
and murdering people. These were hard times. But dammit, I
said to myself, either these people are very brave or very ignorant; either they don't know what they're getting into or
they're irresponsible. That's what I felt. How is it possible, I
thought, that when hundreds of people are being murdered
right now around Ocotal, when the radios are blaring with

news about compañeros being killed, while the Guard is patrolling with helicopters and planes and thousands of soldiers, how is it possible that this man, with nobody here but Andrés and me, is committing himself to a course of action that appears at this moment to be nothing but a very dangerous adventure? Just, but foolhardy. How is it possible that after so much repression and so many deaths, so many defeats, and not just these but the ones they as Sandinistas had suffered with General Sandino, how was it possible that this man, after the death of Don Bacho, could be suggesting that if he weren't so old he would go with me? And since he was too old to survive another campaign he was giving me all his sons?

According to what Augusto Salinas Pinell had told me, Don Bacho Montoya had been murdered, thanks to a guy who had deserted from us and then been captured by the Guard. He had betrayed Don Bacho, and early in the morning the Guard had stormed his shack and started shouting insults. Don Bacho's wife was making black coffee, boiling the water for black coffee, when a lieutenant of the Guard yelled out to her, "Get your ass out here, you filthy old bitch!" The old woman answered back, "Get out yourself, you wretch!" And she took a pan of hot water and threw it at the lieutenant, scalding his chest and whole body. Then all hell broke loose—they started beating and torturing the two old people. They tore the shack apart, dragged them both outside, kicked in the little cooking stove, yanked down the odds and ends they had hanging from the roof—little cups, cheeses, curds; they ripped the sheets off the bed, dumped out all their clothes, hacked apart the cot, and smashed the table and the gourds and the clay pots. They shoved the two old folks out of the shack and tied them to a tree. And once they were tied up, they beat them both to death. Then they took a three-month-old baby out of the ruins of the shack and tossed him up in the air and caught him on the tips of their rifle bayonets as he was falling back to the ground. Then they pulled out the bayonet and tossed him up again. It was a feast of vultures.

And Don Bacho, beaten to death . . . How happy he was, I

remember, when we first made contact with him! And the life that radiated from his whole being when he was leading us through that encirclement. He seemed to be living all over again propelled by the fury he had built up within him all those years since Sandino!

So when Don Leandro talked to me like that, I thought of Don Bacho. It's not that Don Leandro is irresponsible, it's not that he's ignorant, but simply that this was the history of the Nicaraguan people. They had a Sandinista history, a history of rebellion against exploitation, against North American domination. They interpreted rebellion in a primitive, gut-level way; their rebellion was historical and came out of their fight against the Yankee occupation.

It was not irresponsibility; it was history, the honor of the people, the historical rebellion of the people. The Sandinistas were isolated after the death of Sandino, and they started educating their children in that tradition, encouraging that feeling against the occupying Yankees who had invaded and were humiliating us. Poor, barefoot people, but with an extraordinary sense of national dignity, with a consciousness of national sovereignty. That, in essence, was the reality.

I realized there that the Frente Sandinista was forging a tremendous revolutionary determination in its militants, a tremendous stubbornness, a tremendous sense of dignity and combativeness. But these principles were not new; the FSLN had not invented them. This was our historical patrimony, a treasure we were going to bring to light again. And that was the greatest insight and accomplishment of Carlos Fonseca: he took back that history; he took possession of that determination, of that intransigence born of dignity and of sovereignty. What the contemporary FSLN was doing with us and what we were doing with the newer people was nothing more than giving a new context to that historical tradition, that determination, that sense of dignity.

I don't know how, but that day when Don Leandro started talking like that, about giving me his sons, and about Sandino

220

and the Sandinista struggle, all of a sudden I started to feel that Don Leandro was the father, and I realized that in fact he was the father—that Don Bacho and Don Leandro were the fathers of the country. And never did I feel more a son of Sandinismo, more a son of Nicaragua than at that moment. I had been a young student who came to Sandino through books. I had come to Sandino through the study of Sandinismo, but I still had not arrived at the root, the true paternity of all our history.

So when I met that man, when he told me all of that, I felt I really was his son, the son of Sandino, the son of history. I understood my own past; I knew where I stood; I had a country, a historical identity, with everything that Don Leandro was telling me. I wanted to embrace him, to kiss him; and not just because they were going to give me food, and were not going to back out on me but were going to protect me. The magnitude, the dimension was greater. Because, through him, I had recovered my own history, the tradition, the essence of Nicaragua. I had found my genesis, my antecedents; I felt myself a continuation, concrete and uninterrupted. I had found the source of my strength, I now realized. It was Sandino who had been my nourishment, but I had never seen, materially, my umbilical cord—and suddenly it was there. Right before my eyes.

I embraced Don Leandro with a shudder of joy and of emotion. I felt that my feet were solidly planted on the ground; I wasn't in the air. Not only was I the child of an elaborate theory, but also I was walking on something concrete; I was rooted in the earth, attached to the soil, to history. I felt invincible. When we said goodbye I held out my hand to Don Leandro. He gave me his hand, and I remember I took it in both of mine and pressed it tightly. "We'll be seeing each other soon," I said. And he answered, "Yes, I'm old now, but remember, here are all my sons."

Omar Cabezas came of age in the 1960s. It was a decade in which both Nicaraguan and North American society began to disintegrate, and then became reassembled in new, dangerous, and promising ways. But the story of his political commitment, like the story of the entire generation that revolutionized Nicaragua, began in 1911–1912. In those early years the United States government of President William Howard Taft overthrew José Zelaya, the Nicaraguan ruler. Zelaya was an uncompromising nationalist and, no doubt for that very reason, staunchly opposed North American economic and military ventures in Central America, while he tried to unite the region under his own control. Taft removed Zelaya, but the president could not find a Nicaraguan leader who could both cooperate with the United States and survive the resulting wrath of his own people.

Taft solved the problem by sending in the Marines. They controlled Nicaragua until 1925 (as part of the longest U.S. military occupation of the century), left briefly in 1925–1926, and returned in 1926. As they again settled in, however, the Marines encountered their first peasant-based, anti-United

223

States guerrilla resistance. The rebels were led by Augusto Sandino, a short, slim man who had been born in 1895 in western Nicaragua. Sandino had been strongly influenced by the Mexican Revolution, especially by its determination to drive out North American control of Mexican oil resources. After spending some time in Mexico he returned to his homeland in 1926 to lead a few peasant followers in an apparently quixotic struggle against one of the world's great powers.

Sandino was not a Marxist. He thought of himself as a nationalist whose central article of faith was that "the sovereignty and liberty of a people are not to be discussed, but rather defended with weapons in hand." He not only bequeathed that belief thirty-five years later to the Sandinista Front for National Liberation (FSLN), but also left for a future generation his exemplary feat of miraculously bringing the Marines to a standstill. (His guerrillas even survived the first dive-bombing attacks in aviation history.)

By 1932 Sandino's success and the growing criticism at home led U.S. officials to pull out the troops. As Senator Burton K. Wheeler of Montana acidly observed, if the Marines were supposed to fight bandits, they could do more good in Chicago. But the North Americans left behind a U.S.-trained National Guard, under the command of Anastasio Somoza, to maintain order and to preserve United States interests. Sandino had promised to lay down his arms when the Marines left. He did so, and as soon as he did, Somoza killed Augusto Sandino in cold blood. The Guard commander then established a dictatorship that lasted from 1934 until 1956, when he was assassinated by Rigoberto Lopez Perez, a poet from León, Cabezas's hometown. During those two decades Somoza corruptly enriched himself, his family, and the National Guard, referring to Nicaragua as simply "my farm." The dictator systematically destroyed opponents by purchase, imprisonment, or murder. An unquestioning friend of the United States, he received strong support from Washington. The fact that the U.S. Embassy in Nicaragua stood next door to Somoza's palace led Nicaraguans to wonder who actually ruled them.

One enemy, however, could not be destroyed. Nicaraguan university students spearheaded nationalistic, anti-Somoza movements. At times the dictatorship smashed the protests with military force. But for the most part Somoza honored the Latin American tradition that universities were sanctuaries and therefore off-limits to military death squads. The schools thus became recruiting grounds and intellectual seedbeds of anti-Somoza groups. In the words of one Nicaraguan, the sanctuary tradition was "one of the great contributions to the revolution." The National Autonomous University in León (Omar Cabezas's hometown school) helped lead anti-government rallies. The city of León itself had a remarkable and, for Cabezas's own career, revealing history.

Since its founding in 1524 and during its term as Nicaragua's capital until 1852, León had been a proud city of importance and political explosiveness. (That a row of active volcanoes can be seen from the city seems appropriate.) By the 1960s León had been the seat of the country's Liberal Party for more than a century. The party of Zelaya and Sandino, the Liberals historically represented new money, the questioning of tradition, and deep suspicion of North American intentions. Located in the north-central part of western Nicaragua, León waged bitter political wars with the southern city of Granada, which represented the old-monied, more tradition-tied Conservative Party.

In 1852 the capital finally moved to Managua, midway between the two antagonists, but León's political fervor did not subside. It remained especially high at the National Autonomous University of León, which had long been Nicaragua's main institution of higher learning. Here ardent nationalists claimed the legacy of poet Rubén Darío, revered by Cabezas. Darío, who had transformed Spanish literature with his independent thinking and principles of "modernism," is buried in León's cathedral. In this city Somoza had to crush some of the first major student uprisings against his regime in 1939 and again in 1948. In León, FER (the Spanish acronym for Student Revolutionary Front), established by the new Sandinista revolutionaries in 1961, found many recruits, including Omar Cabezas. Students led anti-Somoza movements with uncommon vigor, spirit, and language.

The university's political activities did not quiet when Somoza was assassinated in 1956. The dictator's older son, Luis, carried on the family tradition of greed and political corruption until a sudden heart attack killed him in 1967. Luis's younger brother, Anastasio (also known as "Tacho"), then seized power. Less subtle than his brother and having deep personal ties to the National Guard, the new ruler had his reputation in the United States protected by friends he made while attending a private North American military school and then West Point. Tacho carried the Somozas' tradition of rapaciousness and brutality to new levels. By 1979, when the Sandinistas finally overthrew him, Somoza owned 25 percent of the nation's land (or an area roughly equivalent to Massachusetts), his National Guard officers controlled another 10 percent, and together they monopolized the most profitable industries and rackets—prostitution, the meat industry, real estate, gambling, public transportation, and, of course, tax collection. Not only did Somoza become the United States' most trusted friend in the region, but the U.S. military trained the officers of the National Guard.

As Tacho and his colleagues gathered up Nicaragua's wealth, the number of Nicaraguans who lost their land (and thus their means of survival) increased 1000 percent in parts of the country between the mid-1950s and early 1970s. Presidents John F. Kennedy and Lyndon Johnson poured millions of dollars into Nicaragua through the Alliance for Progress (1961–1970), for example, and the Somoza dynasty diverted the money to its own treasury. The dollars particularly financed capital-intensive export crops (cotton, coffee) whose expansion required driving peasants off the land and into city slums. At the same time, this new agriculture cut down the available amount of staple foods (beans, corn) that Nicaraguans needed for daily diets. The country's economic growth rate shot upward in the 1960s and early 1970s, but it benefited the rich while multiplying the poor. Nor did Tacho channel his new wealth into such social programs as schools. "I don't want educated people," he declared. "I want oxen."

By the mid-1960s, however, Nicaraguan universities were turning out more revolutionaries and fewer "oxen." The Sandinista Front for National Liberation (FSLN) was founded in 1961 by four men—Carlos Fonseca Amador, Tomás Borge, Silvio Mayorga, and Santos Lopez Fonseca, Borge, and Mayorga were young leaders from the anti-Somoza student movement who had been greatly influenced by Marxism and emboldened by Castro's 1959 victory in Cuba over Batista's U.S.-sponsored government. Lopez had been a colonel in Sandino's army and thus formed a vital link to the founders of Nicaragua's struggle for independence. Borge worked especially closely with university students in León. The FSLN had about twenty members in 1962 when the National Guard cracked down and nearly destroyed it.

The Sandinistas thus began a seventeen-year career that would be marked by exhilarating high points and near-fatal low ones. This low period lasted until 1966–1967. The FSLN was a small, isolated group internally. Castro had given them limited moral and material support, but had been far more encouraging to other, less militant leftist groups in Latin America. Ernesto "Che" Guevara left the Cuban leadership and attempted to foment armed revolution in Bolivia (where he was killed in 1967). Guevara's example led aspiring revolutionaries such as Omar Cabezas to glorify "Che" while hardly mentioning Castro in their early writings.

Just when FSLN fortunes seemed dim, a Conservative Party leader, Fernando Agüero, boldly challenged Tacho's run for the 1967 presidential election. A bad crop year in 1966 and the displaced rural workers flooding into urban slums gave Agüero political ammunition. As Agüero's rallies grew, Somoza ordered the National Guard to put a stop to them. People were killed, the Guard closed down opposition newspapers and radio stations, and Somoza overwhelmingly won the presidency. During the turmoil there was an important battle in the northern city of Pancasán. In that battle one of the original Sandinista founders, Silvio Mayorga, was killed, and thus, as Omar Cabezas notes, Pancasán came to occupy a special place in FSLN history. The battle of Pancasán was a military defeat but a political victory. The FSLN's point was made. Civic protest would not work. But new sources of financing had to be found—such as robbing banks, taking "collections" from bus passengers, and kidnapping for ransom.

In 1969 the National Guard trapped and killed five guerrilla leaders. Carlos Fonseca was imprisoned in neighboring Costa Rica. Somoza announced that the FSLN had been destroyed. But he then ironically gave it new life. In 1971 Tacho and Fernando Agüero made a political deal that in reality made Somoza the president for life. Soured on Agüero's Conservative Party opposition, and with the Liberal Party thoroughly corrupted by the Somozas, middle- and upper-class students turned to such leftist alternatives as FSLN. The dictator then made perhaps his greatest mistake.

After an earthquake nearly destroyed Managua in 1972, he and his colleagues looted U.S. relief efforts and then looted their own people by ruthlessly exploiting the rebuilding of the city. The National Guard handsomely profited, but some of its key officers had also left their posts to run for their lives during and after the earthquake. Security had been preserved when the U.S. ambassador, Turner Shelton, flew in six hundred North American troops. Not only had the Guard shown cowardice, but Shelton's action indicated that Somoza depended on outside forces for protection.

Turner, who spoke little Spanish and was not an overly accomplished diplomat, saw his job as helping Somoza at every turn. Reporters only half joked that a Nicaraguan cabinet meeting occurred when the ambassador and the dictator met for their daily drinks. Nicaraguan and U.S. businessmen, however, were not amused by Somoza's extraordinary greed. "He robbed us blind," one North American investor recalled in 1979. By 1974 the middle-class recruits to the Sandinistas received sympathy from others, including even Roman Catholic Church leaders who bitterly and unsuccessfully protested Somoza's blatant fixing of the presidential election of that year.

Throughout 1970 to 1974 (the years when Omar Cabezas trained in the northern mountains to become a Sandinista leader), the FSLN succeeded in fighting its first long-term military campaigns. The Front was gaining because it finally obtained what it most required: peasant support, the same support that had allowed Sandino to survive forty years earlier. The peasants had suffered throughout the 1960s, and the financial dislocations from the 1972 earthquake combined with skyrocketing oil and gas prices in 1973–1975 to decimate the country's economy.

As the suffering of the peasants and slum-dwellers worsened, Roman Catholic priests and nuns had begun to spread the word of "liberation theology," a set of beliefs, emerging from church meetings in Rome and Latin America during the 1960s, that taught the poor they could improve their lives through organized political action. After having cooperated with the rich and the military for centuries, the church was now helping the poor by showing them how to establish "Christian bases" that became political bases as well. The FSLN was positioned to benefit from these bases.

As Omar Cabezas's account graphically illustrates, the Sandinistas devoted their best people to creating and strengthening a "chain" of peasant and slum-dweller support. In addition to this quiet work, the FSLN pulled off a spectacular attack in December 1974 when it invaded a banquet being hosted by a rich Somozan businessman, then held leading diplomats and Nicaraguan officials hostage until the humiliated dictator paid $5 million in ransom, released Sandinista prisoners, and allowed the attackers safe passage to the airport—as Nicaraguans stood along the road to cheer them.

By this time the Sandinista leadership had expanded to include some of the ablest young Nicaraguans: Henry Ruiz (whose code name was "Modesto"), Bayardo Arce, Daniel Ortega, and others, Omar Cabezas among them. The FSLN, by some reports had fewer than 200 soldiers in 1975, and by their own count had a force of between 800 and 1000 soldiers, but the talent was deep enough, and peasant support strong enough, that although Somoza succeeded in killing top leaders (only Borge of the original three founders survived to celebrate the 1979 victory), the "chain" provided new leaders and coherence.

In 1975, however, no possibility seemed to exist for a Sandinista triumph during the next four years. In 1975–1976 a furious Somoza launched an all-out assault on the FSLN that claimed many victims, including Carlos Fonseca, who now became the revolutionaries' most honored martyr. The Guard killed Fonseca in the mountains and then carried his severed head to Somoza as proof, finally, of victory. Internal dissension, moreover, split the Sandinistas into three groups, differing over tactics, but united in their determination to overthrow Somoza's dictatorship. Again, however, Somoza's errors rescued the revolutionaries. His appetite for wealth grew as the nation's economy floundered. Peasant and middle-class support for the FSLN grew especially among the young, who were the products of an astonishingly high 3.4 percent rate of population increase that occurred just when there were fewer goods (and food) available to distribute. More than half the population was under the age of eighteen, and this half was a constant source of fresh support for the FSLN.

Somoza tried to break free of these growing problems by ordering new crackdowns. His brutalities created an uproar in the United States. Some Roman Catholic Church leaders and a congressional group led by Representative Edward Koch

(Dem.-N.Y.) and Senator Edward Kennedy (Dem.-Mass.) pressured the White House to tell Somoza he either had to stop the repression or U.S. aid would be cut. Since Jimmy Carter had made human rights a centerpiece of his foreign policy, the new president was receptive. Somoza grudgingly moved to meet Carter's demands in 1977 and lifted the martial law he had imposed three years earlier.

Tacho's compromise, however, only further undermined his dictatorship. By 1977 he had little other hold than that bought with the National Guard's violence. So, when the repression lifted, opposition grew. Carter's demands, moreover, signaled that Somoza could no longer count on automatic U.S. support when he tortured and imprisoned political opponents. In October 1977 religious, business, and professional leaders formed "The Twelve" to demand Tacho's resignation. The group, promoted by the FSLN in an effort to promote national unity, climaxed a movement of upper class Nicaraguans into the anti-Somoza camp.

At the same time, the "Terceristas," the most moderate and inclusive of the revolutionary factions, led the Sandinistas in a series of devastating military attacks. Somoza responded with a new wave of brutality. Carter again warned Tacho, but on January 10, 1978, one event carried affairs beyond Carter's and Somoza's control. Pedro Joaquín Chamarro, the charismatic editor of the nation's leading newspaper, was gunned down. He was a hero to many Nicaraguans because of his long opposition to the Somozas. Tacho's agents were clearly involved in the killing. The nation erupted in large protest marches, then a two-week general strike, and the first mass spontaneous anti-Somoza uprising seized an important city, Masaya. The Subtiava Indian community in León, which Omar Cabezas knew well, also revolted. Tacho's response included air bombing attacks that took heavy casualties.

The FSLN then launched another spectacular raid in August 1978. They seized the National Palace as Somoza's legislature was meeting and successfully held the nation's leading politicians for a $500,000 ransom and the release of Sandinista prisoners. This victory triggered new uprisings.

Somoza counterattacked with campaigns that included the killing of several thousand civilians. A recently arrived international human rights team recorded the brutalities. Carter again threatened to cut off aid, but his threat now made little difference. About $45 million of U.S. economic assistance had entered Nicaragua during the previous year, and at least $14 million in arms had been given Somoza since 1975. The problem was not a lack of supplies (which could be, and were, easily replenished if necessary by arms from Argentina, Portugal, Israel, and other sources). Somoza's problem was the Guard's corruption and inability to fight effectively. "Tacho," one observer noted, "was more like a gang leader surrounded by his gunmen than an army general."

Such an army could no longer control Nicaragua. The Sandinista factions rejoined in a common front during the spring of 1979 under joint leadership. The events of August and September had suddenly swollen the Sandinista army to four times the size it had been a year earlier. Spontaneous uprisings took towns away from Somoza's control. The revolutionaries began to receive assistance from such neighbors as Costa Rica, Mexico, and Panama. Fidel Castro provided few supplies. The U.S. Central Intelligence Agency verified the Cuban ruler's small role in the final weeks of the war. Castro had helped train and keep united the FSLN leadership. But he knew that more visible actions invited a United States response. "The best help I can give you," he told the Sandinistas, "is not to help you at all."

In late May 1979 the newly unified FSLN launched an all-out offensive. Faced now with a revolutionary victory, Carter tried to piece together a joint U.S.-Latin American intervention that would prevent a total Sandinista victory. Not a single nation in the hemisphere would join him. He then attempted to pressure the FSLN to include more "moderate" members in the new government, including possibly National Guard officers. Even Conservative Party spokesmen dismissed Carter's effort with the comment, "Somoza is the last Marine." The U.S. military withdrawal of 1933 had finally been completed, and the clock could not be turned back.

After a revolution in which 45,000 were killed, 160,000 wounded, 40,000 orphaned, and 1,000,000 left starving, the Sandinistas marched into Managua on July 17, 1979, to claim power. Their provisional government had earlier taken the oath of office in León. Anastasio Somoza fled to Paraguay. In 1980 bazooka shells, fired by unknown assassins, shredded him and his armor-plated Mercedes limousine.

Walter LaFeber
March 1985